ROUTLEDGE LIBRARY EDITIONS: LIBRARY AND INFORMATION SCIENCE

Volume 9

AUTOMATED ACQUISITIONS

AUTOMATED ACQUISITIONS
Issues for the Present and Future

Edited by
AMY DYKEMAN AND BILL KATZ

LONDON AND NEW YORK

First published in 1989 by The Haworth Press, Inc.

This edition first published in 2020
by Routledge
2 Park Square, Milton Park, Abingdon, Oxon OX14 4RN

and by Routledge
52 Vanderbilt Avenue, New York, NY 10017

Routledge is an imprint of the Taylor & Francis Group, an informa business

© 1989 The Haworth Press, Inc.

All rights reserved. No part of this book may be reprinted or reproduced or utilised in any form or by any electronic, mechanical, or other means, now known or hereafter invented, including photocopying and recording, or in any information storage or retrieval system, without permission in writing from the publishers.

Trademark notice: Product or corporate names may be trademarks or registered trademarks, and are used only for identification and explanation without intent to infringe.

British Library Cataloguing in Publication Data
A catalogue record for this book is available from the British Library

ISBN: 978-0-367-34616-4 (Set)
ISBN: 978-0-429-34352-0 (Set) (ebk)
ISBN: 978-0-367-37547-8 (Volume 9) (hbk)
ISBN: 978-0-367-37551-5 (Volume 9) (pbk)
ISBN: 978-0-429-35505-9 (Volume 9) (ebk)

Publisher's Note
The publisher has gone to great lengths to ensure the quality of this reprint but points out that some imperfections in the original copies may be apparent.

Disclaimer
The publisher has made every effort to trace copyright holders and would welcome correspondence from those they have been unable to trace.

Automated Acquisitions: Issues for the Present and Future

Edited by
Amy Dykeman and Bill Katz

The Haworth Press
New York • London

Automated Acquisitions: Issues for the Present and Future has also been published as *The Acquisitions Librarian,* Number 1 1989.

© 1989 by The Haworth Press, Inc. All rights reserved. No part of this work may be reproduced or utilized in any form or by any means, electronic or mechanical, including photocopying, microfilm and recording, or by any information storage and retrieval system, without permission in writing from the publisher. Printed in the United States of America.

The Haworth Press, Inc., 10 Alice Street, Binghamton, NY 13904-1580
EUROSPAN/Haworth, 3 Henrietta Street, London WC2E 8LU England

Library of Congress Cataloging-in-Publication Data

Automated acquisitions: issues for the present and future / edited by Amy Dykeman and Bill Katz.
    p.   cm.
"Has also been published as The acquisitions librarian, number 1, 1989" – T.p. verso.
Includes bibliographical references.
   1. Acquisitions (Librarians) – Automation. I. Dykeman, Amy. II. Katz, William A., 1924-
Z689.A94 1989
025.2'0285 – dc19
                                                                        89-31099
                                                                               CIP

Automated Acquisitions: Issues for the Present and Future

CONTENTS

Preface *Bill Katz*	xv
Introduction *Amy Dykeman*	1

ISSUES TO CONSIDER

The Impact of Library Automation and Electronic Publishing: Toward Distributed Acquisitions *Carol E. Chamberlain*	3
Developments in Automation	4
Impact of Electronic Publishing	8
The Future of Acquisitions	12
Conclusion	14
Triangle Research Libraries Network: Planning for Automating the Acquisitions/Serials Control Functions *Janet L. Flowers*	17
Introduction	17
Background of TRLN	18
The Planning Process Thus Far	19
Advice Regarding Functional Requirements	21
Advice Regarding Evaluation of Vendor Systems	24

Lessons Learned	27
Conclusion	30

Vendor Relations and Automation — 33
    Marcia Anderson
    Donald E. Riggs

Introduction	33
Historical Perspective	34
Library Changes	36
Vendor Changes	37
Advantages to Vendors	38
Perceptions	39
Interdependency	40
Evaluation of Relationship and Communication	41
Strategies for Future Planning	42
Conclusion	43

IN-HOUSE DEVELOPED INTEGRATED SYSTEMS

Life in a Gold Fish Bowl: Or the Changing Nature of Acquisitions Work in an Integrated Online Environment — 45
    Sally W. Somers

Background	46
Information About On-Order Materials	47
Acquisitions in the Online Environment	48
Eliminating Redundancy and Streamlining Operations	51
Merging Acquisitions and LC Copy Cataloging	52
Conclusion	55

The Evolving Structure and Automation of Acquisitions — 57
    Jessie T. Nicol

Acquisitions Organizational Structure	59
In-House Developed Acquisitions System	62

Automated Acquisitions Systems	63
Future Focus for Acquisitions	65
Conclusion	65

NOTIS

A Shared Acquisitions System: The Ties That Bind? 67
Mary Ann Garlough

How to Automate?	68
NOTIS in the SUS	69
The Decision to Share	72
The Acquisitions Subcommittee and Reports	76
A Shared Acquisitions System: Do the Ties Bind?	81
Conclusion	83

Automating Acquisitions at Auburn University 85
Nancy Gibbs

Background	86
Staff Training	86
Integrity of the Database	87
Going Online	88
Problem Sharing	89
Downtime	90
Start of the Approval Program	91
The Advent of Online Fund Accounting	91
Fund Tracking	92
Conclusion	93

Approval Acquisitions and the Integrated Online System 95
Michael Kreyche

Requirements	96
Resources for Experimentation	98
Kent State and NOTIS	100
Microcomputer Solutions	104
Conclusions	106

INNOVACQ

Bringing up INNOVACQ: The Impact on the University of New Mexico General Library   109
    Harry C. Broussard
    Marilyn P. Fletcher
    Chris Sugnet
    Connie C. Thorson

Searching for a New System	111
What UNM Bought	112
Planning for Implementation	113
Personnel Considerations	114
Installation	115
Acquisitions Fund Accounting	118
Acquisitions of Serials and Monographs	121
Interfaces with Other Vendors	122
Impact on Other Areas of the Library	123
The Future	123

In-Process Control of Order Requests for "Out of Print" and "Not Yet Published" Materials Using the INNOVACQ Acquisitions System   131
    Stephen Bosch

Introduction	131
The OP/NYP Problem	132
The INNOVACQ System	133

GEAC

The INNOVACQ and Geac Acquisitions Systems Compared: A Large Academic Library Perspective   143
    Carol Pitts Hawks

Introduction	143
Background—Geac Computers, Ltd.	145
Background—Innovative Interfaces, Inc.	145
System Comparisons	146
Conclusion	161

Ideal and Reality: Automating Acquisitions in a Time of Austerity   163
    Heather S. Miller

Ideal: Automation as a Means of Saving Money	163
Ideal of a Few: The Ergonomic Office	165
Ideal: The Middle Manager's View	165
Reality: Preparation for Automating Acquisitions	166
Reality: Handicapping the Race	171
Reality: Proceeding, Handicaps Notwithstanding	173
Reality: Where We Are Now	175
Reality: What We Wish We Had Known Before We Started	176
Reality: What Happened to Those Ideals?	179
Reality: Implications for Other Libraries	180
Ideal: On-Going Goal	182

Going On-Line with the Geac Acquisitions System: Converting 1970's Clerical Procedures to 1980's Technology   185
    Robert N. Thompson

The Selection of the Geac Acquisitions System and Its Implementation	185
The 1972 Acquisitions System	188
Some Changes Apparent Before Training	190
Some Changes Apparent After Training	192
The New System—Placing Orders	195
The New System—Check-in	197
What We Know So Far	198
Summing Up—Disadvantages	201
Summing Up—Advantages	202

DYNIX

Automated Acquisitions in an Integrated Online System   205
    Pauline J. Iacono

The Ramsey County Public Library	205
Acquisitions	206

The Online System	207
Online Integrated Acquisitions	208
Impact on Technical Services Staffing	213

OCLC

Acquisitions — The Wonders of Automation — 215
Jeanne Harrell

Automation of Acquisitions at Texas A&M University	216
Workflow Using the OCLC Acquisitions Subsystem	220
Advantages and Disadvantages of OCLC ACQ	230
Conclusions	232

MICROCOMPUTER APPLICATIONS

Microcomputer Based Inhouse Acquisitions Program — 235
Helen M. Shuster

Time	237
Support	238
Staffing	240
Choice of Hardware and Software	240
Design of the Database	241
Management Needs	242
Operational Needs	247
Process	256
Conclusion	261

In Pursuit of Shared Access to the CD-ROM, Dialing *Books in Print Plus* — 263
Julie Nilson
Jon LaCure
Anne McGreer

Choosing the Software	265
The Participants and Trial Period	266
Evaluation	267
Final Analysis and Future Plans	269
Other Potential Uses for the System	270
Conclusion	271

**Microcomputer-Based Acquisitions Systems:
Where Have We Come From;
Where Are We Going?** **275**
Norman Desmarais

Early Developments 275
Future Possibilities 283

Preface

This is a new series which will deal exclusively with the delights and problems of acquiring materials for a library. Each volume is devoted to a single, well defined and practical topic of concern to the working librarian. It is directed to a library of any type or size. It is edited for a librarian who has a burning passion to acquire the best at the lowest possible cost in terms of time, energy, and, of course, dollars.

Yes, there are too many publications, particularly in the area of information and library sciences. Yes, many of them could be eliminated without loss to either contributor or reader. Yes, this situation will continue for another hundred years, despite protests by everyone. So, why add another?

Obviously neither the editor nor the contributors think introducing a new title is a grave error. On the contrary they agree with the premise that there is always room for quality. It's a matter of focus and the suggestion that good materials need no rationalization or excuse. Despite the perilous population of numbers, the irresistible will find a place. It is believed this new series will become a passion, as well as a servant for all concerned.

The pages promise to be filled with the good—and the practical. Honor is paid to theory, but for the most part the contributors are asked to consider the humbler, day by day activities of the librarian who inhabits a chilly territory. In this country there is a constant demand by less than patient people. There is never enough staff or money about to fully meet that demand.

The difficulties have no real relation to size or type of library. Nor do they only plague the person who is devoted full time to acquisitions. They are constant problems for the individual who may be in a one person library, or who may be in charge of a highly sophisticated system. It is an exquisite, sometimes pathless zone of combat and peace where there has to be more heroes than martyrs.

© 1989 by The Haworth Press, Inc. All rights reserved.

Librarians from almost any section of the library are deeply involved with what the library purchases, or does not buy, and it is to them, too, that these pages are dedicated. In almost every case, each volume will have more than narrow appeal. It will suggest possibilities for every professional in the library. The ways to success are chartered here.

Each number is given over to a single topic, much in the same fashion as *The Reference Librarian*. Automation is at the heart of this first collection, and budgets will be considered in the second. Other topics will be carefully considered and selected. All will reflect the interests and needs of the working librarian.

The significance, then, of this new series is that it offers an intelligent, less than worn approach to the whole bright bright professional task of acquiring materials. This necessarily means a trip up the road to action, but along the way it is our desire to point out the delights of it all. As one Scot poet put it: "The toils are pitched, and the stakes are set, Ever sing merrily, merrily." At the same time, and this may be the gentle message of this, and every volume to follow: "Ever sing warily, warily."

Bill Katz
Editor

Introduction

Amy Dykeman

This first volume of *The Acquisitions Librarian* focuses on the area of automated acquisitions. Since acquisitions routines were one of the first library functions to be automated as early as the 1960s, what makes this a suitable topic for the present?

Librarians are accustomed to the myriad of choices now available in the library marketplace from integrated and interfacing systems to software packages for a library's microcomputer. Nonetheless, other developments within acquisitions make present automation projects a more challenging endeavor than just converting manual procedures to automated ones. Acquisitions information is now accessible to the public (and to public service librarians) as it appears in on-line catalogs. The distinctions between acquisitions and copy cataloging departments are blurring as the use of often identical bibliographic records occurs in both areas. Furthermore, the use of information received (or transmitted) by means of electronic data transmission or by tape loads into acquisitions systems introduces new dependencies among vendors and libraries.

The "acquisitions circle" has been enlarged (some might say, besieged) by ergonomic and efficiency experts, by sellers of vendor products and system enhancements, and by non-acquisitions librarians. Acquiring a book with a good discount and receiving it in a reasonable amount of time is not as simple as it once was. Or is it?

As a former Chair of the RTSD Automated Acquisitions/In Process Control in Libraries Discussion Group, I noticed that many of these issues were debated at ALA meetings as librarians demanded more from their systems; representatives of book jobbers, subscrip-

---

Amy Dykeman is Assistant Director for Technical Services, Library of Science and Medicine, Rutgers University.

© 1989 by The Haworth Press, Inc. All rights reserved.

tion agencies, and systems manufacturers expressed both interest and frustration in developing all the possible interfaces, products, and reports needed. It is not surprising that certain topics like standards for record transmission and planning for implementation surfaced repeatedly. The articles in this collection describe the hands-on experiences of librarians who have implemented various types of acquisitions systems in this changing environment. In the end, it appears that you can never do enough planning or gather enough information; but the budget year is beginning, the bibliographers have orders to go, invoices must be processed and budget reports produced. The possibilities seem endless for re-evaluating acquisitions work and redefining the role of the acquisitions librarian.

ISSUES TO CONSIDER

The Impact of Library Automation and Electronic Publishing: Toward Distributed Acquisitions

Carol E. Chamberlain

SUMMARY. Two technological developments, library automation and electronic publishing, are having a great impact on acquisitions in academic libraries. Automated acquisitions systems have evolved beyond the fundamental ordering and receiving functions, with the advent of integrated systems, external interfaces with suppliers and local control through microcomputer-based support. Electronic publishing will bring about dramatic changes; among them, a change in focus from the *acquisition* of resources to *access* to information in electronic formats. This growing trend will influence traditional ordering policies, budgets and supplier services. Developments point to a shift toward a distributed acquisitions operation in academic libraries of the future. This shift will bring about a redefinition of both the process and the organization of acquisitions. Ultimately the future of acquisitions will be determined by how successfully operations adapt to the changing technology.

Carol E. Chamberlain is Head, Acquisitions Department, E506 Pattee Library, Pennsylvania State University, University Park, PA 16802.

Dire predictions have been made in the last few years about the impact of technology on technical services in academic libraries. Organization theorists point to a shift of support away from cataloging and acquisitions activities toward service functions such as reference, instruction and collection development.[1] Others herald a return to the "basics" of technical services, without the paper shuffling and highly formalized tasks of the present day.[2] Aveney suggests the dwindling of the traditional cataloging function and the possibility of the actual disappearance of the acquisitions department.[3] Although these predictions may be considered extreme or unlikely to occur in many libraries, it is evident that technological developments are dramatically changing catalog and acquisition operations.

While the technological advancements which transformed the cataloging function into an automated process took place some years ago, the changes being witnessed in the area of acquisitions are generally a recent phenomenon. Acquisitions automation is becoming more sophisticated and at the same time electronic publishing is adding an entirely new dimension to acquisitions service. These two developments are bringing about major changes in acquisitions, in terms of both process and organization. How is automation and electronic publishing changing acquisitions? How will acquisitions adapt to the changes? As Bonk states, the future "is in the way libraries adapt to the electronic environment that is increasingly surrounding them."[4]

An exploration of the impact of acquisitions automation and of electronic publishing signals a shift toward a distributed acquisitions environment in academic libraries of the future, as opposed to the centralized approach prevalent today. This shift will bring about a redefinition of both the process and the organization of acquisitions.

DEVELOPMENTS IN AUTOMATION

Much progress has been made in recent years in the development and enhancement of automated acquisitions systems. At one time the focus of development was on replicating manual ordering and receiving routines within a comparatively isolated context. The integration of the acquisitions component with other internal library systems and with external bibliographic utilities was considered ideal but not reality.[5] Interfaces between library acquisitions systems and book and journal supplier systems were acknowledged as desirable enhancements but not widely available as alternatives to traditional paper-based methods.[6] Most acquisitions systems provided little flexibility in terms of supporting the need for local control.[7] Noteworthy developments in these three areas—integration, interfaces and local control—have taken place within a relatively short period of time. How have they contributed to changes in the acquisitions process?

Integration of Library Functions

The integrated system, such as one which supports technical service functions, circulation and online public access catalogs (whether supported by a single system or by separate, linked systems), has allowed acquisitions to become an open process. No longer is the acquisitions department the sole purveyor of huge paper files containing intricate details about on-order and in-process materials. No longer is the acquisitions department responsible for distributing reams of paper to various parts of the library in order to share information on orders and receipts. Acquisitions data is available online and practically every user can have access to it. As Henderson notes, "citations for materials ordered can be made available in a timely manner, location in the processing flow can be easily identified, and titles are bibliographically accessible in a number of ways."[8] Not only has public access become a reality but also access by library staff has been enhanced. For example, through the fund accounting component of an acquisitions system, collection development librarians can have instant access to up-to-date account data, instead of having to wait for the inevitably out-of-date paper reports of fund balances.

The integrated system has led to a refinement of the preorder search routine. The ability to search library holdings and acquisitions records at the same time using a variety of access points, has reduced the amount of time it takes to perform a typical search while dramatically increasing the quality of the search. Systems offered by bibliographic utilities and systems which support links to national databases provide additional benefits for the searching process. Bibliographic verification and the check for duplication can be done by one individual during a single search session.

However, better and easier access to acquisitions-related data in an integrated environment has resulted in greater responsibility for the acquisitions staff. With acquisitions records accessible in the system, acquisitions staff have become responsible for the bibliographic control of such data. In some libraries the acquisitions staff is responsible for processing functions that were traditionally performed in cataloging departments, such as creating or editing records for incoming receipts from approval plans, or updating catalog records with holdings for additional copies, added volumes, etc. The process is seen as a logical part of the receiving function, as acquisition-type records are transformed into catalog records. This blurring of the distinction between acquisitions and cataloging functions is a by-product of the integration of library systems and represents a major change in the acquisitions process.

External System Interfaces

Interfaces between acquisitions systems and those of library booksellers and subscription agents have become increasingly commonplace. Libraries receive magnetic tapes containing records for materials sent on library approval plans. Invoices from subscription agents and booksellers are provided in a variety of formats including disk and tape. These types of interfaces serve to enhance the acquisitions process by providing data that can be loaded into the library system without requiring manual input or paper handling. This means a savings in staff time and greater efficiency since data are available online more quickly. As Maddox notes, machine-readable data supplied by vendors speed "the *access* to the information . . . but not the *receipt* of" library materials.[9]

Another interface which does serve to speed the ordering process is the electronic transmission of orders to suppliers through bibliographic utilities and turnkey systems. For orders placed with suppliers capable of receiving them electronically, there is no longer a need to generate paper purchase orders. What is needed next is the large-scale application of interactive, two-way communication between library acquisitions systems and supplier systems. Electronic transfer of information on the status of orders, subscription problems, out-of-print searches, stock inventories, etc. has a tremendous effect on an acquisitions operation. Reliance on electronic message systems, paper communication and the postal system would be reduced as would the time-consuming input of status report information and the preparation of reply correspondence. The use of national and international standard formats for the electronic transmission of acquisition and publishing data should ensure continued progress in this area. Compatibility through standardization is a key factor in interface development.

Local Control and Local Options

The last development in acquisitions automation is the provision of local control and local options through microcomputer-based systems. Many turnkey and utility systems offer micro-based acquisitions components that allow for the manipulation and control of local acquisitions records and downloading/uploading features. Local control provides flexibility and supports the need for order, receipt and account data according to individual library requirements. Some libraries have used the microcomputer to achieve local control by creating a homegrown acquisitions system. Commercial systems may not be able to provide the level of sophistication and complexity required, particularly in the areas of budget analysis, forecasting expenditures, and evaluating purchases and supplier performance.[10] Locally-developed systems based on commercial software packages represent a cost-effective alternative. Additionally, libraries are using microcomputers to support certain aspects of the acquisitions process which heretofore have not benefitted from automation. Applications range from the creation of a serials bid database[11] to gift tracking, OP search monitoring, and word processing for daily correspondence.

Local options are further enhanced by the myriad ordering services offered by publishers, booksellers and other information producers. Some are available through commercial database services such as BRS and DIALOG, others are offered by library suppliers.

The ability to place orders online to NTIS, USBE, UMI Article Clearinghouse, Information on Demand and others has given acquisitions departments the potential to vastly improve fulfillment and turnaround time for some categories of orders. It also has brought about a greater reliance on commercial database services which in the past have been used primarily to support the reference function. Electronic ordering services available from library wholesalers and publishers, particularly for books published in the U.S., are providing acquisitions departments with alternatives to the ordering capabilities of commercial library acquisitions systems. The value of the growing array of local options is in the ability to choose a single automated approach or choose any combination of approaches to the acquisitions process. All will improve the efficiency and quality of acquisitions work; and all will make acquisitions more responsive to the technological developments in the area of electronic information resources.

IMPACT OF ELECTRONIC PUBLISHING

Just as developments in library automation have brought about dramatic changes, electronic publications have become an important factor in the acquisitions process of most academic libraries. In the years since Lancaster's landmark study,[12] debate has waned over the demise of the printed word and research supports the widely recognized view that traditional print publishing and electronic publishing will continue to co-exist in the information environment.[13] In 1983 Schmidt noted that

> it is excessive . . . to predict that this newer industry will supercede the traditional publishing industry, which not only maintains a healthy share of the information marketplace, but also exists because of the demand for the physical artifacts of information and knowledge. . . .[14]

As the two formats complement each other, they require an "integrationist approach to their handling."[15] How has the electronic publishing phenomenon affected the acquisitions process? As electronic resources play an even greater role in the information industry, how will acquisitions adapt in the future? These questions warrant an examination of the issue of access instead of acquisition, and of the policy and service implications inherent in the redefinition of the acquisitions process.

Access versus Acquisitions

Electronic publishing encompasses a wide range of computer-produced media, from products such as CD-ROM to online, full-text databases. Acquiring microcomputer diskettes, CD-ROM, etc. has introduced new factors to the acquisitions process and to some extent has resulted in the loss of control. Since these computer-based resources must be used with some kind of equipment, acquisitions staff must be able to recognize and communicate equipment specifications to the supplier (in some cases, the ordering process includes the purchase or lease of appropriate equipment). Many products are available only from the publisher or producer and staff must deal with suppliers that have little or no understanding of library practices. This is particularly evident from the widespread use of license agreements. The acquisitions department as the purchasing agent is usually not aware of the legal terms of the purchase until the product is received, the package is opened and contents reviewed. There is little control over contractual obligations since the terms of liability are not known at the time of order placement. The issue of quality control of receipts is another example of loss of control. Without access to the proper equipment, there is virtually no way to check the quality of the contents beyond observing obvious physical damage. As is the case with other nonprint formats such as sound recordings and microforms, the acquisitions department must rely for the most part on staff at the housing location to check for defects and promptly report problems.

The acquisition of electronically produced resources has posed no insurmountable problems for acquisitions departments. "Parallel" publishing, where information is available in hard-copy format as well as online has further complicated the picture.[16] Historically the online publication has been treated as a service, usually in the reference department, and not as property to be acquired.[17] Intner argues that computer-based services should be coordinated with the parallel hard-copy acquisition in order to achieve some measure of control and avoid unnecessary duplication.[18] However, as Yamamoto states,

> When information is only published online, . . . the product of electronic publishing is not something tangible that can be issued in copies, acquired or marked with the library's ownership stamp. . . . The publication of information in a strictly electronic format aimed directly at end users is the development . . . that is likely to have the greatest impact on technical services.[19]

The issue then becomes one of access versus acquisition. Electronic journals are accessed online and only "published" on demand.[20] There is virtually nothing for libraries to acquire for the collection, at least as far as the physical piece is concerned. The end user will create his or her own product through facsimile transmission of individual journal articles, preprints, etc.[21] Electronic journals are limited at present; Butler asserts that most will continue to be published in print form as long as their level of use demands it and as long as there are subscribers without the ability to use electronic services.[22] However, the worldwide adoption of a standard for the production of electronic manuscripts may provide incentive to book and journal publishers alike. What libraries must address is the issue of who pays for access to electronic information and its on-demand product. It is likely that access to full-text electronic resources will be funded from the library acquisition budget and on-demand prints will be paid for by the end user.

Policy and Service Implications

Online publishing developments have important implications in terms of the scope of acquisitions activities, budgetary policies and sources of supply. Acquisition policies are broadening to include what have traditionally been considered the realm of reference and circulation — access to databases and document delivery.[23] Additionally, as the academic library continues to integrate and make accessible information that is "no longer packaged in neat bibliographical bundles,"[24] it has gone beyond the traditional print boundaries of the library. At some institutions the library and the computer center have been combined administratively to form a "scholarly information center."[25] In such an environment the acquisitions department must participate in campus-wide information resource policies.[26] Even in more traditional settings, many acquisitions departments are involved in cooperative purchases with academic computing units, not only for microcomputer software but also for mainframe-supported data files. With the advent of institution-wide access to online information, the potential is great for acquisitions departments to help formulate institution-wide policies.

There are implications for library budgetary policy. The traditional acquisitions budget has become a comprehensive "information resource budget" which supports not only the purchase of print and nonprint material, but also the access to online publications. The latter "have expanded the services of libraries but reduced the amount of money available for the purchase of books and journals."[27] With the spiraling increases in costs for all types of resources the library must maintain a careful balance among expenditures in all categories. Libraries may charge a fee for the use of some databases, but this has been regarded largely as a fee for service, particularly for bibliographic databases. As acquisitions funds are increasingly used for access to electronic sources, the distinction between a service and a resource in electronic format will become clouded.

Service implications exist in terms of the nature of the relationship between libraries and suppliers. Use of the academic book vendor and subscription agent continues but the traditional sources of supply for print and nonprint materials are not as yet offering their services for online publications. It may be preferable to bypass the vendor and deal directly with the publisher or producer,[28] but as the number and sources of online publications increase, the industry may respond with the emergence of a library vendor specializing in online resources (as opposed to book or serial acquisition). And as Brownrigg et al. note, "as the library stores less and less material in-house on a permanent basis, it will become more and more reliant on the smooth continuance of its relationship with external suppliers."[29] The traditional criteria governing sources of supply, such as discount, service charge, fulfillment rate and turnaround time, may be inappropriate in an online environment. New criteria will no doubt be established. Online electronic publications and their unique requirements present some interesting challenges to traditional acquisitions policy, practice and service.

THE FUTURE OF ACQUISITIONS

Electronic publishing and the development of automated acquisitions systems have had and will continue to have a significant impact on both the process and the organization of acquisitions in academic libraries. What is the likely result in the long term? Acquisitions will operate within a distributed environment which may extend to virtually all units in the library; the traditional organization will focus on specialized services and may require fewer clerical staff. Acquisitions departments will continue as policy-setting units, will work closely with other units on campus (such as academic computing units) and may become the primary negotiator involved in the business aspects of information handling.

Distributed Process

A distributed environment for some aspects of the acquisitions process is possible because automation has made acquisitions and accounting data widely accessible and because electronic publishing has made new forms of communication available online. The process of acquisitions can be distributed among various departments and service units within the library which have the equipment to support it. Because an integrated library system allows for access to national bibliographic databases as well as databases of library holdings, orders, and items expected on approval, pre-order bibliographic searching would not need to be done centrally.[30] Automation also allows sophisticated links between acquisitions and account data, system monitoring of budget balances and access to accounts by dispersed users. Interfaces with library suppliers could facilitate the online ordering of certain categories of materials such as in-print U.S. trade books, technical reports, journal article reprints, etc. from approved library suppliers, or if local microcomputer-based options are available, using designated electronic ordering services. Authorized users in public service units could order these kinds of items because they are relatively easy to obtain and do not require specialized acquisitions knowledge. Budget monitoring would be controlled by the system. Electronic links to supplier systems would facilitate the sharing of status information on outstanding orders, as well as claiming activity.

The application of distributed acquisitions could be extended to include receipt of those items not requiring further processing or, in an environment where the cataloging function is also distributed, it could include receipt of all the above mentioned categories of materials. Acquisition of specialized materials, overall management of the resource budget, policies pertaining to supplier selection and ordering service selection, and the negotiation of contracts would remain the responsibility of the acquisitions department.

The impetus for the shift toward distributed acquisitions is electronic publishing. Access to full-text databases by end users will surpass the acquisition of print materials in some disciplines, particularly the sciences, where electronic journals will become an essential resource. Access to online information is not location dependent; once the acquisitions department initiates a contract with the supplier, the end user may access online journals from the home, office, etc. However, access to online information is equipment dependent and it may be quite some time before most users have access from remote locations. A library's commitment to online publishing implies a commitment to client-centered service units.[31] It is in these library units where end users will access online resources with the support of public service staff.

Organizational Focus

As long as there are books, journals and other materials to acquire, there will remain a need for acquisitions departments, but the focus of the organization will be less on the procurement of a physical entity and more on the business relationships. The organization of acquisition units differs among academic libraries although they are typically organized by format or by function. At one time it was thought that the introduction of automation would lead libraries to change from format-based units to functional units, although survey results do not validate this assumption.[32] Nevertheless, as Schmidt proposes, "it would be preferable to have the research library embrace content over format, with librarians, 'format-blind' as they are now presumably taught to be 'language-blind.'"[33]

There will be need for less staff and smaller departments as the amount of centralized purchasing decreases. However, this reduced staff will require high-level skills, not only because they will be dealing with the more difficult types of acquisitions (e.g., out of print materials, foreign publications) but also because they will be dealing with complex contractual agreements which often will involve other academic units on campus. Staff will require specialized knowledge of the book trade as well as knowledge of the burgeoning number of online information providers who join the ranks as academic library vendors.

As electronic resources continue to proliferate (and as libraries increase their commitments to them), they will take a greater proportion of the library's resource budget. The acquisitions department, in a refinement of its budget monitoring role, may serve to "integrate the business aspects of all . . . activities—accounting, payments, royalty collections, and the like. . . ."[34] It is the acquisitions department which will continue to establish policies consistent with institutional policies regarding acquisition and access to the full range of information resources.

CONCLUSION

The impact of automation and electronic publishing is keenly felt in acquisitions. Acquisitions librarians have been witness to tremendous changes in their operations. "Future acquisitions librarians may not have anything approaching the traditionalists' knowledge of the booktrade . . . but they *will* have the knowledge necessary to make their units competitive in tomorrow's technocracy. . . ."[35]

These technological developments will serve to improve the library's service mission to the scholarly community. Gurnsey notes that it is time that "we recognize that the quality of information is the key—its manner of delivery is incidental."[36] How academic libraries adapt to the effects of new technologies will determine whether their operations come to reflect this philosophy.

REFERENCES

1. Charles R. Martell, Jr., *The Client-Centered Academic Library: An Organizational Model*. (Westport, CT: Greenwood Press, 1983): 5.
2. Edwin Brownrigg, Clifford Lynch and Mary Engle, "Technical Services in the Age of Electronic Publishing," *Library Resources and Technical Services* 28, no. 1 (January/March 1984): 59.
3. Brian Aveney, "Electronic Publishing and Library Technical Services," *Library Resources and Technical Services* 28, no. 1 (January/March 1984): 73.
4. Sharon C. Bonk, "Document Delivery Systems for Books: Online Book Acquisition in the Next Decade," in *Fifth International Online Information Meeting* (Oxford: Learned Information, 1982): 189.
5. Richard W. Boss, *Automating Library Acquisitions: Issues and Outlook*. (White Plains, NY: Knowledge Industry Publications, Inc., 1982): 41-44.
6. Bonk, "Document Delivery Systems for Books," p. 183.
7. Gay D. Henderson, "Automated Acquisitions," in *Crossroads: Proceedings of the First National Conference of the Library and Information Technology Association* (Chicago: American Library Association, 1984): 62.
8. Ibid.
9. Jane Maddox, "Are the Gods Listening?" *Library Acquisitions: Practice and Theory* 11, no. 3 (1987): 213.
10. Helen M. Shuster, "A Versatile DBase III+ Acquisitions Program at Worcester Polytechnic Institute," *Library Acquisitions: Practice and Theory* 11, no. 3 (1987): 241-253.
11. Jeanne Harrell and Gloriana St. Clair, "Revolutionizing Acquisitions Productivity with PCs," *Technicalities* 7, no. 10 (October 1987): 3.
12. F. W. Lancaster, *Libraries and Librarians in an Age of Electronics*. (Arlington, VA: Information Resources Press, 1982).
13. Chih Wang, "Electronic Publishing and its Impact on Print Publishing and Other Selected Library Materials: A Review, Proposal, and Design for Further Research," *The Electronic Library* 5, no. 2 (April 1987): 86-92.
14. Karen A. Schmidt, "Electronic Publishing and the Academic Library," in *Crossroads: Proceedings of the First National Conference of the Library and Information Technology Association* (Chicago: American Library Association, 1984): 182.
15. Ibid., p. 187.
16. Rumi Yamamoto, "Another Interface: Electronic Publishing and Technical Services," *Canadian Library Journal* 43, no. 4 (August 1986): 236.
17. Schmidt, "Electronic Publishing and the Academic Library," p. 184.
18. Sheila S. Intner, "A Question of Medium," *Technicalities* 7 no. 10 (October 1987): 13.

19. Yamamoto, "Another Interface," p. 236.
20. Ibid., p. 237.
21. Patricia Battin, "The Electronic Library," *Collection Management* 9, no. 2/3 (Summer/Fall 1987): 139.
22. Brett Butler, "Scholarly Journals, Electronic Publishing, and Library Networks: From 1986 to 2000," *Serials Review* 12, no. 2/3 (Summer/Fall 1986): 48.
23. Ian Lovecy, *Automating Library Procedures: A Survivor's Handbook.* (London: The Library Association, 1984): 45.
24. Battin, "The Electronic Library," p. 134.
25. Ibid., p. 137.
26. Richard M. Dougherty, "Libraries and Computing Centers: A Blueprint for Collaboration," *College and Research Libraries* 48, no. 4 (July 1987): 294.
27. Stephen R. Geiger, "Electronics in Publishing and the Consequences," *Scholarly Publishing* 18, no. 1 (October 1986): 31.
28. Schmidt, "Electronic Publishing and the Academic Library," p. 184.
29. Brownrigg, "Technical Services in the Age of Electronic Publishing," p. 65.
30. Pamela S. Cenzer, "Decentralized Acquisitions—A Future Trend?" *Library Acquisitions: Practice and Theory* 9, no. 1 (1985): 38.
31. Martell, *The Client-Centered Academic Library*, p. 75.
32. Karen A. Schmidt, "The Acquisitions Process in Research Libraries: A Survey of ARL Libraries' Acquisitions Departments," *Library Acquisitions: Practice and Theory* 11, no. 1 (1987): 37.
33. Schmidt, "Electronic Publishing and the Academic Library," p. 187.
34. Brownrigg, "Technical Services in the Age of Electronic Publishing," p. 64.
35. Scott R. Bullard, "Acquisitions-Ache and Its Relief," *American Libraries* 18, no. 10 (November 1987): 860.
36. John Gurnsey, "Electronic Publishing and the Information Profession," *Aslib Proceedings* 38, no. 10 (October 1986): 340.

Triangle Research Libraries Network: Planning for Automating the Acquisitions/Serials Control Functions

Janet L. Flowers

SUMMARY. The Triangle Research Libraries Network (TRLN) is a cooperative project of the libraries of Duke University, North Carolina State University, and the University of North Carolina at Chapel Hill. Its goal is to provide an integrated online system for the three campuses using a distributed network. The online catalog, which is considered the core of the system, is operational. Other functions are being developed, including acquisitions/serials control. This article outlines the planning process used by the Acquisitions/Serials Advisory Committee to prepare general functional requirements for an ideal automated acquisitions/serials control subsystem. It emphasizes the importance of careful documentation to provide a solid foundation for any direction automation efforts might take. It gives advice for the development of functional requirements as well as for the evaluation of turnkey systems as alternate ways to achieve the goals stated in the requirements. Finally, it describes the lessons learned from the experience thus far.

INTRODUCTION

The Triangle Research Libraries Network (TRLN) is a cooperative automation project of the libraries of Duke University, North Carolina State University (NCSU), and the University of North Carolina at Chapel Hill (UNC-CH). Eight separately administered libraries (including main, law, business and health science libraries) are working together to provide an integrated online system using a

---

Janet L. Flowers is Head of Acquisitions, Academic Affairs Library, University of North Carolina at Chapel Hill, Chapel Hill, NC 27599-3902.

© 1989 by The Haworth Press, Inc. All rights reserved.

distributed network. The online public access catalog and database maintenance functions are operational at all three campuses.

Like many other research libraries, the TRLN institutions are planning for automated acquisitions/serials control. The Acquisitions/Serials Advisory Committee has prepared a general functional requirements document for these functions as a basis for local development. It has also evaluated one turnkey system. While much has been done, much remains to be completed before the planning will result in an operational system. This article, therefore, represents an interim progress report. It describes the lessons learned from our experience and offers advice to others preparing functional requirements or evaluating turnkey systems.

Functional requirements describe *what* the system must do to fulfill the operational needs of the participating libraries. They include the functions to be performed, the data elements required, and the products expected from the system. They do *not* include how the system will work.[1]

BACKGROUND OF TRLN

Staff from the TRLN libraries have documented the history of the network and the bases for its approaches in "The Evolution of a Cooperative On-line Network."[2] A number of factors facilitate their cooperative project. The physical proximity of the institutions is conducive to sharing resources. In addition, cooperative collection development agreements and joint bibliographic projects antedate TRLN by nearly half a century. The three institutions also share similar needs and concerns because of a common research orientation.

The development principles behind the TRLN system are carefully delineated by Joe Hewitt in his article entitled, "The Triangle Research Libraries Network."[3] The on-line catalog, which serves as the basis for the system, is designed to address the needs of large research libraries with complex bibliographic holdings. In March 1988, the TRLN system, known as the Bibliographic Information System (BIS) consisted of an on-line catalog providing author, title, subject, control number, and call number access. There are plans to add keyword and Boolean access later. Beta site testing for the circulation system is expected in the fall of 1988. A decision regarding the option for each library to purchase a turnkey acquisitions/serials system or for TRLN to begin local development of a subsystem is pending.

The TRLN libraries have very different existing acquisitions/serials operations. Duke uses an in-house automated acquisitions/serials control system which is seventeen years old.[4] The Health Sciences Library at UNC-CH uses PERLINE, while the main library has a totally manual system. The library at NCSU has a manual system for ordering but an automated system for payment. The size of the operations to be automated varies. In Fiscal Year 1985-86, one acquisitions department placed 62,000 monographic orders, while another placed 1,200 orders. The organizational structures are also different; some have combined acquisitions/serials units while others have separate departments. The needs and priorities of the individual libraries vary and had to be accommodated in the planning process.

THE PLANNING PROCESS THUS FAR

In November 1984, the Coordinating Committee of TRLN gave the following charge to the newly formed Acquisitions/Serials Control Advisory Committee: "The committee is to develop general level specifications for the acquisitions and serials components of the TRLN system. . . ."[5] The specifications were to describe an ideal acquisitions/serials control subsystem meeting the operational requirements of the participating libraries. Committee members initially assumed that TRLN would use these general functional requirements to develop detailed specifications for its subsystem.

The committee began its work with four objectives. The first was to define an acquisitions/serials control system that could accommodate a variety of complex ordering situations, ranging from single or multiple orders to material in hand. The second was to conceptualize acquisitions/serials control work as one subsystem even though the functions might be handled by different departments. The third objective was to make on order/in process data available through the on-line catalog. The last was to provide flexibility to accommodate the needs of all the libraries without undue requirements on the smaller libraries or restrictions on the larger ones.

After considerable discussion and numerous drafts, the committee produced a report that sets forth the general functional requirements.[6] In conjunction with the TRLN Public Interface Committee, we also prepared a report conceptualizing the relationship between the acquisitions/serials subsystem and the on-line catalog.[7]

Our work was to serve as the basis for further development of a local subsystem. However, due to internal financial considerations and the desire to speed up the process, the committee was asked to shift its focus. Some TRLN libraries needed an acquisitions/serials control system as soon as possible. It also appeared that financial resources might be available to purchase an interim system for use while TRLN developed a local subsystem. We therefore carefully reviewed the turnkey systems available and found one that appeared to meet the needs of those libraries interested in an interim solution.

Our in-depth investigation included preparation of an extensive list of questions for the vendor. A lengthy list of questions for users, visits to libraries having the system, and three days of demonstrations. The questions for the vendor were a modification of the functional requirements document.[8] The committee also prepared a lengthy survey for users containing questions regarding the customer's background, the installation process (implementation and training issues), and documentation. There were additional questions about response time, downtime, system features (such as the size of files, any exceptional routines required by the system and the report capabilities), downloading and interfacing.[9] Finally, after receiving extensive documentation from the vendor, the committee prepared more questions to be covered in the demonstrations.[10]

As a result of this effort, substantial information about the system's capabilities was gathered. The committee then developed a chart to evaluate the strengths and weaknesses of the vendor's system. The grid included such categories as support of MARC, authorization levels, duplicate detection, documentation, training, claiming, cancellation, serials check in, fund control, and reports. Each committee member completed the evaluation grid and shared it with the other members. There were, as was to be expected, variations in the interpretations of the system. For example, those with automated systems were more aware of the steps involved in performing certain actions using the system and were concerned about easy mobility from one screen to another, an issue not as apparent to those without this experience. For those with automated systems, a turnkey system must include at least the capabilities of the one already in place. For example, a library which already has electronic transmission of invoicing information does not want to lose that capability.

Whether TRLN should develop the acquisitions/serials subsystem themselves or purchase a turnkey system to link with BIS is a difficult and complex issue. For that reason, TRLN hired a consultant in March 1988 to evaluate a proposal for local development. The consultant analyzed the functional adequacy and reasonableness of the effort estimates. His findings will be used by the directors of the TRLN libraries, along with a variety of other information, to decide upon the appropriate course of action. The general functional requirements are a central part of the documentation being used by the consultant in this task.

ADVICE REGARDING FUNCTIONAL REQUIREMENTS

Although several stages in the planning process are still ahead of us, we have learned important skills regarding the process. The following two sections will give advice for some of the process-oriented issues in writing functional requirements or evaluating turnkey systems.

Preparation for an automated acquisitions/serials control system, especially in a consortium environment, is a time-consuming process whether the system is developed or purchased. Planning must be done carefully and systematically. James Rush says, "Automation is never a substitute for careful planning and intelligent action. Understanding requirements and selecting the right tools to satisfy them are the keys to successfully implementing . . . automation."[11]

Those involved in acquisitions/serials work already know the complex and detailed nature of our tasks. This knowledge is reinforced when one begins to consider the initial automation or reintroduction of automation into our operations. The planning process is not easy. In hindsight, the following advice may help those acquisitions/serials librarians who have this opportunity ahead of them.

Select Committee Members with the Skills Needed

Look for committee members with a variety of skills. If the members of the planning group have some or all of these skills, the likelihood of a successful planning process is enhanced.

- Knowledge of the functions to be automated is essential, because functional design requires an in-depth analysis of the tasks to be done.
- Good critical thinking skills are vital, because the planning requires follow-through of ideas to their logical conclusion.
- Organizational ability is very important because there is much work to do when preparing functional requirements.
- Technical writing skills are important, because the documentation must be clear and unambiguous to both the vendor and the local systems staff.
- Editorial skills are necessary to ensure that the documentation is consistent in style and format.

Define Functional Requirements Carefully

- Define the functional requirements carefully and systematically. Describe the components expected, e.g., "The bibliographic data component identifies the materials being considered and acquired for the collections of the TRLN libraries. It accommodates all fixed and variable fields defined for the MARC formats for bibliographic data."[12]
- Explain the purpose of the function. For example, in fund control, one purpose may be "to encumber, disencumber, and expend funds/subfunds."[13]
- Prepare a comprehensive, but not necessarily exhaustive, list of the data elements to illustrate the many details being maintained in an acquisitions/serials control system. Place the data elements into logically related groups.
- Define the printed and electronic products expected from the system.
- Define *needs versus wants*. Review the capabilities defined and decide which ones are essential (i.e., needs) and which can be eliminated or delayed (i.e., wants). This step, while

difficult, is necessary when confronted with the reality of what is available and what can be provided.

Document Everything

Keep careful records documenting the process used, the drafts prepared, and the decisions reached. The planning process can be lengthy especially when several libraries are working together. During that time, many decisions will be made, changes will be incorporated, and expectations will be adjusted to a more realistic level. All of this documentation will be useful at various stages of the planning process from the evaluation of systems to the implementation.

The various iterations of our functional requirements document attest to the discussions that were necessary before arriving at a consensus. Keeping a record of the process used and of the decisions made and the reports prepared will enable us to move quickly to the next stage in the planning process, whatever that may be. The author agrees with Carol Chamberlain's assessment that ". . . documentation provided a written testimony of the planning effort and a firm foundation for the subsequent phases of development and implementation."[14]

Use a Top Down Approach to Conceptualization

Work from the broadest to the most detailed level when describing the requirements for an automated acquisitions/serials control system. This enables one to approach the work from a different perspective than that used in the daily operation. Develop discipline by starting with a word then developing it into a phrase, a sentence, and finally a descriptive paragraph. Using this approach, one starts with a conceptual framework which can be fleshed out in an iterative fashion. Use of a top down approach provides consistency in presentation and ensures that every possible angle relating to a particular topic is covered.

Use extreme care in the language. In writing technical specifications, one must not be literary. Be consistent. Always express the same idea or concept in the same way to avoid any ambiguity. Use consistent terminology even when talking about the various versions of the documentation. Using common terminology, even for the drafts of your documentation, will help to keep track of the status of plans.

Involve Staff

Encourage library administration to involve as many staff as possible. This gives a broader perspective on the process and encourages their future involvement. If possible, allow time to receive staff reaction to the work done by your planning group both to critique your ideas and to gain support for them. Get reactions from staff other than those in the departments being automated, for many will have an interest and a need to know what is being planned.

Enlist the assistance of a systems expert to work with your planning group. If this is not possible, spend some time learning more about systems terminology and theory before plunging into your tasks. The more the planning group understands about the way systems are designed and work, the more likely it will understand the consequences of the choices. These choices are vitally important to the users, because they affect the way the system will work and the tasks the users must perform.

ADVICE REGARDING EVALUATION OF VENDOR SYSTEMS

Define Functional Requirements Carefully

- Define the functional requirements carefully and systematically.
- Prepare a list of the data elements required.
- Define the printed and electronic products expected from the system.
- Determine needs versus wants.

Identify Possible Vendors

Identify likely vendors from those listed in the library literature or displayed at professional meetings and by consulting colleagues at comparable institutions. The selection should be based on factors such as the basic capacity of the system, its reputation, and system capabilities. The elimination of systems for review include such factors as inadequate capacity for volume of transactions the operation handles, limited number of customers, or uncertain commitment to future development.

Request Information from Vendors

Use the functional requirements as the basis for your request for information. Include the data elements you have identified as essential. Find out whether the system has a field for each element. If so, determine what the field's characteristics are. If the data is encoded it will cut down on storage but it means staff must remember more codes and requires access to the coding schemes. If the data is structured, it could be useful in validation. If the data is variable but not structured, it is more difficult to search or sort.

Be certain to include appropriate technical questions. Get help from systems staff if you do not have that expertise in your planning group or within your library. Include questions about the hardware, operating system, applications software, system maintenance, and the technical skills required to operate the system. Spell out the requirements for interfacing the vendor's hardware/software with the local system.

Prepare Questions for Users

Ask users which feature of the system pleases them the most. Also ask them about their disappointments. Include a what-did-I-forget-to-ask question. Those who are working in a manual environment may well overlook features that are commonplace to those working in automated environments. For example, in our survey, several users reminded us of the importance of carefully deciding how and when to purge the files, an implementation consideration we might have slighted.

Arrange Demonstrations of Systems

Plan the demonstrations of the systems very carefully. There are three major considerations: attendees, content, and decision-making roles. First is who to include in the sessions. Of course, the staff from the acquisitions and serials units must be included. In addition many other staff from other departments as well as the public will be affected by the automation of the acquisitions/serials control functions. For example, the collection development librarians will be interested in what management data is available through the system. The public services staff will want to know what the user will see and how easy it will be to interpret, while catalogers will want to know about using the system for in-process control. The system must meet their requirements, too.

The second issue is the content of the sessions. Be careful not to remain at such a general level that the vendor gives a canned presentation. Structure the sessions so specific questions prepared by the library can be raised. Allow adequate time for follow-up and full comprehension of how the system works.

The third issue is the participants' role in the decision-making process. Can they express opinions and reservations? To whom? In what format? The time for demonstrations is limited so it must be carefully scheduled to provide maximum information regarding the system.

Visit Other Libraries

If possible, visit libraries using the systems in which you are interested. Or, if you are developing a local system, visit other libraries to see what you like or do not like in existing systems. Try to get first-hand experience in using the system. Ask the users to describe their workflow, their frustrations, and their recommendations. Ask them for caveats based on their experience.

Prepare a Final Evaluation

After gathering information about the system from the vendor, other users, and demonstrations, evaluate the system carefully in the light of your own needs. There are at least five questions to answer when assessing the suitability of any turnkey system to meet the needs of a consortium seeking a vendor product to use in conjunction with the local system.

- Does the system meet the general functional requirements defined by the library?
- Can the system accommodate the number of records/transactions required by each operation?
- Can a single system serve all of the libraries or are separate systems necessary?
- Can the system be networked and linked with the local system and, if so, how easily?
- What will the system cost the libraries and can they afford it?

Compare and analyze the features of the systems systematically. Use clearly defined priorities so if the vendor does not meet system requirements, one will know whether the deficiency is a critical one. Prepare a precise definition of the contents of acquisitions/serials control records in the local on-line system before beginning a discussion about the interface between a turnkey acquisitions/serials control system and the local one. Try to obtain a clear idea of the technical requirements for an interface.

LESSONS LEARNED

After many hours of work, including much discussion of our needs, the following lessons can be taken from the experience thus far. Although these lessons were learned in the context of a consortium environment with the intent of designing a local system, they may be relevant for others planning an automated system.

Capabilities List versus Design Document

Despite advice from the systems staff, the committee had difficulty separating *what* the system should do from *how* it should do it. As a result, we included some design assumptions in our functional requirements report. There were two unfortunate consequences of this. One was the writing of the report took longer than would have been necessary if we had remained strictly with functions, an area which we knew well. Another was that, when we needed to use the report as the basis for evaluation of a system, the design assumptions were irrelevant. Therefore, we had to adapt the report. The report would have served equally well for local development or a turnkey evaluation if it had been confined to capabilities. We advise a strict definition of the functional requirements document. It should list the functions to be performed, the relevant data elements, and the products required. Leave the design to the systems staff!

Similarity of Functional Requirements

As described earlier, there are many differences among the libraries involved in this planning process. Nonetheless, one lesson learned—after we had reached mutual understandings regarding local terminology—was that we all need essentially the same functions for our operations. Recognition of this fact took some time as we compared local variations in practice and concerns. In time, however, we recognized that, when stripped to the basics, our needs were fundamentally compatible. This, of course, reinforced the perception that mutual work on this project was of benefit to us all.

The committee also discovered that it was easy to treat both monographic and serial acquisitions in the same manner. The single major exception to this is the area of serials check-in where there is a need for repeatable fields to provide historic records of receipts. In most other areas, we found that the same functions, data elements, and products applied. We suggest that a combined approach to the design of automated acquisitions/serials control can be a time-saver as well as a method to ensure compatibility and uniformity between the two areas.

Necessary Tradeoffs

It is now clear to the committee that any system, whether developed locally or purchased, will have some undesirable features and will lack something wanted. Also, due to funding, staffing or other considerations, the implementation of a system must often be done in phases. Tradeoffs must be weighed against one another. Ease of use must be balanced against the need to provide for every possible situation that can occur in an acquisitions or serials environment. Speed of access must be balanced against the cost of indexing and storing the data. Report generation may well require downloading to allow the flexibility desired and to save storage costs in the main system. In short, no system will have all of the features listed in an idealistic document. We suggest, however, that many of the features wanted can be obtained with careful attention to selection of a system or design of a local one.

In preparation for the consultant's evaluation, another committee, with systems expertise, amended our functional requirements document to a more realistic level. One adjustment was to specify that data output needed to be in common formats. In other words, the libraries must agree among themselves about the forms used, the reports expected, and coding. The second change was the delaying of electronic links with vendors. Although the eight libraries use many vendors in common, the cost of the system requirements to interface with several of these are prohibitive at this time. We would suggest seeking the advice of systems staff when attempting to pare down expectations. They can give insight into the consequences of the capabilities requested.

Either local development or purchase of a turnkey system can be used to meet the needs defined in the functional requirements stage. Briefly, local development of a sub-system gives the library greater control over the features provided than does a turnkey system. It also allows the use of the same hardware being used for the rest of the on-line system, thus reducing the number and types of terminals with which the user must contend. Local development also results in the use of the same command structure and search keys as that of the on-line catalog. Finally, a local sub-system can permit faster update of files. In some cases, such modifications may be made online.

A turnkey system offers the library a product that is already tested. It may be available to users faster than a locally developed system. This depends in part upon the waiting period to install the system and to interface it with the local system(s). With a linked system, necessary delays in showing transactions in the public catalog must be included in operational decisions. Each option involves tradeoffs which must be assessed before decisions can be made.

The *develop versus purchase* choice also involves developmental concerns such as enhancement of the on-line catalog versus local development of the acquisitions/serials control system. Is it more important, for example, to develop Boolean searching capabilities or authority control for the on-line catalog or to add acquisitions/serials control functions? Decisions of this kind affect the entire library, thus complicating the decision-making process. Given limited time and money, one choice must be weighed against the other.

Throughout the planning process, the political and economic realities at each participating library affect the decisions reached as well as whether they are acted upon. Libraries must operate within the constraints of the financial and staffing resources available. TRLN libraries include both private and public institutions, each with different sets of constraints, sources of funding and demands upon those resources. The priorities of multiple libraries at various stages of development and needs relative to automation must be balanced. Dealing with the many tradeoffs requires taking a wider perspective on the functional requirements and making tough decisions within the context of the local situation.

CONCLUSION

The issues surrounding the automation of acquisitions/serials control functions are complex. The planning process can be frustrating and time-consuming. However, it is exciting to plan for a system (whether local or turnkey) to perform tasks more easily and efficiently while also enhancing the services the library can provide. Careful formulation of the general functional requirements (i.e., capabilities) required for automated acquisitions/serials control gives the library the ability to act more quickly upon decisions made after reviewing the tradeoffs involved.

REFERENCES

1. James Rush's books on evaluation of acquisitions and serials control systems provide detailed descriptions of the requirements for those two functions and are a good resource for the library beginning this process. James E. Rush Associates, Inc., *Library Systems Evaluation Guide: Acquisitions*. (Powell, Ohio: James E. Rush Associates, Inc., 1984) and *Library Systems Evaluation Guide: Serials*. (Powell, Ohio: James E. Rush Associates, Inc., 1983).
2. Gary D. Byrd et al., "The Evolution of a Cooperative On-Line Network:

Lessons from the History of the Triangle Research Libraries Network," *Library Journal* v. 110 (February 1, 1985), pp. 71-77.

3. Joe A. Hewitt, "The Triangle Research Libraries Network," *North Carolina Libraries* v. 42 (Summer 1984), pp. 68-72.

4. Thomas W. Leohardt, "The Duke University Library Automated Acquisitions System," *Library Acquisitions: Practice and Theory* v. 5 (1981), pp. 185-191.

5. Letter to TRLN Acquisitions/Serials Advisory Committee from Joe A. Hewitt dated June 19, 1985.

6. TRLN Acquisitions/Serials Advisory Committee, "BIS Acquisitions/Serials Control Subsystem: General Functional Requirements," May 1986.

7. TRLN Public Interface Committee, "Acquisitions/Serials Information and the On-Line Catalog," February 15, 1987.

8. TRLN Acquisitions/Serials Advisory Committee, "Questions Regarding Functional Requirements for an Automated Acquisitions/Serials Control System," October 7, 1986.

9. TRLN Acquisitions/Serials Advisory Committee, "Questions for . . . Customers," October 13, 1986.

10. TRLN Acquisitions/Serials Advisory Committee, "Questions for Demonstrations," November 11, 1986.

11. James E. Rush, "Automated Serials Control Systems," *Serials Review* v. 12, Nos. 2-3 (Summer-Fall 1986), p. 101.

12. TRLN Acquisitions/Serials Advisory Committee. "BIS Acquisitions/Serials Control Subsystem: General Functional Requirements," p. 5.

13. Ibid, p. 17

14. Carol E. Chamberlain, "Automating Acquisitions: a Perspective from the Inside," *Library Hi Tech* Consecutive Issue 11, v. 3, No. 3 (1986), pp. 57-66.

Vendor Relations and Automation

Marcia Anderson
Donald E. Riggs

SUMMARY. Automation of acquisitions functions and vendor-supplied automated systems and services have changed the nature of library and vendor relations. Automated support services give vendors an edge in a competitive marketplace, but may be costly in terms of overhead. Libraries may enjoy the convenience and efficiency that vendor-supplied automated support offers, but must remember that the vendor's product (books/journals/learning materials) and service is of primary importance. Automated support services have heightened the sense of interdependency between libraries and vendors. Libraries must periodically evaluate a vendor's product, service and automated support in relation to their own strategy for the future. Vendors will continue to increase the variety and sophistication of the automated support services they offer. Libraries must ensure that they retain their freedom of choice among vendors.

INTRODUCTION

Automation of the various acquisitions functions has afforded many advantages to libraries and vendors. Mechanical devices have been used for decades by libraries and vendors for greater efficiency in procurement and distribution activities. However, only in the past eight to ten years, has the level of sophistication in systems and in libraries spiraled, causing greater demand for automated interaction with and services from vendors. The development of automated acquisitions functions is a bit like a whirlwind—so much is

---

Marcia Anderson is Head of the Acquisitions Department and Donald E. Riggs is Dean of University Libraries, Arizona State University, Tempe, AZ 85287.

Several vendors were interviewed on their perceptions of the role automation plays in the relations between vendors and libraries. Some of their thoughts are included in this article. The authors are grateful for the vendors' cooperation.

© 1989 by The Haworth Press, Inc. All rights reserved.

happening, so quickly on both a national and international scale. The situation resembles the very early years of serial data control. Fasana described the situation as ". . . virtually impossible to keep abreast of current happenings; it is almost like burying your head in the sand to interpret or find a logic in many of these events."[1]

Veaner gives three major reasons for automating: "To do something less expensively, more accurately, or more rapidly . . . [or] which can no longer be done effectively in the manual system because of increased complexity or overwhelming volume . . . [or] which cannot be performed in the manual system. . ."[2] Much has been written on the reasons why libraries automate their acquisitions activities. However, the literature reflects little on the vendors' rationale for automating functions. Essentially, vendors automate various internal functions for many of the same reasons cited by libraries. Many vendors developed billing/invoicing and ordering systems in order to more effectively manage their internal operations, and thus, provide better service to their customers. Some vendors developed automated systems specifically to market to libraries. Internal needs and external competition were the driving forces behind vendor automation activities.

The many advances made in technology have permanently changed acquisitions operations, making them streamlined and efficient. Libraries and vendors are, and should be, proud of the progress made in automating these complex and labor-intensive functions. Although many acquisitions-related technological issues await resolution, many improvements have already been realized. One area radically changed by automation is that of library/vendor relations.

HISTORICAL PERSPECTIVE

Through the mid-1960s, the computerized acquisitions' applications used by libraries and vendors were primarily off-line technology employed to achieve basic control of data and/or to create various types of lists. Batch processing of data into the computer (usually overnight) was the most common method of creating and updating a database. Very little computerized interaction between libraries and vendors occurred. After the mid-1960s, the immediate entry of individual transactions via terminals (connected directly with a vendor's computer) became possible. Twenty years later, online systems, intelligent terminals, visual display units, minicomputers, large disk stores, advanced programming techniques and sophisticated telecommunications have all contributed to the creation of elegant systems which are far easier to use and much more effective than their manual counterparts.[3]

Libraries and vendors are rushing to apply this revolutionary technology in a myriad of ways. They have chosen to make use of the new technology to resolve many of the complexities of the various acquisitions/serials functions. For example, the function of serials claiming has been radically modified by the advent of automated systems. The claim function is most definitely a two-way responsibility, i.e., the responsibility of both the library and the vendor. A journal not received creates a gap in library service. When a library places a request with its journal vendor for action on a missing journal, a "claim" function has been performed. Modern technology has eliminated much of the labor from the claims process. Online serial control systems save hours of personnel time by automatically determining which journal issues have not been received and printing claims ready for mailing. Second and third claims are automatic and easily identified for further action. For a number of years, vendors have used data processing techniques for communicating journal claims to publishers. Many libraries communicate directly with their journal vendors via a terminal linked to the vendor's system. These online capabilities have not only saved staff time, but have tremendously enhanced interactions and relations between vendors and libraries. Automation of claim functions has changed what was once viewed as a sometimes "win-lose" situation to a "win-win" situation for vendors and libraries.

The application of automated technology to acquisitions/serials operations has most assuredly benefited both vendor and library. Former Librarian of Congress Daniel Boorstin offered the following perspective on the computer and information control:

> The last two decades have seen the spectacular growth of the information industry—the frontier spirit in the late twentieth century. A magic computer technology accomplishes the dreariest tasks in seconds, surpasses the accuracy of the human brain, controls production lines and refineries, arranges

inventories, and retrieves records. All this makes us proud of the human imagination.[4]

LIBRARY CHANGES

The automation of acquisitions functions and vendor support services creates many changes in library operations. Much has been written on the effect of change on library personnel. High stress levels and fear of change are natural byproducts of implementing an automated system/support service. Library administrators know that change is essential to the effectiveness of organizations, but, the human preference for maintaining the status quo remains strong. Staff concerns for job security and complexity of job tasks after automation must be addressed. Library administrators must be proactive in creating a climate in which the transition from a manual to an automated system is made with as much ease as possible. Planning for a change to an automated system must include a sensitivity to the human element.

Vendor interactions and relations are also an essential concern in planning and implementing an automated system. Prior to automating acquisitions/serials operations, a library should ask the following questions:

1. What impact will the new system have on order/receipt/payment procedures in relation to our vendors?
2. What communication problems will the new system create (or reduce) with our vendors?
3. Is our system compatible with our vendors' systems? If not, what can we do to prevent a reduction in level of service?
4. Have we notified all of our vendors of the unique characteristics of our new system?

Automation of acquisitions/serials functions and the availability of automated vendor support systems has changed, in a very basic way, how many libraries view vendor services. Expectations are greater. Libraries now expect a vendor to offer automated support, e.g., downloading of invoice and bibliographic information into the libraries' system. Indeed, several years after automating acquisitions operations, some libraries may no longer be staffed to handle all manual record entry or invoice processing. In addition, the tight economic conditions of the past fifteen years have encouraged libraries to demand "more" for their limited funds. Today, libraries are asking for healthy discounts, excellent service and vendor-supplied automated support.

VENDOR CHANGES

In some cases, vendors have been more progressive in designing and implementing automated systems than have some libraries. Lack of funds has prohibited many libraries from purchasing and implementing an online acquisitions/serials control system. Marketplace competition has forced many vendors to develop automated systems. Like libraries, vendors must ask questions when considering the investment in an automated system. The following are some examples:

1. Will our system interface with the various systems of our client libraries?
2. How shall priorities for hardware/software development be determined?
3. How much influence should any single customer, or group of customers, have on decisions relating to our automated capabilities?
4. Should we contract for our computing services, purchase turnkey software, or develop software within the company?
5. How will we continue to effectively interface with our clients as they upgrade their own hardware/software?

As the nature of the vendor's business changes, i.e., marketing automated support systems in addition to the basic book/journal products and services, the vendor's sales representatives must also change. As the most visible and available of the vendor's services, the sales representative usually has a very close relationship with client libraries. In addition to understanding the issues related to books and journals, a sales representative must be knowledgeable about automated support for libraries. A representative who is not, will not be well received by sophisticated acquisitions/serials personnel. To date, most vendor sales representatives have more than adequately adjusted their "pitch" to include intelligent discussion of automated support for library operations. At times, a sales representative may need to refer library personnel to the vendor's system development staff. Such referral is appropriate for the more sophisticated questions of computer-to-computer interfacing. The representative, however, must be able to engage in a knowing discussion of the capabilities and limitations of the vendor's automated system/ services. Libraries expect vendors to help them, to "consult" with them, and to suggest methods of manipulating data now available from automated support systems. Libraries want assistance in maximizing the capabilities of their own system and/or the vendor's automated services.

ADVANTAGES TO VENDORS

A vendor realizes several definite advantages by automating operations and providing automated support services to libraries. Increasing the efficiency of operations is, perhaps, most important. Labor costs and space constraints are major considerations to both libraries and vendors. Automation of labor-intensive internal operations, e.g., order entry or billing, reduces overhead costs for vendors. Book/journal vendors operate in a highly competitive marketplace and, thus, are constantly searching for better ways to serve their customers. Vendor-supplied automated support/systems may offer a competitive edge unmatched by another vendor. In some instances, vendors automated their internal operations of necessity and only later realized that, with very little additional investment, much of their system or support services could be marketed to libraries.

One of the chief benefits from automated services to be realized by vendors is the improvement in relations with libraries. Sophisticated management report capability allows the vendor to closely monitor accounts. Instead of waiting to be informed of a problem by an unhappy client, the vendor is now aware of the problem and can take quick action to correct it. A vendor can see at a glance if a degradation in service has occurred over a given time period. If turnaround time is slow or the fulfillment rate is low, the system can assist in analyzing the data and efficiency and effectiveness can be improved. Alternatively, if need be, data supplied by the system can be used to counter a client's claims of less than expected service.

Implementation of and sustaining effective automated systems/services is not an easy task for vendors. Many vendors find that they require a "small army" of trained, and many times highly paid, staff to support automated services. The profit margin on books and journals is generally narrow and many vendors question whether they can be expected to provide a full range of sophisticated automated services to libraries. While the "front-end" of services provided by the vendor may be a client's dream, the "back-end" may be a debacle for the vendor in terms of research/development and staff costs. Nonetheless, automation activity among vendors indicates that the advantages of offering automated support to libraries outweigh the disadvantages.

PERCEPTIONS

The emergence of automated systems has changed the perceptions of vendors and librarians. Initially, automated systems and vendor-supplied automated support services were embraced most enthusiastically by library directors. When questioned, many vendors state that the systems appealed especially to the elitism of academic library directors. Personnel in acquisitions/serials departments were often reluctant to abandon manual operations and to forego "personal contact" with account representatives and customer service personnel. In addition to this normal resistance to change, many staff members felt that they now were performing tasks that vendor personnel once performed, e.g., data entry and database searches. Staff in other areas of the library, for example, collection development or cataloging, perceived a loss of control as there was often fewer paper forms and a greater dependence on the vendor's database for information. However, as automated services increased in sophistication and library staff realized the benefits of so much information at their fingertips, resistance was generally transformed into enthusiasm and demands for more service and access.

Vendors perceive automated support systems/services as part of a "better mousetrap." The services provide a way to tie the library more closely to the vendor, in effect, to sell more books/journals to the library. If the library has purchased a vendor system, the system is completely geared to that vendor and the library is virtually a "captive customer." However, even libraries which own a system independent of book/journal vendors, may find that they are bound very closely to a vendor. Implementing an interface between the library's and vendor's systems can forge an extremely comfortable and mutually advantageous working relationship between vendor and library—one that a library may find difficult to break.

Many vendors view automated support services as a cost they must bear in order to market their products (books/journals) to libraries. Libraries often regard automated vendor support as their right and do not feel that they should be made to bear the costs for these services. However, as the demand for new and more complex services grows, vendors may request that libraries contribute to research and development and on-going costs. They may increase their charges for books/journals in order to offset the cost of automated support requested by their clients. If these occurrences arise, the relationships between vendors and libraries will become more complex as libraries seek imaginative ways of maintaining their purchasing power without relinquishing the automated support and services they now rely on. The opportunity exists for a creative vendor with a "better mousetrap."

INTERDEPENDENCY

Despite the fact that the relationship between libraries and vendors is, by nature, "adversarial," i.e., purveyor of goods versus consumer, there has always been a sense of interdependency between the two entities. Automated support services have heightened this interdependency. When a library avails itself of a vendor's automated services, the decision to change vendors becomes more complex than a simple change in where orders and claims are mailed. Installing, testing and utilizing a system/service supplied by a vendor creates a bond between vendor and library. The vendor becomes attuned to the library's internal processes. Vendor-supplied hardware is often installed in the library. Lease and service agreements may exist for hardware/software. Relationships are established, via telephone and electronic mail, with vendor support staff. A library may provide input on system enhancements to the vendor. All of these circumstances serve to tighten the relationship between library and vendor. The convenience offered by a vendor's automated services to a library may cloud the issues of service and reliability.

The choice to change vendors requires a "disengagement period," often lasting over one year, while hardware is removed, systems replaced, internal processes adjusted and personal relationships established elsewhere. Needless to say, this process can be traumatic for both the library and vendor. The desire to avoid such a change can sometimes be strong enough to cause a library to accept less than excellent service or products.

Under these circumstances, the library must be a "good consumer" and maintain a balanced perspective. It is important that they not abdicate responsibility of choice to a vendor. They must evaluate the total vendor package of service, product and automated support. If service, reliability and product are anything less than excellent, a library must be willing to disassociate from a vendor, no matter what vendor-supplied automated support/services they have enjoyed.

EVALUATION OF RELATIONSHIP AND COMMUNICATION

An effective working relationship between a library and a vendor is best maintained if it is evaluated on a regular basis. A thorough evaluation of service, product and automated support/services should occur approximately every three years. Scrutiny of service and product should emphasize reliability, delivery of goods, turnaround time, cost for product and shipping, customer support services, etc. When evaluating vendor-supplied automated services, questions should focus on the following: (1) How is the system contributing to the overall achievement of acquisitions goals, e.g., lowering costs, saving staff time, increasing efficiency, getting books/journals to users more quickly? (2) Are reasonable standards of system performance being met? A library should establish a set of standards allowing for both specialized local needs and accepted vendor constraints. (3) Does the automated system/service still fit into the library's overall technological plan? Is the system compatible with new or existing library systems, is the cost/benefit ratio still favorable, what are the possibilities for interfacing with other library systems, what is the time frame for establishing such an interface?

The above questions can be used for evaluation purposes by either libraries or vendors. Evaluation instruments and results of systematic evaluations can be shared between libraries and vendors. The value of effective communication in maintaining strong vendor/library relations cannot be underrated. Technological interactions between libraries and vendors comprise a very important form of communication. Expanded online services and capabilities, management reports, etc. are really forms of communication between vendors and libraries. As the use of these "automated" forms of communication grows, libraries and vendors must ensure that system operations serve to enhance communication, not to impede it.

STRATEGIES FOR FUTURE PLANNING

The future of vendor-supplied automated systems/services in acquisitions activities will require critical thinking on the part of both vendors and librarians. Four basic questions should be asked: (1) What is the current situation in regard to the automated service/system? (2) What is the desired future for the service/system? (3) What factors might inhibit the realization of these future plans? (4) What action can be taken to achieve both the library's and vendor's goals and objectives vis-à-vis the automated system/service?

Collaborative strategies should be formulated between the vendor and library. Every strategy employed by the two groups should be consciously designed and regularly assessed. Strategies should be stable, flexible and adaptable. Vendors and libraries should collaborate on personnel strategies, growth strategies, financial strategies and innovation strategies.

CONCLUSION

The arena of library/vendor relations has been significantly changed by the advent of automated systems and support services. Automation has forged a closer relationship between libraries and vendors and brought a new competitiveness to the library marketplace. While enjoying the convenience and increased efficiency automated services provide, libraries must keep sight of the fact that they are consumers of a vendor's basic products (books/journals/learning materials), not simply consumers of automated support services. The "bells and whistles" of automated systems/services cannot serve to mask an inferior product.

In an effort to gain a competitive edge in the marketplace, vendors will continue to supply and to enhance automated services and systems now available to libraries. If development costs rise, however, some vendors will be unable to bear the cost of automation, in addition to maintaining high levels of service. These vendors may choose to cut automated services/support and attempt to compete solely on the basis of their products. Lacking a sound product, some vendors will not be able to retain their customers. Libraries will benefit by an increase in innovation and in the range of services offered by vendors.

Relations with vendors should continue to be measured in terms of competitive pricing, reliability in delivery, and customer support. Libraries should retain their freedom of choice among vendors and be willing to disengage from one vendor if superior products and services at a competitive price are offered by another vendor. The shift of large amounts of business from one vendor to another will certainly continue as libraries evaluate vendor products and services and review their own automation goals.

The key to successful future relations between vendors and libraries in regard to automated support services is careful planning between the two entities and open communication. Compatible automated systems and services is also necessary. There will inevitably be some "give and take" during discussion and decision on the "desired fruits" from the automated system. When two actions performed jointly produce a larger result than they would if performed independently, synergy exists. (An example of "synergy" is 3 + 3 = 7.) It is an important element in collaboration between libraries and vendors. However, synergy will not just happen; it must be planned for and made to happen.

REFERENCES

1. Paul Fasana, "Serials Data Control: Current Problems and Prospects," *Journal of Library Automation* 9:319-33 (March 1971).
2. Allen Veaner, "Major Decisions Points in Library Automation," *College and Research Libraries* 31:299-312 (September 1970).
3. P. A. Thomas, "The Use of Computers," in *Serials Librarianship*, edited by Ross Bourne (London, Library Association, 1980).
4. Daniel Boorstin, *Gresham's Law: Knowledge or Information* (Dallas, Somesuch Press, 1980).

IN-HOUSE DEVELOPED INTEGRATED SYSTEMS

Life in a Gold Fish Bowl: Or the Changing Nature of Acquisitions Work in an Integrated Online Environment

Sally W. Somers

SUMMARY. The integrated online automated system is a recent development in libraries. The implementation of the integrated MARVEL system and the decision to display order information to all staff has had a great impact on the nature of acquisitions work at the University of Georgia Library. Integrated systems offer the opportunity to reduce or to eliminate redundancy of effort among technical services staff. Two areas for which this opportunity exists are searching—both preorder and precataloging—and LC copy cataloging. If these changes were implemented, the result would be a blurring of traditional technical services department lines.

What is the potential for change brought about by an integrated automated system within a library organization? More specifically,

---

Sally W. Somers, is Head, Acquisitions Department, University of Georgia Libraries, Athens, GA 30602.

© 1989 by The Haworth Press, Inc. All rights reserved.

how has automation affected the work of an acquisitions department? In a larger context, how will technical services organization and activities be affected by this automation?

BACKGROUND

The University of Georgia has a decade of experience gained from working on its integrated system MARVEL. I would like to use our experience to examine the impact of integrated files on the operation of acquisitions and to explore the possibilities offered by our system for reorganization of staff involved with collection development, acquisitions, and cataloging. Since the acquisitions module was the first to be developed and implemented, acquisitions experiences with automation are extensive and, I believe, typical of what might be expected at a large university library.

Actual development and implementation of integrated online systems has been accomplished largely in the 1980s although the concept of these systems has been discussed for years. One definition of an integrated automated system is a bibliographic database shared by all applications and functions which permits users to access the different functions without logging off one subsystem and logging on to another.[1] In practical terms the typical integrated system contains a common file of bibliographic records and effectively handles activities including acquisitions, cataloging, circulation, and an online public access catalog. Integrated systems generally fall into two distinct categories—distributed systems which are developed and supported by a vendor and in-house developed systems developed by and for a local environment. Examples of the former are NOTIS or GEAC while the latter are the Pennsylvania State University LIAS (Library Information Access System) system or the University of Georgia's MARVEL system (Managing Resources for University Libraries).

The MARVEL system supports functionally integrated activities for collection development, ordering, receiving, fund accounting, circulation, and an online public access catalog. System design was begun in the mid-1970s; implementation began in 1978 with the functional areas for processing materials (collection development, ordering, receiving and fund accounting); circulation was brought up in 1981; the online catalog in 1984; and the loading of our OCLC tapes began in the fall of 1987. A cataloging module was specifically omitted during the initial design because according to one of the system designers, "information in the OCLC database was superior to what could be produced locally" and ". . . the OCLC system was well established, whereas an in-house cataloging system would take years to develop and implement."[2] Although the system does not support cataloging activities online, developmental work has been completed and implemented permitting us to load and to maintain online our OCLC cataloging records. All functional areas share the same bibliographic database thereby eliminating file redundancy. The system is divided into two distinct parts with activities specific to circulation or acquisitions accomplished in the processing system in functional areas devoted to those tasks. Within this portion of the system records are updated and manipulated as needed; the online catalog portion of the system does not permit updates.

INFORMATION ABOUT ON-ORDER MATERIALS

Whether a library is automated or not, a major function of the organization is to acquire material for the collection. On-order titles have always been of great interest to library staff and patrons, and libraries traditionally tried to meet this interest by providing information about these materials. In a manual environment this information generally was a slip from the multipart order form which was filed by main entry in the public catalog. On-order information provided by a batch automated system frequently took the form of a computer-generated listing of all on-order titles; access generally was solely by title. Titles which went into a cataloging arrearage became a problem because the title might be in the library for months or even years with no access to the fact that it was available, even though not cataloged.

By contrast an integrated system provides a great deal more information and flexibility about on-order materials. Because in the MARVEL system we choose to display all processing information, it is possible for library staff and patrons to track a title from the time it is first selected for purchase until it is received for the collection. It is also possible to ascertain call number and specific location information as well as to determine whether it is available for circulation or not. Access provided by the online system offers a major advantage over a manual system since there are the multiple access points— by author, title, or series.

Library staff have access to order information which in the typical manual environment would be available only to acquisitions department staff. This information includes the date of order, the vendor to whom the order was sent, whether it was a "rush" or regular order, the most current vendor report, the number of times and the dates that the title was claimed, the reason and date a title was cancelled, the date of receipt, the amount we paid, and the date the call number was entered in the system. Call number information available online means that the cataloging department has released the title for shelving in the stacks.

ACQUISITIONS IN THE ONLINE ENVIRONMENT

How is the acquisitions department affected by the decision to display information previously not generally available to all library staff? A quick flip answer is "life in a gold fish bowl," a "life" in which all activities are under constant scrutiny. Gone are the days when the on-order file, the in-process file, and the payments file were the domain of a group of staff whose primary duties included pulling order slips and matching them against title pages. A more serious and considered answer is better information for patrons and staff regarding on-order titles. The decision to display all order information has made it essential that the acquisitions department remain current in all aspects of our work. The number of days that a title remains in the queue before a purchase order is sent to a vendor, the number of times a title is claimed, status reports from vendors, and the delivery time for titles are of paramount interest to many individuals throughout the organization. It is axiomatic that a well-run acquisitions department should be as current as possible in all aspects of its work; however, the effect of having order information available online tends to focus attention wherever information is not timely.

The acquisitions program at the University of Georgia is a large one and acquisitions department staff who are accustomed to working with large numbers of purchase orders and incoming materials tend to view the program in broad terms while other staff and patrons frequently are interested in one specific title. For example, acquisitions staff tend to think it is important that 300 purchase orders were sent to Vendor A on Tuesday; that we posted 150 status reports yesterday; or that we received a shipment of 15 boxes from Vendor A this week. Other library staff frequently represent a very different viewpoint because it makes no difference to them if we just got a shipment of 500 titles from Vendor A, if the title that s/he is interested in was not among the 500 nor has a status report regarding availability been posted. It also makes no difference if the status report is in a basket waiting to be posted—for all intents and purposes we have not received one.

Acquisitions supervisory staff faced several challenges when the MARVEL processing system was implemented. Introducing the system and training staff in new procedures after years of operating on a totally manual system could be anticipated. An unanticipated result of automating and displaying order information was the questioning of decisions which previously had been unquestioned because they had not been general knowledge and few staff within the organization were aware of them. Three activities which previously were primarily the concern of acquisitions staff which generated a great amount of interest among library staff included vendor performance, claiming, and posting of status reports. Vendor performance had never been a concern because few staff had access to vendor information nor was it easy to calculate the amount of time that it took for a vendor to supply the item. Going through a large on-order slip file for the purpose of ascertaining this type of information was not a task that most staff engaged in willingly more than once or twice. Claiming was an activity which frequently was done at irregular intervals; however, no one seemed to mind because few knew how or when the process occurred. On a manual system this labor-intensive activity frequently was "saved" for slow times of the year. The information contained in status reports generally was available only to acquisitions staff. Occasionally a selector might check to see if a status report had been received for a particular title, but this was not done routinely. As questions arose about our practices and procedures, they caused us to examine many long-standing procedures. Overall, this scrutiny has been beneficial because it caused us to analyze all aspects of our workflow and to search for ways to stream-line and to improve it.

Bibliographers and other staff experienced a similar learning process as they came to realize that many standard acquisitions practices were sound and well grounded. The advantages of acquiring materials from book jobbers, both domestic and foreign, was one aspect of the acquisitions program about which selectors had to learn. It took time for them to realize that even the most efficient foreign vendor is unable to consistently ship materials so that they reach the library in less than two to three months and frequently it takes much longer; that the publisher who advertises that a title is ready for immediate shipment is unlikely to ship the title the same day that he receives the purchase order; and the library order sent direct to the publisher may take significantly longer to fill because publisher distribution systems are set up to handle multiple copy orders.

Although one could assume that the interest in acquisitions data would focus primarily on order data, in our organization this has not been the case. Online we have had a decade of firm order data (order records and accounting information) as well as an equal amount of payment data for all serials. Locating specific payment information within the large number of payment records associated with all serials proved to be cumbersome and unwieldy as well as using an enormous amount of storage in the operating system. Because acquisitions staff assumed that ten-year-old or even four-year-old data would be of little general interest, a proposal was presented to remove noncurrent order and payment data (over three years old) from the online environment and to archive it onto microfiche. The ensuing dialog regarding both the amount of data to be removed as well as the advisability of removing anything other than the very oldest payment data has once again brought home the understanding that files, which are updated and manipulated solely by staff within the acquisitions department, are no longer the sole domain of that group.

ELIMINATING REDUNDANCY AND STREAMLINING OPERATIONS

If an integrated system eliminates file redundancy, it also points out with startling clarity redundancy and repetition of effort among staff. Systems capabilities offer the possibility of eliminating this redundancy and streamlining operations. If this opportunity is utilized, one possible outcome is a blurring of traditional technical services departmental lines. In an automated environment it is potentially more efficient to call a record up once and to manipulate it as fully as possible at that time. Staff may be more effectively utilized if they are trained to complete similar activities. Whenever changes of this nature are implemented, they may have an even more profound impact on the organization than those caused by integrated files.

Searching is a task in which several functional areas traditionally have duplicated efforts. In an online environment searching the database whether for preorder duplicate check or precataloging duplicate check is just that—searching the database. Since there is a common file of bibliographic records to be accessed, the techniques used for searching the database are similar whether the task is a preorder or precataloging search. Preorder searching has been combined with other similar searching tasks as libraries recognized the advantages gained by eliminating duplication of effort. Libraries as diverse in size as Pennsylvania State University and the University of Idaho have combined preorder searching with precataloging searching. Penn State, utilizing its LIAS system, combined acquisitions searching with copy cataloging and retrospective conversion.[3] The University of Idaho using the Washington Library Network combined the preorder search with the precatalog search and placed these activities in the cataloging department.[4] Both organizations cite more efficient use of terminals and elimination of duplication of tasks as chief reasons for combining these functions. Although both of these organizations shifted preorder searching into areas primarily associated with cataloging, searching also could be accomplished by a unit operating within an acquisitions area. The key to success lies in the level of training, not in the area performing the tasks.

MERGING ACQUISITIONS AND LC COPY CATALOGING

As a library becomes more involved with automation, activities traditionally associated with copy cataloging offer additional opportunities for merging of functions. At the University of Georgia we have discussed the possibility of shifting our Library of Congress copy cataloging to acquisitions staff who would verify that the correct title had been received, add a barcode in order to create the basic circulation record, key in accounting data, and accept and add Library of Congress cataloging copy to the record. At the time the call number is accepted, spine labels could be produced from equipment which attaches to terminals. These books could then be sent directly to a unit responsible for affixing the labels and completing shelf preparation thereby getting the titles to the patrons much faster since they would never move through a cataloging unit per se. The MARVEL record would be accessed only once and both receiving and cataloging could take place at that time.

Instituting a reorganization of this magnitude would require that a number of preliminary changes be in place and functioning effectively. The card catalog would need to be closed because there would be no card production associated with the LC copy cataloging. Holdings information for OCLC would be tape loaded. It would be essential that staff have online access to authority systems and that these systems be updated regularly with both national level data and with local data which varied from LC. Currently our LC copy catalogers in the cataloging department verify only personal names, and acquisitions staff would need access to these authority files for that activity; resolution of problems with call numbers and corporate names would continue to be accomplished by cataloging staff. A regular schedule for loading the MARC tapes from the Library of Congress into the MARVEL database would need to be functioning. Since about 75-80% of our new materials are cataloged using LC copy, a significant portion of our new titles would fall into this category.

Although the proposal to have acquisitions staff do entry level copy cataloging sounds revolutionary, this suggestion is not as startling as it may sound because entry-level staff in both acquisitions and cataloging currently verify, accept, and change records within well-defined parameters. Acquisitions staff accept the order record and change and update specific information in the record or correct a title and LC copy catalogers accept the LC cataloging record and update fields such as physical description or imprint.[5] The scope of work completed by acquisitions staff would be expanded but the nature of the work—that is, accepting a record within well-defined parameters—would remain the same.

While changes of this nature offer savings in time and better utilization of staff, much preliminary work needs to be accomplished before they could be instituted. Personnel and technical services organizational issues are complex because the traditional lines separating acquisitions and cataloging would be removed were this organizational pattern implemented. Myriad details need to be worked out, staff training procedures reviewed and the organization prepared for changes of this magnitude. A major reorganization of work flow goes to the very heart of staff jobs and if the organization were not prepared carefully the results could be turmoil and chaos.

System-imposed restrictions present an even greater hurdle than personnel-related ones. Perhaps the decision which has had the most serious long-term system implications was the decision that MARVEL was not to be in the MARC format. One of the system designers justified the decision because

> ... it was deemed best to start with a clean slate, without being bound to the MARC format, as MARC had been designed for a specific purpose—cataloging—and did not lend itself to record keeping for other functions, such as ordering, receiving, and accounting.[6]

Although a decade after implementation the MARVEL system is MARC compatible, the amount of effort expended to achieve compatibility has been costly and long. A second decision having severe repercussions was omitting a module devoted to cataloging activities. Until recently little work normally associated with cataloging has been accomplished online in MARVEL. There was no updating of receiving records with cataloging-level data until we achieved the ability to load our OCLC cataloging tapes into MARVEL; instead, system users accessed order and receiving records. We are just now beginning to wrestle with the many issues involved with cataloging in an online environment. One clear advantage to this process is that we have learned a great deal from our years of operating acquisitions online; hopefully many of the mistakes associated with designing and implementing the acquisitions modules can be avoided.

How would acquisitions staff be affected if changes in preorder searching and in cataloging books with LC copy were instituted? Changes would be immediate and profound. The most immediate change would be the blurring of defined departmental distinctions. Three distinct areas—preorder searching, acquisitions receiving, and LC copy cataloging—each having highly specific tasks possibly could disappear or be radically changed. Although I have written about staff who are responsible for receiving material and entering payment data also cataloging LC copy titles, staff whose chief responsibilities include cataloging books could just as easily have the responsibility for accepting titles and entering payment data. Whichever group had the responsibility, the activity would remain the same—updating and manipulating the same records.

Another major change to acquisitions staff would be in the level and type of training required. If the staff member working in an automated environment has a different type of job than his counterpart working in a manual environment, the staff member working in an area responsible for accepting cataloging copy for books as well as receiving them would need to be more knowledgeable about cataloging, including the MARC format and authority files. One result of the change possibly might be increased job satisfaction because of more complex responsibilities which could result in a more interesting position.

Although the managers within our organization have talked about the possibility of these organizational changes, implementation remains at least several years in the future. If the amount of time required to effect MARVEL/MARC compatibility is any yardstick, we are several years away from significant changes in organization or combining of tasks. We have yet to actually close our card catalogs. We are proceeding with retrospective conversion and with loading these records into our automated system. Administrative interest and impetus could go a long way toward urging us to make these changes sooner than expected.

CONCLUSION

One conclusion which seems irrefutable is that integrated files change dramatically the way that data traditionally thought to "belong" to the acquisitions department is updated and processed. It is imperative that the staff be as up-to-date with ordering, claiming, posting status reports, cancelling orders, and accepting titles and posting payment data as possible because this becomes important information to system users.

Differences must be accommodated in the manner that selectors and acquisitions staff evaluate the effectiveness of an acquisitions program. Bibliographers who serve as the link between faculty and patrons seeking a specific title have a different orientation than does an acquisition librarian who thinks in terms of the total number of orders or the number of books sent, the speed of delivery, and the number of problems in comparison with the overall size of the shipments. The two viewpoints are not mutually exclusive but an understanding needs to develop.

As the level and complexity of automation increases, the likelihood that traditional departmental organization patterns will remain intact diminishes. Automation focuses attention in a manner not possible in a manual environment on similarity of tasks. Since file redundancy is eliminated and the record appears only once the same record is accessed, manipulated, and updated; in terms of efficient utilization of personnel it may be good management to use the same staff to perform similar functions or to access a record once and to manipulate it as fully as possible. The result of these changes in workflow can cause a dramatic reorganization within a technical services area with traditional departmental designations crumbling.

Just as acquisitions staff have adapted and become accustomed to their gold fish bowl existence resulting from shared files, they will continue to adapt to new workflow and to new and different job responsibilities. As long as the integrated online automated system continues to develop, the nature of all library work and technical services activities in particular continue to change.

While it is true that librarians a generation ago scarcely could have conceived of the changes considered commonplace today, it is likely that the next generation of librarians will be profoundly different from librarians today. It is equally likely that technology will remain one of the major causes of these changes. Who can predict what the staff member involved in acquiring materials will be doing in order to accomplish this task in the next generation?

REFERENCES

1. Brian Aveney, "Electronic Transmission in Acquisitions Systems," *Technical Services Quarterly* (Spring/Summer, 1985), 2:17-31.
2. John Christofferson, "Automation at the University of Georgia Libraries," *Journal of Library Automation* (March, 1979), 12:22-38.
3. Suzanne Striedieck. "And The Walls Come Tumblin Down: Distributed Cataloging and the Public/Technical Services Relationship—The Technical Services Perspective," *1984 Challenges to an Information Society*. White Plains, NY: Knowledge Industry Publications, 1984. p. 118.
4. Conversation with Mary Bolin, Head of the Cataloging Department, University of Idaho Library, *January 10, 1988*.
5. Conversation with Barry Baker, Assistant Director for Technical Services, University of Georgia Library, March 18, 1988; Conversation with Katha Massey, Head of the Cataloging Department, University of Georgia Library, March 21, 1988.
6. Christofferson, p. 23.

The Evolving Structure and Automation of Acquisitions

Jessie T. Nicol

SUMMARY. One of the least studied, and least understood, areas of librarianship is acquisitions: the ordering, claiming, and receipt of library/informational materials. The traditional tasks in the acquisitions function have been very broad. Acquisitions tasks are labor intensive and until just a few years ago, all acquisitions work was performed manually. Although there have been arguments for decentralized acquisitions, to achieve efficiency and accountability, ordering, receipt and payment must be monitored by a single entity. This is supported by a 1985 survey of 28 libraries. Automation of acquisitions has been slow in development. Because of the slow development of turnkey systems, many libraries developed in-house systems, many of which are still in use. Virginia Polytechnic Institute and State University's Newman Library uses an automated acquisitions system which was developed in-house in the late 1960s. There have been many benefits, although the system has a number of imperfections. If there is a term that may be used to describe an efficient and desirable automated acquisitions system, it is flexibility because no two libraries can or should perform the same activity alike. Acquisitions will be faced with evolving developments in electronic publishing and the future focus of acquiring information, whether in print hard copy from traditional sources or through telecommunication direct from the author, will be effected through automated on-line systems.

One of the least studied, and least understood, areas of librarianship is acquisitions: the ordering, claiming, and receipt of library/informational materials. Acquisitions is the part of a library which requires a knowledge of librarianship and the practices of the publishing companies, vendors, and the book trade. It is the core, the

---

Jessie T. Nicol is Head, Acquisitions, Newman Library, Virginia Polytechnic Institute and State University, Blacksburg, VA 24061-0434.

© 1989 by The Haworth Press, Inc. All rights reserved.

activity for acquiring information necessary for a library to fulfill its service function of providing information to its clientele.[8]

Automation of acquisitions has been slow in development. There are a number of reasons, two of which are the complexities of acquisitions tasks which have demanded time and expense in development of systems, and the evolving organizational structure in the performance of the acquisitions tasks. In a 1985 survey of 28 libraries I conducted, it was interesting to learn that only seven libraries used an automated acquisitions system but 75 percent had an on-line catalog. Of those libraries with automated acquisitions systems, six had automated ordering, four used automated serials check-in and two, automated binding. Automation itself will cause further changes in the organizational structure of acquisitions, something which the in-house systems and early vendor-developed systems have indicated.

There are very labor intensive tasks in acquisitions which require much typing and filing. In the current period of library financial retrenchment and with smaller percentages of the operating budget going to acquisitions, there has been tremendous pressure on acquisitions personnel in the acquiring of materials.[2]

Just a few years ago, all acquisitions work was performed manually. In general, it is still performed manually. Out of desperation and a desire to provide on-line acquisitions information service to the library's clientele, a fair number of libraries developed in-house automated acquisitions modules. Some of these are still in use; however, their efficiency varies greatly. These were developed mostly as an interim step until turnkey systems became available. A majority of these systems are in batch mode and operate on a general purpose mainframe computer. Most of these early systems were not comprehensive acquisitions systems in their development because of technological, financial or political problems.[1]

In general, automation of acquisitions has received less attention than other library functions. Although there are many elements that enter into the slow development of the automation of the acquisitions function, two of those reasons are the nonrealization of the service benefits of the acquisitions function, its complexity, and the lack of a uniform organizational structure for performing the acquisitions task.

"The move toward integrated systems is belated in some ways

since acquisitions automation in libraries is now more than two decades old. But it is now coming very quickly and will play a very significant role in our future activities."[2] This statement was made in 1980 by one of the most knowledgeable librarians in the field of automation. Acquisitions automation of a sophisticated sort began in the mid-1960s.[2]

As we near 1990, there are several automated acquisitions systems on the market, a few of which interface with a library's system if the library uses the same system for other library functions. There are others which perform most of the tasks needed in the acquisitions operation but which do not interface with a library's on-line catalog. Now that other service functions have been automated and are in the process of becoming highly-developed, attention is focusing more on the automation of serials check-in and acquisitions functions for fully-integrated library systems. However, software vendors have not been willing to devote the time and expense necessary to develop the complicated software to handle the complex tasks of acquisitions. Until recently there was little available in vendor or network-supplied acquisitions systems or services. There are systems on the market for both functions, however, these are rare considering the length of time that has elapsed since the beginnings in the mid-1960s.[2] Several well-known systems available are NOTIS, GEAC, INNOVAQ. Several of the other early acquisitions were the Baker and Taylor BATAB system of 1969, WLN in 1978, CLSI, and OCLC. NOTIS, first operational in 1971, included both acquisitions and cataloging. Serials receiving was designed into the system as an integral part of acquisitions.[2] Although automated acquisitions functions are a giant step forward, when software cannot interface with a library's on-line catalog, it deprives a library's clientele of valuable information.

ACQUISITIONS ORGANIZATIONAL STRUCTURE

The traditional tasks of acquisitions have included participating in collection development activities, serving as liaison with academic faculty in selection, bibliographic searching, ordering (all formats of library materials), receiving and checking in all materials ordered, payment authorization, and mail receipt and distribution.

In some libraries, other activities include receipt and acknowledgement of gifts, binding and book repair, and disposition of discards.

Although there have been arguments for decentralized acquisitions, to achieve efficiency and accountability, ordering, receipt and payment must be monitored by a single entity.

After bibliographic searching and order information is entered into a part of a library's database, the interim file must be given a final review by Acquisitions prior to ordering. After revision by Acquisitions, the record then may become part of the on-line catalog/database and searchable by normal index keys. This would provide for centralized management of bibliographic and financial information and may also assist in the transition from manual to an automated environment.[3]

In 1985 UCLA and Stanford University had well-established routines for decentralized ordering and searching processes. At both universities' libraries, the acquisitions department has final authority for receiving and payment functions.[3] In a 1984 survey[8] it was reported that 57 percent of responding libraries stated that monograph and serial acquisitions are organizationally separate and at one time, proponents of serials departments argued that advanced bibliographic skills were necessary to handle problems with title changes, frequency changes, and claiming.[8] However, in an unpublished survey I conducted of medium-sized libraries in 1985, 89 percent combined these activities into one acquisitions department. Of 28 questionnaires distributed in the 1985 survey, there were responses from 80 percent. According to the 1984 survey, integrated acquisitions areas performed somewhat less of preorder searching and did more work in marking, editing, etc.[8]

In this survey, of 28 libraries, 19 respondees performed the functions of bibliographic searching, ordering, receiving, check-in, and payment. Eleven received and distributed mail, ten handled discards, and only six performed the binding function. It is interesting to note where some libraries have dispersed some of the traditional acquisitions functions in other library areas. For instance, at one library in California, the acquisitions librarian has the title of Collection Development Librarian; ordering and receiving are performed in that department. At one university in North Carolina, acquisitions was merged with the Cataloging Department in 1984, a unit responsible for all monographic works. Monographic materials are searched, verified, and ordered by the Order Section, a division of the Cataloging Department. A separate serials department handles ordering, receiving and check-in of all serials. However, the Cataloging Department catalogs all serials.

At a college in New York, bibliographic searching is performed in the Cataloging Department and payments are authorized by a separate payment department. At a large university in Virginia, bibliographic searching is performed in the Cataloging Department and payment is authorized by a totally separate department. Mail receipt and distribution is performed by the department that handles payments and, binding, although formerly in the Cataloging Department, is now part of public services. The binding unit is near the area where all currently received periodicals are shelved. At one college in Virginia, serials ordering and check-in have been performed in a serials department. Other acquisitions functions have been dispersed to various other areas of the library, but the library is now planning to return all ordering and receiving and check-in to a single acquisitions department.

These are only a few, medium to large-sized, libraries that have chosen different ways of fulfilling the acquisitions function. However, the overwhelming majority of libraries responding to the 1985 survey maintained the acquisitions functions in the traditional way by an acquisitions department with a librarian as head. Twenty-two libraries responding to the survey employ one or more professional librarians in acquisitions with a range of one to ten. Forty-one percent believe the greater part of acquisitions tasks is professional, 35 percent believe the greater part of acquisitions tasks is business or management-oriented, and 23 percent believe that acquisitions tasks are evenly split between professional and business-oriented tasks. When this question was posed differently, 68 percent felt acquisitions tasks were an even combination.

Twenty-two acquisitions librarians responding to the questionnaire participate in selection of materials for the library, act as liaison with other librarians who participate in collection development, make budget decisions, and negotiate with publishers and vendors.

Fifty percent of the acquisitions librarians believe that collection development differs from acquisitions, that collection development is the actual selection of materials and collection measurement, the analysis of and policies for these functions. The same 50 percent believe acquisitions is the function of physically acquiring materials and participating in collection development. Four respondees believe collection development and acquisitions are the same function. In 81 percent of the libraries, librarians other than the acquisitions librarian participate in collection development and 54 percent of acquisitions librarians serve as liaison with academic faculty in collection development. With decentralization, "the role of acquisitions librarian would require greater coordination and communication with other library areas."[3]

IN-HOUSE DEVELOPED ACQUISITIONS SYSTEM

Virginia Polytechnic Institute and State University's Newman Library Acquisitions Department uses an automated acquisitions system which was developed in-house in the late 1960s. It is a module designed for batch processing and runs on the IBM 3084. The database used is IMS and the program is primarily written in COBOL. Much typing and filing is eliminated with use of this system, and, also, by the use of only a few vendors from whom to acquire library materials instead of ordering direct from thousands of publishers. After entering orders into a database, they may be edited, status reports added and receipts recorded. Bibliographic searching is performed by using an on-line bibliographic utility and transferring the information into the acquisitions database by rekeying.

Orders are edited by the Acquisitions Department, part of which includes assigning a search code for duplication, a fund check code, a claim date, and a vendor code. Each weekend purchase orders are printed out by batch mode. These are then verified the first part of each week and mailed to suppliers. The Acquisitions Department monitors each fund account by accessing a separate accounting database. Upon arrival, all materials are checked in on the acquisitions database. Status reports are also entered into the on-line order record. However, none of this information is available to the public service area. Although the biggest advantage in using this in-house developed acquisitions module is the termination of some paperwork, other benefits have been the automatic claiming and batch printing of purchase orders. However, batch processing of these purchase orders slows the process of ordering. The whole ordering process requires three full weeks.

Some imperfections with this in-house developed module are that (1) there is no safeguard against deleting receipt information which may cause a claim to be automatically issued thus causing problems with the vendor and much time in resolving the problem, (2) it is very difficult to generate any management reports, (3) there is too little space in some fields which requires the use of many abbreviations, (4) no editing may be performed on an order once it has been printed which requires a large number of cancellations and reorders, (5) there is no highlighting capability which causes some vital information to be overlooked, (6) it does not interface with the library's on-line catalog, (7) it is old and must be treated very carefully, and (8) access is limited to either the purchase order number or an in-house "VV" code. If neither code is available, then the order cannot be accessed.

AUTOMATED ACQUISITIONS SYSTEMS

If there is any single term that may be used to describe an efficient and desirable automated acquisitions system, it is flexibility. An automated acquisitions system should be extremely flexible if it is to provide the operational features needed in efficiently acquiring information and in having that acquisitions information accessible to a library's clientele. Any restriction designed into an automated acquisitions system that limits its ability to perform, instantly makes it less than desirable. For many years, developers of these systems have asked acquisitions librarians "Should the system be able to do this . . . ?" The answer is always "yes"! No two libraries can or should operate in the same way or perform the same activity alike. This is the result of administration restrictions, of purposes, of goals and objectives, of differing ideologies of individual librarians.

Although many librarians still operate under the maxim of "librarianship as a noble calling," anyone in today's library and information environment or calling who chooses to ignore efficiency and accountability, may find himself in a minority. The whole concept of providing information is changing very rapidly. Implementation of an automated acquisitions system is a catalyst for change. Workflows and procedures must be evaluated and modified. Communication patterns must be improved because the rate of change is accelerated.[3] Already those institutions which have not upgraded their operations may fall behind in providing the services or fulfilling the purpose for which they exist. An automated acquisitions system should provide for entry of a title to be ordered by any of a library's clientele, interfacing with national database/s for bibliographic searching and for downloading records, for interfacing with a library's on-line catalog, for a process of assigning a vendor, setting a claim period, for printing purchase orders batch and on-demand, for ordering on-line from a vendor/publisher, for automatic printing of claims, for automatic recording of order status information taken from the on-line ordering system or manually, for entry of order receipt, and pay status, for access to account funds balances, encumbrances and for manipulation of funds. The system should also provide for the receipt, duplication searching and acknowledgement activities for gift materials and materials received and exchanged through a planned exchange program and for the handling of approval plan titles. It should interface with all other activities in the library, including the serials check-in and binding modules so that all information is available on-line to the clientele. The acquisitions system should provide for the capability of compiling and printing of management reports in any sequence desirable.

Just as predictions were made in the early 1970s that the printed book would become obsolete by the early 1980s, so were predictions made that the automation of acquisitions was upon us. As we know, developments have been slower than expected in many areas. Although there has been a concentrated effort to develop bibliographic systems, in other functional areas, the effort has been considerably less. When vendors of automated library systems concentrate their energies on acquisitions and serials check-in systems with more zeal, there is no doubt the library and information world shall benefit from fully-integrated systems.

FUTURE FOCUS FOR ACQUISITIONS

Two characteristics of traditional paper publishing have been permanence and linear sequence. Permanence guarantees preservation. Acquisitions will be faced with evolving developments in electronic publishing as authors publish and disperse their own works. Electronic publishing is volatile and transient. This is expected to have a great impact upon the whole future mind set about information and its acquisition.[5] In the future, the focus of acquiring information, whether in print hard copy from traditional sources or through telecommunication direct from the author, will be effected through automated on-line systems.

CONCLUSION

In the evolution of acquisitions organizationally, a number of structures have been used. However, a number of institutions have returned operations to the traditional structure. As with any task, there is more than one way to accomplish the tasks of acquisitions. Although developments in automation of acquisitions have been very slow, there has been progress. In-house automated systems have provided valuable assistance up to the present, however, greater efforts are required to bring the automation of acquisitions up to expectations and needs. Libraries must realize this automation soon in order to adequately fulfill their service function of providing information and access to information and to cope with new developments in the computerization of publishing.

REFERENCES

1. Bierman, Kenneth J. "Vendor Systems and On-Line Ordering." *Journal of Library Automation* 13:3 (September 1980): 170-181.
2. Boss, Richard W. "Automated Acquisitions Systems: Keynote Address." *Journal of Library Automation* 13:3 (September 1980): 156-164.
3. Cenzer, Pamela S. "Decentralized Acquisitions—A Future Trend?" *Library Acquisitions: Practice and Theory* 9:1 1985: 37-40.
4. Furlong, Elizabeth J. "A Case Study in Automated Acquisitions: Northwestern University Library." *Journal of Library Automation* 13:4 (December 1980): 222-240.

5. Hjerppe, Roland. "Electronic Publishing: Writing Machines and Machine Writing." *Annual Review of Information Science and Technology* 21, 1986: 123-166.

6. Line, Maurice B. "National Libraries in a Time of Change." *IFLA Journal* 14:1 (February 1988): 20-28.

7. Norwood, Frank W. "Telecommunications and Education in the 1980s." *Journal of Library Automation* 13:4 (December 1980): 281-282.

8. Schmidt, Karen A. "The Acquisitions Process In Research Libraries: A Survey of ARL Libraries' Acquisitions Departments." *Library Acquisitions: Practice and Theory* 11:1, 1987: 35-44.

9. Vigil, Peter J. "The Software Interface." *Annual Review of Information Science and Technology* 21, 1986: 63-86.

10. Woods, Richard. "The Compatibility of Library Systems." *Journal of Library Automation* 13:4 (December 1980): 244-250.

11. Nonpublished survey by questionnaire of 28 medium-sized libraries in 1985 conducted by Jessie T. Nicol.

NOTIS

A Shared Acquisitions System: The Ties That Bind?

Mary Ann Garlough

SUMMARY. In order to function effectively, a library acquisitions department requires a means to manage its budget and generate financial and collection management reports. An automated acquisitions system can be an efficient means to do this; an automated system shared with other libraries can be an efficient use of resources as well. Since libraries operate in diverse environments and have diverse needs, however, system-imposed uniform practices and the compromises made in choosing system-wide options offset some advantages of sharing. Florida's State University System libraries, which are sharing a centralized NOTIS system, are seeing first-hand the consequences of sharing.

Once upon a time in the golden days of yore — the 1960s — academic libraries had reasonably adequate acquisitions budgets. At that time the great attraction of an automated acquisitions system was the provision of an efficient means to acquire materials in order to expend the budget by the end of the fiscal year. Today the situation is quite different. While libraries still need to expend the bud-

---

Mary Ann Garlough is User Services Librarian with the Florida Center for Library Automation, 2002 NW 13th St., Suite 202, Gainesville, FL 32609.

get by the end of the fiscal year, the money is not as plentiful as before and the cost of materials has risen. In order to spend the limited funds wisely, acquisitions librarians have become more interested in collection development and fund management information, whether for their own use or for that of others in the library or parent institution.[1]

One would think it would not be too complex a task to define the information that libraries (or at least academic libraries) need, and to devise an automated acquisitions system that could store, manipulate and report the necessary data as well as manage purchase orders, claims and the other housekeeping tasks associated with the acquisitions process. In reality that is a difficult task, if the experience of Florida's State University System (SUS) libraries is an indication. Even within this publicly funded system of nine universities that theoretically follow uniform procedures, the libraries' acquisitions departments manage their funds and collections quite differently internally. They all prepare reports for a variety of departments and organizations at the library, university, state, and national levels. These reporting requirements influence what data is stored, how it is manipulated, and how it is reported for each library.

HOW TO AUTOMATE?

Obviously, several options are available to a library to automate its acquisitions procedures. A library can develop locally a dedicated acquisitions system to suit its requirements; such a project requires a considerable commitment in time and money for development and maintenance, however. If a vendor-produced dedicated system is used instead, development cost savings are offset by the compromises that are usually necessary to use the pre-defined records and reports, although some customizing is usually possible, depending on the system. If the acquisitions module of an integrated library system is used, the acquisitions department must coordinate activities and prioritize needs with other departments in the same library or with other libraries within the same institution. The difficulties (and savings) are compounded when that integrated system is shared among several institutions, as in the SUS.

This article will discuss sharing an integrated system, specifically the NOTIS system.

NOTIS IN THE SUS

NOTIS is an integrated library system developed by Northwestern University Library and now enhanced, maintained and marketed by NOTIS Systems, Inc. of Evanston, Illinois. The NOTIS software includes catalog maintenance, circulation and acquisitions modules as well as the online public access catalog, called LUIS.

The University of Florida in Gainesville (UF) acquired the NOTIS software in 1981 and adapted it to suit local conditions. By 1983 UF was using catalog maintenance, LUIS and acquisitions. (The integrated circulation module was not available until 1986.) In 1984 the Florida legislature funded a plan to automate libraries in the nine state universities, which are Florida Agricultural and Mechanical University (FAMU), Florida Atlantic University (FAU), Florida International University (FIU), Florida State University (FSU), University of Central Florida (UCF), University of Florida (UF), University of North Florida (UNF), University of South Florida (USF), and University of West Florida (UWF). The libraries' collections have unique strengths, so to encourage sharing those resources, the plan called for the libraries to use the same software system. The SUS Board of Regents chose the NOTIS software that UF was already using as the system for all state universities. Responsibility for NOTIS was transferred from UF to the Florida Center for Library Automation (FCLA), which was created to support the system-wide use of NOTIS.

By the fall of 1986 records from OCLC archive tapes had been loaded into databases; training on catalog maintenance and searching had been completed; and LUIS had been implemented for the eight additional universities. These were the only functions the libraries were required by the Board of Regents to implement. Whether and when to implement NOTIS circulation and acquisitions were left as local library decisions. Several of the SUS libraries did decide to implement acquisitions, and accommodating their different needs and practices on NOTIS presented several challenges.

NOTIS System Structure

In NOTIS a database is known as an "institution group." An institution group has a single set of indexes and holds certain files in common, among them an authority file. An institution group contains one or more "processing units." The processing unit corresponds to a library processing center and is the level at which catalog maintenance and acquisitions occur. Each processing unit has its own copy of the same bibliographic record for an item. Although processing units within an institution group share the same set of indexes, each unit's bibliographic record has its own entries. Further, each institution group has assigned to it one or more "service units," the level at which circulation occurs. The result of this structure is a union catalog which permits decentralized responsibility for processing and circulation.

In library organization terms, an institution group with one processing unit corresponds to a library with no branches or with multiple branches whose materials are all processed centrally. An institution group with multiple processing units corresponds to a library system composed of independent libraries that have their own budgets and process their own materials, all of which are overseen by one ultimate governing authority.

Each "record" for an item is loaded into a processing unit and is actually composed of several types of records linked together by a key, which in NOTIS is the bibliographic record key. Bibliographic and copy holdings records are required by NOTIS. The first contains the descriptive and subject cataloging information; the second contains the location, call number and copy information. Optional records for detailed volume holdings, circulation, and acquisitions information are linked to the copy holdings record.

NOTIS Acquisitions Subsystem

One acquisitions record, the order/pay/receipt (o/p/r) record, is linked to a copy holdings record. The o/p/r contains all of the order information pertaining to that copy of that title: order history, vendor information, commitment, payment, receipt, and any other notes associated with the acquisition of that copy.

The other online components of the NOTIS acquisitions subsystem are vendor records, fund records, and invoice records. The vendor record stores up to four vendor addresses for ordering, claiming, paying for, and returning materials. Batch programs print the appropriate addresses on purchase orders, correspondence and vouchers. The fund record contains summary information about the fund, including allocation, expenditures, commitments, allowable overcommitments and overexpenditures, and effective dates for the fund. The invoice record is the online equivalent of the vendor's paper invoice and gathers together in one record all the payments posted online to one invoice.

Codes entered in o/p/r and invoice records link them with the appropriate fund and vendor records. The system creates links between pay statements in o/p/r and invoice records; i.e., links are maintained not only at the record level, but also at the line item level within records. Updating an order or invoice record online updates the appropriate linked fund records and line items in other records through complex online programs operating in background mode.

Acquisitions in Relation to the Institution Group

As previously mentioned, the o/p/r record is linked to an item's copy holdings record, which is maintained at the processing unit level. Thus, the o/p/r record is unique to a processing unit. The vendor file is an institution group file; all processing units share the file and can share vendor records if they so desire. A fund record is also stored in an institution group level file, but it is assigned to and can be used by only the processing unit that created it. The code that identifies a fund record is library-assigned, but it must be unique within the institution group. An invoice record is also stored in an institution group level file and is assigned to a single processing unit, but its unique identifier is a system-assigned sequence number.

Nature of the SUS NOTIS Installation

The NOTIS installation for the SUS is a unique arrangement. Other NOTIS installations that serve consortia generally set up one institution group for the entire consortium; each consortium member has its own processing unit. The advantage is a union index that enables a user to find all consortium copies of, for example, *Books in Print* with just one title search. There are also some data processing and storage advantages as a result of less duplication in indexes and institution-group sharing of some files.

In contrast FCLA set up a separate institution group for each university, which gives each university greater autonomy in managing its database. The disadvantage is that an online catalog user must perform nine searches to find the SUS's complete holdings for a particular title. The user's ability to find the whole system's holdings of *Books in Print* in one search was perceived to be less important than the user's need to discover quickly and easily whether just the local university library has it, because the universities are spread out from Pensacola to Miami, a distance of over 600 miles. (The SUS does see the need for a union index. FCLA implemented an author/title union index in August 1988.)

Because the NOTIS acquisitions files exist at the processing unit or institution group, not installation, level, the SUS type of installation offers the maximum flexibility in a shared NOTIS system.

THE DECISION TO SHARE

In June 1987 only UF was using NOTIS acquisitions, but a majority of the other SUS libraries were interested in implementing acquisitions. Of the others, most were using manual acquisitions systems, one was using a locally developed mainframe system, one was using BATAB (a Baker & Taylor batch acquisitions system), and one was using the OCLC mainframe system. For all libraries, NOTIS acquisitions was attractive as an alternative that was part of an integrated system already operating in the library and required no local funding to install.

Of the libraries that have decided not to use NOTIS acquisitions, one has a locally developed mainframe system, the other the minicomputer-based INNOVACQ. These libraries do see advantages to operating acquisitions in the same system that the other library departments use, but their existing automated systems have certain features that NOTIS does not offer. More importantly, converting to another acquisitions systems is a time-consuming, labor-intensive and wearing process; the new system must offer the acquisitions department solid advantages to inspire a desire to change to it.

The first two libraries outside of UF to decide to implement acquisitions were ones in danger of losing their current automated acquisitions systems. USF was using OCLC's mainframe-based system (which was later announced to have an indefinite lifespan). FIU's locally developed system resided on a UNIVAC computer which their campus computer center was going to stop supporting. USF implemented NOTIS acquisitions July 1, 1987. FIU began a test the same month to run in parallel with their existing system.

So what have been the UF, USF, and FIU experiences in sharing acquisitions?

Constraints of Sharing: The Data Files

Since each university has its own institution group, the disadvantages of sharing NOTIS acquisitions have been minimized for the SUS. Most of the system restrictions encountered in acquisitions would exist even if each campus had its own copy of NOTIS. Acquisitions departments would still need to negotiate and coordinate with other departments in the same library on matters such as bibliographic record creation, detailed holdings displays, and monographic series management. A university with independently operated libraries, e.g., a main and a law or medical library, would still require decisions on whether to share vendor records, who should maintain them if they are shared, and how to identify each library's records by code if they are not shared.

Slightly different issues arise regarding fund codes, but again these issues would exist if each library ran its own copy of NOTIS. Unlike a vendor record, a fund record cannot be shared by multiple processing units; the system assigns it exclusively to the unit that created it. Even so, the code that identifies the record must be unique within the institution group. The system can identify and report out funds by processing unit, so there is no system requirement that the fund codes themselves contain a processing unit identifier. However, coordination among acquisitions departments is necessary to allow each processing unit's acquisitions department to assign meaningful fund codes to its records in confidence that its codes will not duplicate another's.

A consortium that is using a single institution group installation would encounter the same problems across institutions that the SUS libraries encounter across libraries within an institution. Within an institution that had independently operated libraries, the constraints of sharing data files could be significant. The institution's libraries probably would share a processing unit, so probably would share a single bibliographic record for the same item (which may have a greater impact on cataloging than acquisitions). Each independent library would have its own orders for its own copies and each could have its own vendor records. Devising fund codes that contain a library identifier or otherwise identifying a fund record as belonging to a given library would be essential; fund records for all of these libraries would be assigned to the same processing unit, so the system could not sort them at that level.

Constraints of Sharing: Security

Most security for acquisitions is set at the processing unit level. Decisions such as whether a location within a processing unit can acquire serials is determined at the location level by the affected library. The library also determines the addresses that can be "billed to" or "shipped to" through its processing unit's o/p/r records. An invoice or fund record, as mentioned before, is assigned exclusively to the processing unit that created it. Sharing the system in the SUS installation has little impact in these areas. Ramifications for member institutions could be significant for a consortium using a single institution group installation.

Further protection for records is provided by the operator ID assignments and definitions. For example, a cataloging ID cannot create or update an order record, a serials check-in ID cannot create orders, and the acquisitions supervisor ID for one processing unit cannot create fund records in another processing unit. These operator ID assignments and definitions have caused inconvenience for SUS acquisitions departments that are using NOTIS. The NOTIS security tables for the SUS are complex and too large to permit a separate ID for each library staff member, which might be possible in a much smaller operation. Instead, FCLA has set up IDs for four functional responsibilities: acquisitions supervisor, regular acquisitions staff, serials check-in staff, and vendor file maintenance. Since the security tables exist at the installation level rather than the institution group level, the same operational definitions are in force for the same staff functions throughout the SUS. There is no ideal definition that will suit all needs, because acquisitions department organization and workflow vary among the libraries. Acquisitions departments therefore find themselves adapting local operations to the operator IDs rather than vice versa. (As an aside, some of these problems would exist within a single institution group, single processing unit installation. For example, acquisitions and cataloging departments differ over whether acquisitions staff should be allowed to edit fully cataloged bibliographic records.) The operator ID assignments and definitions have less to do with installation type than with the number of operator IDs required.

Additional protection from unauthorized changes is provided through terminal tables, which identify the processing unit or units whose records a terminal can update. Even if a person knows the processing unit code and operator IDs that permit updating another processing unit's records, he or she still would not be able to update those records unless using a terminal with update access to that other processing unit. These tables even disallow viewing o/p/r records belonging to another processing unit, which many acquisitions staff regard as a disadvantage; they would like to refer to another library's orders for vendor, price, or receipt information when processing their own orders. They could view one another's orders if they were in the same processing unit in the same institution group or if the terminal table security were bypassed, but both options are out of the question for SUS libraries, which have twenty-five processing units and over a thousand terminals. A consortium using a single institution group would have a slight edge here; all of the libraries in the same parent organization that shared a processing unit would be able to view one another's orders.

Constraints of Sharing Squared: Reports

Despite the fact that the nine universities have a Board of Regents in common and must follow State of Florida financial regulations, their library acquisitions departments manage finances and organize acquisitions information very differently. Some variations are due to the size of the library operation, while others are due to practices of campus or college accounting authorities (which is true even for different libraries within the same university). For example, some libraries must use ranges of purchase order numbers that the central accounting authorities assign; others assign the numbers themselves. In all of the libraries, money that is committed but not spent by the end of the fiscal year must go through a process called "certifying forward" so it won't be lost, but the way that money is actually spent in the new fiscal year varies by library. The larger libraries tend to have more breathing space in their operations in general, perhaps due to the difficulties of a campus agency overseeing a large library operation in detail.

The most significant differences occur at the fund allocation level. A library receives money pre-allocated to a few broad categories, such as "Books" or "Foundation." Acquisitions departments then subdivide the money for library materials according to intra- and extra-departmental needs. These internal-use funds are defined and receive allocations in accordance with the library's organizational and physical arrangement as well as the subject and research emphasis of its parent body. Reports on these internal funds should meet financial management, collection management, and external reporting requirements.

Many of these variant practices can be handled in NOTIS through data entry in locally defined fields. The difficulty in any shared environment is designing fund and collection management reports that will make the required information available in a format usable by all participating libraries. The SUS libraries dealt with some of these issues in preparing for NOTIS acquisitions.

THE ACQUISITIONS SUBCOMMITTEE AND REPORTS

USF and FIU were scheduled to implement NOTIS acquisitions with the beginning of the new fiscal year on July 1, 1987. That coincided with the implementation of NOTIS 4.4, which introduced online fund accounting and the associated fund and invoice records. The new fund and the redesigned o/p/r records contained locally defined required and optional fields. Questions arose among the three 4.4 users-to-be (UF, USF and FIU) of how to use which fields. Since the majority of the SUS libraries had expressed interest in eventually implementing NOTIS acquisitions, it was agreed that all the libraries would be included in the field definition process to ensure their needs were considered. The mechanism for the process was a thirteen-member acquisitions committee composed of representatives from the nine main, two law, and two medical libraries.

Since its inception, FCLA has relied heavily on input from advisory committees in making decisions about how the system should be used. FCLA expertise is in how the system does, should, or could (maybe) work. The libraries' expertise is in how to apply that to actual operations. It is primarily through the advisory committees that the two groups pool knowledge and ideas to arrive at the best way to implement NOTIS when options are available.

The Acquisitions Committee was authorized by the SUS library directors to determine the best utilization of the redesigned acquisitions module and gauge the level of cooperation and coordination required. Of major concern in light of the limited number of NOTIS acquisitions reports available with 4.4 were what reports FCLA should produce. The challenge was to define data fields in NOTIS o/p/r and fund records so that a minimum number of FCLA-written reports would generate the most useful information possible for all of the libraries. At the same time the definitions needed to be flexible enough to accommodate local variations in practice. At the committee meeting held in April 1987, the cooperation among the representatives from the thirteen diverse libraries was exemplary as they looked beyond their current local practices to what their essential needs were and how NOTIS could fulfill them.

In the interest of supporting maximum flexibility, the committee designated one local use field in the o/p/r record for subject code use, then left the remaining local-use fields to be defined as each library wished. Several locally defined fields in the fund record were left to FIU, UF and USF to define cooperatively as necessary because the use that the online system and batch programs would make of these fields was unclear at the time.

Most of the committee's energy was consumed in defining the fund code field. FCLA had made a commitment to produce a detailed fund report, which was not available from NOTIS Systems with the 4.4 release. If a single field could be analyzed to generate an informative report, the libraries would be free to define other fields strictly according to local needs and not be bound to uniform practices for the sake of an SUS-wide report. FCLA also wanted to avoid replicating the proposed NOTIS Systems fund report, which would sort and subtotal on several complete fields, as opposed to analyzing the content of any field. The fund code field was recommended for analysis because it is the only field that appears in the three records that contain accounting information—o/p/r, fund, and invoice, which would make possible data manipulation across record types.

The SUS Fund Code Format

The fund code is the unique identifier for a NOTIS fund record; it is used to retrieve the record in the online file and to link it with commitments and payments made in o/p/r and invoice records. It may be up to nine characters long, and as mentioned before, it must be unique within the institution group. Since a fund code is entered for every commitment and payment, it is in the interest of accuracy and ease of staff use to keep it short and easy to remember.

The libraries' existing allocation schemes were examined to determine the feasibility of designing a fund code format that would satisfy all needs. The committee found that allocation definitions could be clustered into eleven broad categories, of which each library used from two to six. They agreed to use a six-character fund code that is brief enough for efficiency, yet long enough to accommodate the allocation categories. The categories were grouped into four levels; each character in the code was assigned to a level.

The committee members took local requirements into account in their agreement. Several libraries use multiple categories within a level, which determined the number of characters assigned each level. The letters A-Z and numbers 0-9 may be used in the fund code field; libraries using multiple categories in any one level decided that the resulting number of options in the one- and two-character levels were sufficient to cover their needs. The group agreed that if a library does not use one or more levels, it should use the fill character "Z" in those positions; "Z" rather than zero was designated the fill or place holding character in recognition of the importance of zero in several libraries' allocation schemes. To enable libraries with less complex allocation schemes to use shorter fund codes, it was agreed that final Zs could be dropped from a code; the fund report program would assume left justification and complete the six-character code with Zs as necessary.

The levels, their categories, and the fund code characters assigned to them are the following.

Level 1 (fund code character 1) could mean:
branch, site or campus
or
funding source

Level 2 (fund code character 2) means:
college

Level 3 (fund code characters 3 and 4) could mean:
department
or
subject
or
collection
or
academic or research program
or
library function (e.g., binding, computer services)

Level 4 (fund code characters 5 and 6) could mean:
material type or format (e.g., monographic series, AV)
or
request source (e.g., approval plan)
or
vendor

The committee agreed to rely on the libraries implementing 4.4 first to make adjustments to the code as necessary.

The FCLA Fund Report

All of the libraries intending to implement NOTIS acquisitions agreed to adhere to the format, but that did not guarantee that they wanted the information reported in the same way. UF assigned to each level meanings that were independent of the other levels in the code. USF assigned meanings that were dependent on the other levels. (FIU delayed implementation.) A report useful for UF was close to meaningless for USF; a report useful for USF was more complex than UF initially thought necessary.

FCLA wrote a report that analyzes and subtotals the four levels of the fund code by commitments, expenditures, and balances in several ways. An easy-to-interpret table reports subtotals for each value in each level across all funds and independent of the other levels. Complex charts report subtotals for each value in each level in combination with all other levels, e.g., subtotals for the level 4 code for microfiche across all funds in a processing unit, across all funds within the same level 1 code, across all funds within the same level 2 code, across all funds within the same level 3 code, and so on.

Other Reports: Present and Future

As of fall 1988, the Acquisitions Committee has not met again to discuss additional reports, partly because implementing acquisitions was the primary concern at the time. New reports have appeared on the scene from various sources, however. FCLA wrote a generic invoice-based fund report that sorts invoice pay statements by fund and provides otherwise unavailable information on the individual payments that make up the expenditures on a fund. NOTIS Systems, Inc. released its fund report that sorts and subtotals on fields other than the fund code and complements the fund report FCLA wrote. In development by FCLA is an outstanding orders report that provides information on commitments by fund.

Now that the basic acquisitions survival reports are being generated, acquisitions departments are requesting reports that reflect more and more their local requirements. For example, even if every library wants a new title list, every library will define differently the elements that should be in the list, how the list should sort, and what it should look like. It is frustrating for the libraries not to receive the needed reports and frustrating for a central agency such as FCLA or NOTIS Systems not to receive uniform specifications.

In response to this dilemma, NOTIS Systems released a program that extracts data from order records and presents it in a form that a library can manipulate locally to generate reports. The SUS libraries are being surveyed in order to determine whether FCLA should write additional reports, concentrate on extracting data files for the libraries to manipulate as they will, or some combination thereof. There is great interest in downloading data to library microcomputers for a library staff member to manipulate using whatever accounting or statistical program is available locally. The more an SUS library can manipulate data for itself and be less dependent on centrally produced reports, the more flexibility it has in using NOTIS acquisitions. This would be a boon for libraries with complex needs and the staff to manipulate data to produce reports. Libraries without these needs or resources could continue to rely on the centrally produced reports.

A SHARED ACQUISITIONS SYSTEM: DO THE TIES BIND?

The SUS libraries are admittedly limited in certain ways by using a shared, centralized system. The primary emphasis of FCLA activities is to use computers to improve resource sharing, and this SUS installation that uses a single copy of the NOTIS software was designed with that in mind. In contrast, if each university were running its own copy of NOTIS and had its own programming staff, only local needs would need to be considered in determining priorities or designing reports. Acquisitions departments would have an easier time manipulating the system as needed to generate data that their programmers could manipulate through locally designed programs.

The constraints of sharing the NOTIS acquisitions system are nevertheless minimal for the SUS, with the exception of reports. The basic NOTIS file structures and record designs are flexible enough to handle a variety of acquisitions department requirements. The SUS type of installation — one institution group for each university — allows a great deal of flexibility while still sharing the system. Security is sufficient to protect each independent library's records from accidental or intentional corruption by unauthorized users. The libraries are restricted by the pre-defined operator IDs, but not to a serious extent, judging from libraries' reactions.

The severest sharing-imposed limitations on the SUS libraries are in the area of reports. FCLA does not have the manpower to write a complete set of tailored reports for each SUS library, though it can provide a core set of reports for all libraries. A library that is going to use the centrally produced reports must accept the generic report format. The SUS libraries are further restricted in their fund code designs if the FCLA-written fund report is to generate the maximum useful information. However, these limitations will decrease in the future as NOTIS Systems, Inc. and FCLA move toward giving each library its acquisitions data in a file that can be manipulated locally, thus freeing libraries from the need to coordinate data input for the sake of universally usable reports.

The libraries gain in some important ways from sharing a system. There are economies of scale in a large, centrally administered, shared system. In the Florida case, members of the legislature had strong interest in fostering resource sharing; funding for independent local systems would have been harder to obtain and renew each year than for the more politically popular cooperative venture now existing. In addition, FCLA's NOTIS operations are funded directly by the legislature, not by the individual libraries. If each library had its own system, not only would the system costs come from individual library budgets but the total costs spent on individual systems would be larger. With nine institutions to support, FCLA can justify librarian and programmer staffs large enough to allow the specialization that results in better maintenance, troubleshooting and development services overall than would be available with the usual library systems office staff. At a less technical level, the formal cooperative structure makes information sharing easier through the committees and through contacts made via FCLA activities.

CONCLUSION

The advantages of sharing an automated acquisitions system probably outweigh the disadvantages for the SUS libraries, if for no other reason than the cost savings. There is no clear-cut answer to the question of whether the advantages of sharing a system would outweigh the disadvantages for other libraries. Much depends on the nature of the system, how it is installed and managed, and how it is funded. No system is perfect; any system, shared or unshared, requires compromises. The question becomes which method of automation has the most favorable benefit to compromise ratio.

REFERENCES

1. R. W. Boss, *Automating Library Acquisitions. Issues and Outlook* (White Plains, NY: Knowledge Industry Publications, Inc., 1982), pp. 3-4.

Automating Acquisitions at Auburn University

Nancy Gibbs

SUMMARY. Automated acquisitions has been a reality at Auburn University for over four years. Staff training and procedures were changed in order to accommodate this reality. Auburn has experienced most of the good points (increased access) and some of the bad points (downtime) of automation. Auburn has been able to overcome most problems and concerns with cooperation from the department and strong support from other libraries using our same automation system. In turn, we have been able to assist newer libraries with their automated acquisitions.

Automated book acquisitions at Auburn University Libraries has been fully implemented and online for over four years. With the advent of online fund accounting, installed in October 1987, the same feelings of frustration, isolation, helplessness, lack of understanding, and lack of support, experienced by the staff when AUL first installed the online system returned. Although the Acquisitions Department staff experienced a 60% turnover of staff within the past four years, the feelings experienced by new and old staff members are familiar; having been encountered at every level of each job task and appearing to be a normal part of "coming up and going online."

Nancy Gibbs is Approval Plan Librarian, Auburn University Libraries, Auburn University, Auburn, AL 36849-5606.

© 1989 by The Haworth Press, Inc. All rights reserved.

BACKGROUND

Auburn University Libraries (AUL) purchased NOTIS, a totally integrated online system developed at Northwestern University Libraries, in the fall of 1983 and initial bibliographic records were loaded in May 1984. Technical service departments were the first to work with the NOTIS system. Terminals were added for public use and later for use within the two branch libraries. The final two NOTIS components, an automated circulation system and an automated acquisition fund accounting system, were brought online in October 1987.

Initially, the AUL database contained 240,000 records input from Solinet tapes for the years 1976 through 1984. During the next two years, the size of the database was augmented every two to three months as retrospective conversion (RECON) tapes, produced at SOLINET, were loaded into the database. Within this year, the NOTIS system contains over 700,000 bibliographic records with accompanying holdings screens, item records, order screens, and volume holdings screens where appropriate. RECON anticipates loading the final tapes from the card catalog into the database by late 1988.

STAFF TRAINING

In an effort to ease NOTIS into the Acquisitions and Catalog Departments, committees comprised of both librarians and support staff were formed to analyze present and anticipated online work flows with an aim towards preventing problems. These committees allowed staff in different departments to learn how their individual concerns and online work procedures might impact upon another department's work load. They offered library staff a way to express feelings of bewilderment and frustration brought on by a new system.

Previous to NOTIS all order information was typed on a multi-part form and one copy was filed in the public card catalog. With the advent of NOTIS, the usual order information (i.e., title, publisher, vendor, etc.) appeared online in an entirely different format. Technical services librarians assisted in the training of public service librarians to interpret this new order information. The dialogue between librarians at these sessions helped to break down the natural barriers existing between the divisions regarding future acquisitions procedures. Some public service librarians have not kept up with learning the refinements to these order screens. Consequently, many public service librarians find it easier to seek assistance from acquisition or serial librarians rather than interpret the order screen themselves.

NOTIS Systems, Inc. staff held initial training sessions for departmental staff. Although documentation came with the system, it was certainly necessary to have a more complete understanding of the online system and its accompanying capabilities and terminology in order to access and interpret what Auburn had purchased.

A longer second NOTIS training session for the technical services staff would have been valuable. It was necessary to save a portion of our allotted days of NOTIS staff training to the time the automated circulation system and acquisitions fund accounting system became available online. Although preplanning and post planning were brief and somewhat harried, the staff made the correct choices; no one wished to change any major decision.

INTEGRITY OF THE DATABASE

With an automated system such as NOTIS, the initial bibliographic record input into the database is the final record upon which every other online task is based. The creation of this one bibliographic record became a primary duty in a department that previously had only secondary control of the card catalog. Who it is that inputs that bibliographic record into the database and how that task is accomplished are questions that become critical to the entire online operation. What occurs in the Acquisitions Department has a direct impact on all other departments which share that same bibliographic record. The responsibility for the integrity of the online catalog is now shared by the Catalog Department and the Acquisitions Department.

The impact and importance of creating that bibliographic record in NOTIS can be enhanced with training and communication between all staff members within the department. Staff that once used the card catalog to determine if a title was owned are now imputing records into the database. An understanding of bibliographic fields, name authority, and the intricacies of a MARC record need to be explained and understood before staff feel comfortable performing this task. A new phase of staff training emerged when Acquisitions went online.

From this same bibliographic screen, now visible to the library public as well as those accessing the system by a campus dial-up connection, the reference librarians will provide service to patrons throughout the main library and its branches. Each time an acquisition task is performed online, messages on the screen, viewed by the public, change to reflect different tasks completed. For example, when an order is first downloaded into NOTIS, the message on the public service screen states a title is in the preorder process. This message is updated after an order is created and mailed to a vendor. It is updated after a title is received and checked-in in Acquisitions, again after a book is cataloged, and finally after the title is ready for circulation.

GOING ONLINE

The Acquisitions Department decided the automated acquisition system would be used beginning with the fiscal year 1984-1985. Staff had four months to become familiar with the NOTIS automated acquisition system before going totally online at the start of the new fiscal year in October 1984. All check-in and ordering for new orders would be done online from that point forward.

During these four months, a somewhat dual acquisition system became operational. Some outstanding and all new orders with an anticipated arrival date after October 1st were loaded into the automated system in order to familiarize staff with this part of the procedure. When possible orders are input by transferring bibliographic records from OCLC into NOTIS via a transfer procedure.

The transfer procedure required: additional computers (Telex 476L); cables attached simultaneously to printers and OCLC terminals; new procedures to accommodate new routines. The actual process of transferring (or downloading), was an initial nightmare because all OCLC fields did not transfer directly, response times were very slow due to local problems. Transferred records could be wiped out with one inadvertent key stroke. Staff members held lists of OCLC fields which required changing and deleting before the transfer process could be completed.

Unfamiliar formats, such as those for maps and audiovisual materials, had to be mastered quickly in order for the acquisitions staff to continue to order materials at a reasonable pace for end-of-year purchases. These tasks became time consuming and frustrating.

The staff continued to check in books under the old paper system. However, more orders were checked in online as the end of the four months lessened. This transition allowed the Acquisitions check-in unit responsible for that procedure also to become familiar with procedures for single monographic works, added volumes, and more difficult material.

Each procedural change necessitated revisions to already sketchy in-house staff manuals. Contrary to popular thought, coming online seemed to increase paperwork in Acquisitions at Auburn rather than diminish it. (We provided screen printouts in books that benefited cataloging and serial personnel, and this added to our processing time.) The staff experienced frustration as each change occurred and they soon realized librarians did not have instant answers to their questions and problems. When librarians did have answers, the solutions were subject to change three days later when the consequences of some actions became apparent. These procedures and changes mandated that orders, books, multi-volume sets, and invoices be set aside until problems could be researched and solutions found.

PROBLEM SHARING

Acquisitions librarians reached for the telephone frequently to call the NOTIS systems offices or another library presently using NOTIS. These contacts began a form of network sharing which has evolved into a strong group of similar-sized libraries sharing ideas with each other. Over the years Auburn has gained from this resource sharing and has in turn provided newer NOTIS users with training materials and assistance in an effort to avoid like problems.

Networking has also proven helpful to librarians considering the purchase of NOTIS. Visiting book vendors have observed our technology and discussed our procedures with other librarians. Major research and government libraries as well as present and future NOTIS librarians have visited Auburn to gain a better understanding of our system. This recognition has been equally gratifying to Auburn's acquisitions staff.

After the first few months, online acquisition at AUL began to work smoothly. AUL has been fortunate in having an above average complement of computer terminals. Specialized furniture, ordered for these new terminals, began to arrive and work stations were organized. This crowded but practical work environment evolved during the transition. The acquisitions staff soon fell into a comfortable routine varying only when interruptions beyond the department's control intervened.

DOWNTIME

Computer downtime was and is still the most frustrating problem for staff; downtime is the one problem over which Auburn University Libraries has the least control. AUL uses the campus computer mainframe and bad weather, campus construction, or extraordinary usage can cause the system to crash. Occasionally the computer center also finds it necessary to take down a portion of the system for quick repair. When a new component of NOTIS is installed, tested, or initially brought online, the potential for downtime is greater: staff are unfamiliar with functions; bugs need to be worked out of the system; overloads can develop quickly.

The plus side of downtime is new staff have the opportunity to learn non-terminal library skills. This in turn changes the way staff are trained in the department. When downtime occurs staff must be assigned other duties as they can no longer transfer bibliographic records, create orders or check-in books. Acquisitions librarians at Auburn maintain a mental list of non-terminal jobs for these times. Advanced planning for downtime is vital to good working relationships within the department.

START OF THE APPROVAL PROGRAM

Because the automated acquisitions system was performing smoothly after the first six months, AUL initiated a large approval program which brought innovations to the automated acquisition system.

Vendors supplying Auburn with approval books were chosen partially because of their promises to provide MARC records on computer tapes for books sent on the approval plan. Although this innovation took some preparation time on the part of vendors, these tape loads are now a reality and staff use them consistently. Initially, titles coming on approval were downloaded into the NOTIS system in the same manner as for titles ordered in the firm order department. Downloading individual titles quickly became an impossible task because the approval program was processing over 1,500 titles monthly with a staff of only two full time employees using one check-in terminal and one OCLC-TELEX terminal.

With the advent of the MARC tapes loading time for approval titles input into NOTIS was reduced to little more than the time needed to load a tape at the computer center. Processing time for approval titles has been reduced by one half while providing immediate access to new material. With 85% of the titles in an approval shipment in the database and accessible online, the impact of these tapes to the public becomes immediately apparent. Students and faculty can now access the online system and be advised that approval titles, which have no previous order record in the database, are in-process and will soon be available for charge-out purposes.

THE ADVENT OF ONLINE FUND ACCOUNTING

When Notis Online Fund Accounting (NOFA), the newest component of automated acquisitions was demonstrated many member libraries asked for enhancements in fund accounting. Academic libraries must conform to institutional business procedures so individual libraries may have difficulties with standard packages. Testing of NOFA was performed at a member library which reported on its success at NOTIS user group meetings.

When Auburn actually started to order and check-in titles under

NOFA, many of the four-year-old frustrations resurfaced. Although the staff did not need to relearn the complete acquisitions system, enough changes had been made to require hours of staff training and practice. The downloading operations were not changed under NOFA but all order and receiving activities were affected.

NOFA's greatest impact was felt in the check-in and bookkeeping units. Before fund accounting the bookkeeping unit was using a largely manual or paper accounting system. Bookkeeping is now performed online and these staff members needed NOTIS training in order to understand concepts of the system.

Changes in check-in under NOFA had a great impact also. A NOTIS internal invoice must be established when a staff member begins to check-in titles on an invoice. As each title is paid for, the payment is recorded on the NOTIS invoice record (NIR) screen. After all titles have been paid for, the NIR payment should equal the payment on the vendor's invoice. If a mistake is discovered, corrections can be made to the NOTIS invoice record but not to the item payment record. (These changes are automatically corrected on the individual records when invoices are approved online in the bookkeeping unit.)

Adjusting to this invoicing procedure initially was difficult; it is easy to make a key stroke error or accidentally place a decimal point in the wrong position when recording prices and figures. If there were major problems, departmental policy dictated that only acquisitions librarians could try to correct the problem invoices so we could assure a "trail" through the computer operations explaining what occurred and how the problem was solved.

AUL has also found when the system went down, invoices and payments made to specific invoices may need reworking. Often, payments made do not have time to attach to an invoice in the split second the computer goes down. When the online system appears "shaky" but not totally down, check-in procedures are monitored more closely in order to avoid such problems.

FUND TRACKING

NOTIS online fund accounting will make tracking of expenditures an easier task. There are now statistical programs, such as

SAS, which interact with our NOTIS acquisition screens to extract all types and forms of data. Through the expenditure class code assigned to each title, the SAS programs can examine and review these codes for budgetary purposes.

Auburn hopes to use this program to examine types of material purchased on different book and serial funds. For example, analysis can be made to ascertain how much money was expended for microfilm on all book funds; or, how much money was expended for back issues of new periodicals on all funds from the College of Math and Science or the College of Liberal Arts. There is a limit to the number of codes used under each fund, hampering the analysis of some data. Auburn is trying to work around this problem with limited success.

At present, our expertise in analysis of this data is limited by our inexperience with the SAS programs. However, AUL anticipates using these programs more fully in the future. There seems to be meaningful possibilities to gather and analyze this type of budget data expeditiously before a new fiscal year budget is developed for future expenditures.

CONCLUSION

NOTIS automated acquisition has greatly changed procedures at Auburn University Libraries acquisitions department. There are fewer all paper jobs; procedures are streamlined, patrons can learn the status of orders more quickly, and there exists the capability to analyze our expenditures in new ways for cost benefits. However, there have been times when these changes have caused staff frustration, books not being processed in a timely manner and orders delayed. The end result has been rewarding, getting there is sometimes difficult.

Changes have occurred with staff but these have been mostly positive changes. Acquisition staff now clearly see a relationship between their job and other's within the department, technical services and the public service areas. This has made the staff more cognizant of their responsibilities and confident in performing those job duties. Staff have learned when new procedures are implemented there is a shakedown period which is natural and a routine will shortly be established. As Acquisitions staff become more familiar with automated acquisitions, the frustration levels have been reduced or modified to the point where workflows have jelled; orders and books move through the department with relative ease.

Currently, Auburn University Libraries appears limited in efforts to anticipate computer downtime. Staff members have learned to accommodate to this situation and our ability to predict slow response time or downtime has increased. With this awareness has come the capability to assign new or different tasks before problems arise.

Auburn has found it most helpful to talk with other acquisitions librarians from similar sized academic libraries. In the past, NOTIS Systems, Inc. occasionally has grouped a portion of the user's meetings in this manner. It is hoped this will continue to be a more integral part of these meetings. Hopefully, networking between member libraries will continue to grow and organize into specific user's groups based on library functions and library size. Member libraries have also suggested regional user's meetings be held before and after major library meetings.

Sharing of ideas, internal procedure manuals, expertise on hardware and software, and voicing feelings of pleasure and disgruntlement are vitally important to the success of any automated acquisitions system. Without the strong support of departmental staff and member libraries sharing information, automating acquisitions would be difficult.

Approval Acquisitions and the Integrated Online System

Michael Kreyche

SUMMARY. Approval vendors have developed products and services that simplify the management of approval acquisitions in libraries with manual systems. As libraries install integrated online systems new products and services from the dealers and enhancements from the systems vendors are needed to match the old manual efficiencies and to take full advantage of the automated system. The library community needs to define and articulate its needs, create a demand for the products it requires, and promote inter-vendor cooperation to facilitate their development. As this process unfolds, a certain amount of improvisation and experimentation is necessary. Some of the issues faced in implementing approval acquisitions at Kent State University with the NOTIS system are described to illustrate typical problems.

Over the years book vendors have developed the approval plan into an efficient acquisitions method. Pre-printed 3" × 5" multiple-copy order forms, ready to be dropped into a library's files, make it a simple matter to incorporate shipped titles into the library's processing routines. Slips for other books of potential interest allow a library to place supplemental orders almost effortlessly. Books received on approval may be returned with a minimum of paperwork, thanks to self-issuing credit memos. Approval vendors can also provide statistical and financial reports that are useful to library administrators.

The services that approval vendors offer depend heavily on two technologies; the relatively simple one of multi-part forms, and, of

---

Michael Kreyche is Technical Services Automation Coordinator, Kent State University Library, Kent, OH 44242.

© 1989 by The Haworth Press, Inc. All rights reserved.

course, computerized data processing. This happy combination of technologies has served both the book vendors and libraries extremely well, but in different ways. Libraries have benefitted most directly from the paper products generated by the vendors' automated systems, while the vendors have had all the power and flexibility of the computer at their disposal.

Fortunately this situation is changing as libraries become increasingly automated. Librarians are becoming accustomed to having access to data processing equipment instead of simply being indirect beneficiaries of someone else's machine. As library systems proceed in the direction of integration of functions, expectations continue to rise, while paper files and peripheral manual systems become less and less acceptable. The time has come to take a look at how approval plans can be managed in the context of an integrated system, and what parts librarians, dealers, and systems vendors can play.

The key to the success of approval acquisitions in manual systems (collection development considerations aside) is the use of vendor-generated records that the library can manipulate with ease. Applying this principle to integrated online library systems means that records used for acquisition of approval titles ought to become a part of the library catalog itself. Timely access to these records can provide direct benefits to administrators, staff involved in cataloging, collection development, reference, and circulation, and even to patrons. For faculty and collection development staff it can mean greater control over the review process; for acquisitions staff it means that a single search can verify that an order being placed will not duplicate a title received on approval or already part of the library's collection; for patrons it means that needed materials can be identified even before they are cataloged and fully processed; for catalogers it can mean a head start on their work; for administrators, it means the potential for readier and more comprehensive management reports than a vendor can supply.

REQUIREMENTS

What will it take to make these possibilities reality? First of all, a certain amount of data has to be acquired and gotten into the system in an efficient manner. Secondly, the system must provide useful access to the data, and the ability to modify and manipulate it. Thirdly, the system must be able to generate output that can be passed back to the vendor. Data is central to the whole process, and the requisite elements may be categorized as bibliographic description, order information, or invoice information.

Description is essential for identification of a bibliographic entity. If a reasonably complete cataloging record cannot be procured, at least the author, title, edition, publisher, and any available control numbers should be included. This should be supplemented by some kind of status and/or location element to indicate that the item has been received for approval. Order information is the data that the library needs to control the acquisition and initial processing of the material. It includes identification of the vendor, invoice number, price, and funding source. Invoice information is the invoice number and date, invoice amount, discount, and an itemization of individual titles and miscellaneous charges.

These different data elements may be structured in any number of ways in a system. Although the number and nature of the record types, their linking and indexing, and storage techniques may vary considerably, the types of data and their interrelationships remain basically the same, and any library system that boasts an acquisitions function must provide for them and their manipulation. If a system can handle normal acquisitions functions, it should also be able to handle approval acquisitions, which is essentially a simplified special case.

Data for ordered materials enters the system in bits and pieces over a period of time. Some kind of bibliographic description must be created before the order can be placed. This description will have to undergo at least some minor revision before an item can be considered cataloged, and often it is scanty and inaccurate. The data categorized above as order information always starts out as tentative: price and terms may be other than expected or another vendor may have to be sought if one is unable to supply an order. In any case, this data is uncertain and the invoice information is unknown until the paperwork for the item is received from the vendor.

In contrast, consider the case of approval materials. Much of the data is constant, and virtually all of the variable data is furnished by the vendor at one time — normally in the form of order slips and invoices, but thanks to the vendor's own automated system, it can also be in machine-readable format. This situation—a logically complete body of data in machine-readable form for a significant quantity of materials arriving at regular intervals—lends itself well to automated data entry rather than manual keying, and is analogous to the use of preprinted slips in manual files.

Unfortunately book vendors, systems vendors, and libraries are giving this opportunity relatively little attention. A few libraries are actively engaged in projects to exploit the situation, but only one account, from Auburn University, has appeared in the literature thus far.[1] Book vendors have been approached for help in resolving problems and are responding willingly, but there seems to be little coordination and communication among all the parties. Apparently the only public forum so far has been an RTSD RS discussion group.[2]

Perhaps the explanation for the lack of widespread enthusiasm is that manual approval procedures work so well that there is little motivation to explore new ground, or that there is some reluctance to abandon or change a proven technique, especially when integrated library system vendors have no special features to offer in their stead. Whatever the case may be, the time has come to delineate the concepts of approval plan management in the integrated on-line system. It is important for librarians to take the initiative and articulate generalized solutions to which book and systems vendors can respond. Experimentation can play a useful part in formulating problems and their solutions, and the resources to do this kind of work are readily available.

RESOURCES FOR EXPERIMENTATION

The book vendors certainly have a great deal to offer. In addition to their considerable experience with automation, they are the source of most of the needed data. At this point, though, there is quite a bit of diversity among vendors in what they can supply. A number of them offer records that contain order or invoice data. Although the bibliographic description in these records is minimal, it is the same data, or derived from the same data, that appears on slips and invoices, so it should suffice for acquisitions purposes.

These records may be in MARC format, a variation of it, or in the vendor's own internal format. In any case the raw material is there.

A second type of record is also available. Vendors that are able to provide catalog cards based on the Library of Congress MARC database also should be able to provide the MARC records themselves, and a number of them are doing so. These records pose several problems of their own, though. First of all, the vendors can never find records for every title they supply, and due to the currency of the material they handle, many of the records are CIP level. Secondly, these records do not contain any of the order and invoice information mentioned above.

Although at present the library interested in machine readable records for approval materials must choose between an incomplete set of cataloging records, or a complete set of order/invoice records with minimal bibliographic description, it is undoubtedly only a matter of time before vendors begin to offer a product that combines the features of both types.

The system vendors provide other important resources: the hardware and software that the library has to work with. Here the problem of variability is more serious than with the vendors. Integrated library systems are much more complex than those employed by book vendors, and designs differ radically from one vendor to another. These systems are also in a relatively early and dynamic stage of growth, and developers are beleaguered with demands for a wide range of new features and enhancements.

An additional resource that is often taken for granted is the recognition of the need for standards in library-related industries and the numerous precedents for standardization. Most notable among these is the MARC format, which has proven its utility and versatility over two decades. Yet another resource, which may be underestimated in the context of large systems, is the proliferation and decentralization of data processing power—in a word, the microcomputer. The development over the last few years of inexpensive mass storage, faster CPUs, impressive programming products, and mainframe links make these machines very powerful and useful tools.

KENT STATE AND NOTIS

The balance of this discussion will focus on some of the issues of implementing the acquisitions component of the NOTIS system at Kent State University. NOTIS is an IBM-based integrated system developed at Northwestern University. Currently the system is marketed and supported by NOTIS Systems, Inc., a corporation wholly owned by Northwestern. Ongoing development is shared between NOTIS Systems and the Information Systems Development Office of Northwestern University Libraries.

The system was installed at Kent in the spring of 1986. In the summer of 1987 the main card catalog was closed, retrospective cataloging records were loaded, and current cataloging was moved to the NOTIS system. In December of 1987 the main library's circulation went online, and in February of 1988 serials check-in activities migrated to NOTIS after machine conversion of the library's OCLC Local Data Records. Implementation of acquisitions, the major remaining function, is just beginning.

More than half of Kent's monographic acquisitions budget is spent on a comprehensive approval plan, so much thought has been given to optimizing the handling of this material under the automated system. Initially Auburn University's technique of acquiring LC MARC records for its approval materials directly from the vendor and batch loading them into the system provided a great deal of inspiration. During 1986 and 1987 a program to evaluate approval vendors was undertaken at Kent, and one of the criteria applied was the ability of the vendors to provide machine readable records for titles furnished on approval. After an initial screening of written responses, three vendors were selected to make presentations on campus, and all of these proved willing and able to provide these records, even if they had not yet initiated this service for other libraries.

System Description

At this point a simplified explanation of the relevant aspects of the NOTIS system design is in order. Because of NOTIS' integrated nature, the bibliographic file serves as the foundation of the acquisitions component of the system as well as of the online catalog and circulation functions. A bibliographic record may be a partial or full cataloging record using standard MARC tags, or it may be a brief provisional record using a smaller set of NOTIS-defined 9xx tags, but in either case it merely provides bibliographic description and access, and carries little or no local data. Another type of record, the "copy holdings" record, contains elements relating to the local status of the bibliographic record plus a "copy statement" for each copy of the title that the library has owned or ordered. The copy statement contains location, call number, processing status, and a set of links to other types of records—and thereby to various functions of the system.

Of these other record types, the order/pay/receipt record (which will be referred to here as simply the "order record"), is the focus of the acquisitions component of NOTIS. The order record is normally created to generate a printed purchase order; later it is updated to indicate receipt of the item, and ultimately, once the invoice is in hand, the actual cost is entered. Batch programs read the order file periodically to generate fund reports, action lists for potential claims and other problems, and claim notices and other types of correspondence. For approval materials, though, no purchase order is printed; and, since receipt and payment data are available at the time the record is created, the entire acquisition process can be represented in the record in a single step.

From the description of the system it is apparent that before any acquisitions activity can be performed, two records—bibliographic and copy holdings—must first be established. There are three ways of creating these records in NOTIS: keyboard input, online transfer from another system, and batch loading. The first two methods are typically used for current work, while the batch loading program was primarily written for the initial creation of the database. Auburn University's imaginative use of this program on a regular basis to create bibliographic and copy holdings records for its approval titles yields a significant reduction in manual input, though the necessity of keying in the order records remains.

Approval Implementation at Kent

Given the relative importance of approval acquisitions at Kent, there was an early commitment to adopt the Auburn technique and to develop it further, if possible. Initially batch loading of bibliographic data was seen as a possible mechanism for reducing the library's dependence on OCLC for cataloging copy. A plan evolved whereby the library would use the vendor supplied LC MARC records for cataloging whenever possible. Instead of manually searching and updating these same records in OCLC's Online Union Catalog, the library would utilize OCLC's tapeloading service to set holdings from copies of the records acquired from the dealer.

The anticipated benefits of this plan were threefold. First, elimination of online OCLC updates for approval material would free staff time for other work. Second, the number of OCLC terminals and the concomitant costs would be reduced. Third, the difference between the per-record charge for setting our holdings online ($1.19 during non-prime time) and that for tapeloading ($.15) would represent a significant savings, even taking into account the vendors charge for the LC MARC record (another $.15 or so).

Unfortunately OCLC's current pricing structure makes these seemingly sensible efficiencies difficult, if not impossible, to achieve. In order to take advantage of the tapeloading service an OCLC library must change its membership status, for which it is penalized with higher per-terminal charges. The increase in these charges is such that it offsets the anticipated per-record savings and, at least at Kent, the reduction in terminals necessary to make the switch worthwhile would entail difficult decisions to restrict staff and patron access to OCLC terminals.

Although the hope of using vendor supplied cataloging records to achieve OCLC savings has been abandoned at Kent for the time being, the convenience of using them to streamline acquisitions workflow was considered reason enough to implement the batch loading technique for materials received on approval. At the same time, consideration of the acquisitions enhancements included in version 4.4 of the NOTIS software, which was released in mid-1987, served to turn the emphasis back towards acquisitions.

Acquisitions Emphasis for Batch Loading

The two principal new features of the system, fund accounting and invoicing, each brought another new record type to NOTIS. In addition the format of the order record was altered to permit interaction among these three record types.

The fund records, which are typically entered into the system at the beginning of the fiscal year, contain several fund identifiers, an allocation amount, commitment and expenditure balances for the fund, and various other data elements that govern the use of the money in the fund. When an order is placed by creating an order record, a certain amount of money in a specified fund is committed, and the adjusted balance is reflected immediately in the online fund record. Later, when the title has been received and the actual cost is known, the commitment balance is reduced and the expenditure balance increased accordingly.

Before the actual charges can be entered, though, an invoice record must be created. This record parallels a paper invoice, but its creation involves only the entry of data that identifies the paper invoice, the invoice total, and the discount applicable to the invoice. Then, as charges are entered on the order records for each title on an invoice, the system posts them to the invoice record as well as the fund record. Miscellaneous charges — postage, for example — may be entered directly into the invoice record. When the sum of all charges equals the invoice total, the system allows a terminal operator to approve the invoice for payment, which causes a payment voucher to be printed.

Prior to the 4.4 enhancements there was no reason to create an order record for returned approval titles, but now the link to the invoice record imposes certain demands. If order records are only created for titles accepted by the library, the resulting line items in the invoice record will not balance the invoice total. To make the invoicing feature of NOTIS work with approval shipments, some accommodation must be made.

With a low rate of returns it would require little extra work to enter order records for returned titles, but at present Kent is experiencing a very high rate of returns. This is primarily because the approval program is still in need of fine tuning after a complete revision of the library's profile and major changes to the reviewing procedures in 1987. Yet even in past years when the return rate was normally very low, there have been occasional mid-year budget cuts which precipitated high return rates. The temporary solution to the problem will be to make a single entry for the total of the returns in the invoice record. This will balance the record, but summarizing what ought to be individual items in a single amount on the record is a dubious practice.

The ultimate solution, of course, is to take advantage of the vendor's order and invoice data in machine-readable form and avoid keyboarding any of it, whether for titles that are kept or those that are returned. The ability to load this data into the appropriate records is really a fundamental step that would represent a significant new level of integration as well as efficiency,

If it were only a matter of using the vendor data to create new records to put into NOTIS, the problem would be relatively simple. Assuming that order data could be incorporated into one or more fields in a MARC record, the batch loader that creates bibliographic and holdings records could be modified to create order and invoice records as well. The difficulty lies in preserving the integrity of the complex relationships among the order, invoice, and fund records. With a strong enough demand from libraries and interest on the part of vendors, NOTIS could no doubt produce batch programs to solve this problem in time, but a fair amount of more basic development work on the acquisitions component of the system is still underway.

MICROCOMPUTER SOLUTIONS

Meanwhile, there are books to buy and libraries to automate. Given the resources mentioned earlier in this discussion, some worthwhile experiments and perhaps even some relatively quick solutions to the problem of automating the entry of approval order data are within reach.

Micros are becoming ubiquitous in libraries, and they frequently do double duty as terminals connected to the library's online system. At Kent State there are a number of IBM PCs and compatibles equipped with boards that emulate IBM mainframe terminals. They are used with memory resident software that is capable of maintaining a mainframe session regardless of whatever other software is running on the micro. A "hot" key combination enables the user to switch back and forth instantaneously between PC and mainframe sessions, suspending one while the other is active.

There are several software packages available that can access the emulator board's screen memory and keyboard functions to interact with online mainframe applications (some packages will also work with modems and dial-up links) while making use of the micro's own processing capabilities and I/O resources as well. Two of these are called Autokey 3270[3] and Gateway PC.[4] These packages include programming languages that can turn the micro into an intelligent terminal that utilizes data residing in the micro to perform functions built into the mainframe application.

The possibility of creating such an application to load vendor data for approval materials is an intriguing one. Perhaps its greatest appeal is that it would take advantage of existing online system functions instead of requiring the development of new mainframe batch programs to duplicate them.

The scale of such an application, too, seems more appropriate to a microcomputer. At Kent weekly approval shipments typically contain from 100 to 300 titles. Even at its relatively slow speed a microcomputer could process this amount of data in less time than it would take to deliver it to the computer center and get the necessary batch job scheduled and run. The storage medium poses no particular problem, either. A 5 1/4" DSDD diskette can hold several hundred full MARC records, and the experience at Kent State has been that a variety of vendors, including book dealers, are perfectly willing to supply MARC records and other data on floppies instead of on tape.

Developing such an application is clearly not a trivial task, though it is within the capabilities of the advanced amateur programmer or a computer science student. One problem with this approach is that the instructions sets of the languages used to control the terminal have certain limitations, so some pre-processing of the input data would be inevitable. Fortunately there is a good selection of powerful yet inexpensive languages available for microcomputers. The QuickBasic version 4.0 compiler,[5] for example, offers a remarkable programming environment and a number of useful language extensions. A language that deserves attention in library circles for its unparalleled string handling capabilities is SNOBOL4, which is also intrinsically fascinating. Generally neglected for the past decade or so except for brief mention in introductory computer science classes, several versions have become available for micros in recent years. The SNOBOL4+[6] implementation includes some extensions, a very complete and flexible set of I/O functions, a large library of programs, and comes with an excellent tutorial and reference manual. A freely distributable version without some of the extras is also available from the same source at a nominal price.

Although the matter of loading order data is the central issue in automating approval acquisitions in NOTIS, there are others as well. Just as the library receives slips for titles not actually shipped, it might be desirable to load bibliographic records for these titles as well. Although there is no technical problem with this, it raises some practical questions. Is it really desirable to include such records in the library's catalog? Perhaps it would be better to load them into a separate file. In either case, some method of purging these records from time to time would be desirable. Yet another issue is the transmittal of credit memos to the vendor for returned titles. At present returns have to be entered online as well as listed on the vendor's paper form. Some method of generating paper or machine-readable records for the vendor from the online records would be a logical feature.

CONCLUSIONS

Libraries that use approval plans and are implementing integrated systems have a clear need for products and system functions to facilitate the management of this type of acquisitions. Approval vendors seem fairly responsive to the needs of libraries with integrated systems, and perhaps have an interest of their own in promoting automated transactions with libraries. There may be a tendency among them, though, to go their own ways in seeking to develop a competitive edge. Systems vendors are in the position of struggling to balance priorities and to keep up with library concerns.

Like other facets of online integrated library systems, the automation of approval acquisitions is likely to remain a partially fulfilled dream for some time to come. Although the responsibility for progress is a divided one, librarians can and should assume the burden of leadership. They need to identify weaknesses in the systems they use, exploit their strengths, improvise creatively, and above all articulate their requirements and press them on the vendors. They also have a collective role in determining the bounds and parameters of standardization and cooperation among vendors.

REFERENCES

1. Gibbs, Nancy J., "LC MARC Approval Tapes at Auburn University," *Library Acquisitions: Practice & Theory*, vol. 11, no. 3 (1987): 217-219.

2. Kreyche, Michael, "Use of Approval Plans with Automated Acquisitions: The RTSD RS Automated Acquisitions/In-Process Control Systems Discussion Group," *Library Acquisitions: Practice & Theory*, vol. 11, no. 3 (1987): 207-208.

3. CDI Data Communications Corp., 2803 Butterfield, Suite 250, Oak Brook, IL 60521.

4. SCA Products and Services, Inc., 353 Lexington Ave., New York, NY 10016.

5. Microsoft Corporation, 16011 NE 36th Way, Box 97017, Redmond, WA 98073-9717.

6. Catspaw, Inc., P.O. Box 1123, Salida, CO 81201.

INNOVACQ

Bringing up INNOVACQ: The Impact on the University of New Mexico General Library

Harry C. Broussard
Marilyn P. Fletcher
Chris Sugnet
Connie C. Thorson

SUMMARY. During a search process that spanned a year, and an installation that took a few weeks, the University of New Mexico General Library replaced an antiquated acquisition system with INNOVACQ. This paper tells the story, from the criteria developed for the RFP to the effect on the people and procedures when automation brings rapid change. Implementing the system involved coordination between separate serials and acquisitions departments, between technical services areas and a large group of collection development personnel, between a central library and four branch libraries, and between two autonomous libraries sharing the same system. Modifi-

---

Harry C. Broussard is Systems Librarian, Marilyn P. Fletcher is Head, Serials Department, Chris Sugnet is Head, Cataloging Department, and Connie C. Thorson is Head, Acquisitions Department, at the General Library, University of New Mexico, Albuquerque, NM 87131.

cations made to augment the turnkey system, transitional strategies to ease the impact of changes in the work environment, creative adaptations of the standard options in the functional modules, and implications for the future are all covered in detail.

For the first time in eight years, the 1986/87 annual reports of the Acquisitions and Serials Departments in the University of New Mexico General Library did not plead for a new automated acquisitions and serials control system in the new fiscal year. The new year found UNM the proud guardians of a new system and the happy discarders of an antiquated system. The General Library brought up INNOVACQ, the automated system marketed by Innovative Interfaces, Inc. in Berkeley, California, at the very end of the old fiscal year, and would spend the next year fine tuning the system and the workflow until everything reached maturity. Getting to this point was not entirely easy.

The General Library system at the University of New Mexico is composed of the Zimmerman Library and four branch libraries: Centennial Science & Engineering, Fine Arts, Parish Business Library, and the Tireman Learning Resources Library. UNM is a member of the Association of Research Libraries, with a total collection of 1.7 million volumes, and an annual materials budget of approximately $350,000 for monographs and $1.2 million for serials. Collection development is managed by a group of 5 coordinators who work with 30 subject selectors throughout the library system. The coordinators and selectors communicate closely with the academic community through individual contact with faculty and with faculty liaisons named by the academic departments. Monographic materials are ordered through the Acquisitions Department, which comprises sections devoted to Searching, Ordering, Receiving & Claiming, and Gifts & Exchange. Serials are ordered by the Serials Department's Serials Acquisitions Section and are received and added by the Serials Check-In Section. Serials started using the Faxon Datalinx system for ordering, claiming, and electronic mail in 1984, and both departments use OCLC for record verification. From 1976 to 1987 the Acquisitions and Serials departments relied on a batch mode system, using key tape machines, called BATAB. BATAB was implemented at UNM on the university's IBM mainframe, and served both to generate orders and to create the "book history" microfiche that was used throughout the system to keep track of ordered and received materials.

SEARCHING FOR A NEW SYSTEM

Because the General Library must adhere to various purchasing acts that are state law in New Mexico the process of buying a new system had to begin with an elaborate Request for Proposal (RFP) to system vendors. Writing the RFP started in the spring of 1985 and continued throughout the next year. The final document consisted of 57 pages of detailed questions covering the specific functional needs of both the General Library and the Law Library, which had joined with General during the writing process when it became necessary for them to plan for the day when OCLC would no longer provide the online serials and acquisitions modules that Law relied on. The length of the RFP was partially the result of having two autonomous libraries sharing the same system. The RFP was sent to 23 vendors in early 1986, and bids were due in August of the same year. It was somewhat disappointing that only 3 vendors responded, and one of the three only responded to the serials component of the RFP.

Having only 3 respondents did not appreciably shorten the time required to evaluate the bids. The evaluation committee had 14 members, and each read and critiqued each proposal according to a specific list of criteria (see Appendix A) provided to vendors as part of the RFP. Part of the evaluation process consisted of having a representative from INNOVACQ visit the campus for two days of system demonstrations. The overall system design and the variety of functions impressed staff from both libraries.

After additional questions concerning various functions in INNOVACQ had been answered, many calls were made to libraries where the system was installed and in use. The customers reported that they were pleased with it, reinforcing the evidence from other sources, including articles in the professional literature, the most specific being an article by Sara Heitshu[1] listing the reasons why the University of Michigan chose INNOVACQ and one by Shirley Leung[2] on implementing the system at the University of California,

Riverside. The evaluation committee forwarded a recommendation that INNOVACQ be purchased for both the General and Law libraries. An installation date of June 1, 1987 was negotiated with the company.

WHAT UNM BOUGHT

Because the system was to replace four other systems (BATAB, manual check-in and bindery preparation systems, and a machine readable serials database with public microfiche holdings list) it was decided to acquire the largest number of terminals possible. The CPU is comprised of 16 slave processor boards (with 32 ports) and two 150Mb disk drives. A system printer, tape cartridge drive and buffers for the OCLC ports complete the equipment at the "central site," which is a desk top located centrally in the Acquisitions Department. Other equipment includes 5 label printers and 3 local printers for report generation.

Some of the terminal locations differ from the original plan, primarily due to the extensive record creation needed to implement serials check-in. Some reassignment is planned after that task has been completed. The ports are currently allocated as follows:

- 9 in the Acquisitions Department
- 8 in the Serials Department
- 5 in the Law Library
- 3 in Reference Department areas
- 2 in the Science/Engineering Library
- 1 in the Government Publications Department
- 2 shared between the Business Library, Education Library, Fine Arts Library, and Special Collections in the General Library
- 1 for use by BNA and other vendors via dial modem
- 1 for system maintenance by Innovative Interfaces, Inc. via dial modem

The price of the system was partly a function of the numbers of various kinds of records UNM anticipated storing. The system currently is capable of storing 136,000 bibliographic records, 120,000 order records, 20,000 check-in records, 750 vendor names and addresses and 600 fund codes. After 10 months of operation the records occupy about 29% of the available space.

System maintenance includes a weekday backup of all transactions to two tape cartridges and a weekend backup of the entire database. (Two tape editions are kept of the database, one of them in another building.) Half of the indexes are checked by a vendor-supplied program on alternate weekends.

The potential to network the system was particularly noteworthy. Because the two libraries are about a quarter of a mile apart, and because campus politics favored proof of "compatibility" with other campus systems, it was imperative that the Law Library be able to communicate with the Central Processing Unit in the General Library via the University's Ungermann-Bass NetOne local area network (LAN) and the Campus Data Control Network (CDCN). The network being used at the University of California at San Diego is also driven by Ungermann-Bass, and since UCSD had linked their INNOVACQ sites on it, UNM decided to put the system on the LAN. This campus-wide network allowed for effective telecommunications between the main library, the branches, and the Law Library.

PLANNING FOR IMPLEMENTATION

Before the new system was installed, a number of library committees were formed to prepare for implementation. The major committee, called the INNOVACQ Implementation Committee (IIC), was composed of the department heads from Acquisitions and Serials, the Systems Librarian, and the Law Library Technical Services Head. IIC was primarily responsible for setting up the initial codes to be entered into the system before implementation. The Acquisitions and Serials Librarians worked on the fund designations and location and other codes. Planning without any previous experience with the system was tricky, but the manuals provided with the system helped in establishing specific work procedures. Most of the internal procedures were entered into word processing programs in order to facilitate continual revision.

Another committee, the Serials Start-Up Committee, began to investigate the best way to load bibliographic data for serials. Since a bibliographic record must exist in the system before a check-in or order record can be created and attached to the bibliographic record, it was imperative that as many current serials as possible be entered into the system quickly. Options included farming out the downloading of records to a "tape massage" vendor, but this was deemed too expensive. UNM's systems librarian devised a program that transfers MARC serials records from the LS/2 (DataPhase ALIS II) circulation system, in use since 1984, to the INNOVACQ system using INNOVACQ's OCLC linking software. Thanks to this unique program (described in detail in Appendix B) 7,000 current serials records were transferred automatically. Plans were then initiated to download the inactive serials titles in the near future. At this point the planning for use of the system by two autonomous libraries took on added significance. The Law Library agreed, for example, to use the percent sign (%) as the first character in fields designating funds, locations, and vendors. This character alerts anyone working in the system that the record belongs to Law, and has prevented General Library staff from inadvertently using Law's funds.

Bibliographic records that have no order or check-in records attached to them are more problematical, but a solution that worked was to put "LAW" in the location field if there is going to be only the bibliographic record to represent the title. Another significant concern was that of space for the hardware. This consideration was complicated by the fact that at first the Law Library had to do its work at the General Library because the LAN was not installed in the General Library or the Law Library. The Acquisitions Department had no more space to use than it ever had, but, by creating pods of back-to-back terminals, mounting the CDCN boxes to a column above the system printer, etc., the staff made it possible to squeeze in all the new equipment.

PERSONNEL CONSIDERATIONS

Presley and Robinson,[3] Johnson,[4] and others have recently written about the effect a new automated system may have on library personnel. They point out that it is a complex issue involving redistribution of work and subsequent reclassification of positions, and they also focus on the morale problems that often surface during the implementation process. In anticipation of this, long before the system contract was signed, the University's personnel office was notified that possible changes in position responsibilities would be tied to the system. Several possibilities that were not under consideration in the beginning were restructuring departments or eliminating positions. After the system was bought, and installation was underway, a number of positions did get reclassified, or upgraded. Some of these were: the searchers, data entry clerks, and a position to direct the creation of new records for the checklist. The searchers, for example, continued doing all the work they had previously done, but they added some new functional responsibilities: data entry, downloading portions of bibliographic records from OCLC to create order records, and assigning vendors. Some new positions were added, using existing vacancies that were upgraded also. The position of INNOVACQ Coordinator was created at this time to take over the system maintenance and reports generation, and to be the installation liaison with the company, etc. In addition to these jobs, the full-time coordinator provided valuable assistance in training, ordering supplies, liaison with the vendor and with the University computing center regarding LAN configurations and problems, replacing and shipping terminals and CPU parts, moving cables, and general problem diagnosis and correction. In retrospect, the library could have used the coordinator from the day the system was turned on. Later, after implementation, another searching position was added.

Coping with a new system was a challenge for some of the staff, though most were eager to have the new system and well aware that changes would occur daily until the procedures and workflow settled down. As described below, the system takes about a week to install and to start implementing full work routines on, and a week is not the slow implementation schedule recommended by Johnson.[5] The issue of possible reorganization was put on the "back burner" partially in response to the feeling that this would be too much too fast in an already fluid, ambiguous environment.

INSTALLATION

Unpacking the crates from INNOVACQ, wiring the terminals to the CPU and the backup unit, etc., took approximately 8 hours. The initial configuration was accommodated in the Acquisitions Department. A company trainer spent about a week in detailed sessions with selected staff who then took on the task of training the rest of the staff. Data entry began very soon after the initial training ended. The fact that on the first day of implementation there did not exist a specific set of internal procedures covering all local workflow options caused concern on the part of some staff. Department heads tried to warn the staff of this in advance and to reassure everyone that changes would be made and that documentation would follow. The ideas and procedures developed during the planning phase either worked as expected or needed some modifications, and flexibility was the key to the latter. After the first week, the system started receiving heavier use as more staff were trained. Staff members directly involved in acquisitions and serials records creation and maintenance received intensive training at the terminals, and local procedures proliferated and changed almost daily. A pragmatic approach was a necessity, and the trade-off in terms of getting a much better system more than made up for the inconvenience.

There was a great deal of curiosity about the system on the part of staff who did not work directly with the functional modules. Orientation sessions were conducted over a period of several months. The sessions were geared to specific needs of the personnel involved. Thus, the collection development coordinators and the selectors were given a thorough session on how to search the system and how to interpret both the bibliographic and financial information. They were also introduced to the capabilities of the system to create lists (see Figure 1) which could be profiled by a selector on an internal form and carried out by the INNOVACQ coordinator. These had to be run in the evenings, when the system use was lower. Several terminals were placed in the Reference Department and public access areas so that collection development personnel could easily and quickly see financial information online. The management reports available from INNOVACQ were immediately attractive. Coordinators and subject selectors had available from any terminal an up-to-date summary of their book and serial funds status. Reports utilizing Boolean searching strategies were available on a regular basis, including fund name, selector name, location, call number, or a combination of any indexed field. Regularly printed financial

FIGURE 1. Political science recent acquisitions for the week of January 1, 1988.

Modelski, George, ed.
EXPLORING LONG CYCLES.
Boulder, Colo: Rienner Publishers, 1987.

Thee, Marek, ed.
ARMS AND DISARMAMENT: SIPRI FINDINGS.
Oxford: Oxford Univ. Press, 1986.

Shenfield, Stephen.
NUCLEAR PREDICAMENT: EXPLORATIONS IN SOVIET IDEOLOGY.
London; New York: Routledge & Kegan Paul, 1987.

Carnesale, Albert, ed.
SUPERPOWER ARMS CONTROL: LESSONS LEARNED FROM EXPERIENCE.
Cambridge, Mass.: Ballinger Pub. Co., 1987.

Locke, John.
SECOND TREATISE OF GOVERNMENT.
Indianapolis, Ind.: Hackett Pub. Co., c1980.

Ceadel, Martin.
THINKING ABOUT PEACE AND WAR.
Oxford: Oxford University Press, c 1987.

Velikhov, Yevgeni, ed.
WEAPONRY IN SPACE: THE DILEMMA OF SECURITY.
Moscow: MIR Publishers, c 1986.

Hucko, Elmar M., ed.
DEMOCRATIC TRADITION: FOUR GERMAN CONSTITUTIONS.
Leamington Spa, UK: Berg Pubs., 1987.

Rosenblum, Nancy L.
ANOTHER LIBERALISM: ROMANTICISM AND THE RECONSTRUCTION
 OF LIBERAL THOUGHT.
Cambridge, Mass.: Harvard University Press, 1987.

Chapman, William.
INSIDE THE PHILIPPINE REVOLUTION.
New York: W.W. Norton, c 1987.

Mandelbaum, Michael.
REAGAN AND GORBACHEV.
New York; Vintage Books/Council on For Rel/Random House, 1987.

status reports were explained to the selectors, and assistance offered in how to use them for monitoring and planning purposes.

After the orientation of the selectors, other personnel were invited to participate in training and orientation sessions. Branch libraries were given a basic overview with emphasis on searching, financial information, and serials check-in functions. At least one of the branches, the new science library, was slated to use only the INNOVACQ system for access to serials information. Older, established branches had set up their own Kardex files. The government publications section was interested in setting up online check-in records for popular, current depository titles. Their staff was trained in the creation of check-in records and an agreement was negotiated on the number of government publications records that would be input. Finally, brief overview sessions were offered to any interested library employees. These sessions concentrated on searching the system for bibliographic information and on interpretation of payment information. Everyone who participated in the training was informed that the system functioned as a "search only" tool unless an individual had direct responsibility to change or manipulate the data. Searching was the least password-protected function in the system. Ordering and receiving were generally password-protected, with access available only to staff working in acquisitions or serials. System maintenance functions were very tightly controlled, being accessible only to the department heads, the systems librarian, and a few selected staff members, the INNOVACQ Coordinator being one.

ACQUISITIONS FUND ACCOUNTING

Another consideration was fund accounting. It was necessary to keep the money separate since the funding to the two libraries comes from separate budgets. In the accounting reports, therefore, "clusters" were set up one of which has only Law Library information and one of which has only General Library information. Within the clusters, sub-clusters were established, and then finally the funds were placed in their proper sub-cluster.

An explanation of the decision on how to handle funds might make this clearer. In the past the General Library allocated money to agencies such as Education or Science. There were, of course, more specific funds within these agencies, but money was not allocated to them. In INNOVACQ, however, money was allocated to each fund, placing much greater accountability on the individual selector. In the past, overexpenditure of a given selector's budget was common. In the new system the funds were clustered (see Table 1) to put like subjects together under one heading. For example, Social Sciences is still a cluster or agency, but under it money is allocated to Anthropology, History, Political Science, Sociology, etc. By clustering these funds together, it was possible to keep track of the spending of the Social Sciences selectors on a regular basis, making the job of the Social Sciences Coordinator a little easier. Most of the funds were closely related to subjects and those subjects were, for the most part, divided into three separate funds. The previous "Political Science" fund, for instance, in the new system became "POLI" for subscriptions and standing orders, "POLI2" for title-by-title and approval form selection orders, and "POLI3" for straight approval plan book selections. The specificity of the funds allowed for much greater control of the budgets, an important facility in a period when rising serials subscription prices necessitated holding a percentage of each fund back as a contingency to cover subscription overruns in the latter part of the fiscal year.

When the funds were set up, there was also the option for putting in such information as selectors' names and how much was allocated for subscriptions and how much for standing orders. Also part of the fund record was the subfield group. Every order record got a subfield type. It could be such things as "book," "approval," "standing order," or "periodical" and was defined by the library. By putting the correct character for the subfield in the order record, the money encumbered and then subsequently spent for a given item was recorded to the proper subfield of the fund. A selector could then go to her/his fund and see that so many dollars had been spent for periodical renewals.

The activity in the funds was recorded for the selector in hard copy in the fund activity report that was printed each week, or more frequently if necessary. This report went to the selector and showed every transaction, regardless of its function, that occurred in a given fund since the last report. Another nice feature of the system was that a percentage could be programmed in that would cause the data entry operator to be alerted if a given fund was over, say, 75% spent and encumbered.

TABLE 1. Financial status: Social Science.

Social Science(28)	FINANCIAL STATUS : GENERAL LIBRARY			
	APPROPRIATION	EXPENDITURE	ENCUMBRANCE	FREE BALANCE
1> Anthropology	$34,007.45	$11,828.12	$3,093.55	$19,085.78
2> Communicative Disorders	$6,853.26	$1,272.14	$248.30	$5,332.82
3> Ethnic Studies	$16,304.35	$6,852.11	$329.46	$9,122.78
4> Geography	$11,524.70	$3,805.48	$728.05	$6,991.17
5> History	$45,511.45	$10,765.16	$3,620.39	$31,125.90
6> Newspapers	$32,494.79	$13,062.02	$2,697.11	$16,735.66
7> Political Science	$35,906.68	$10,494.87	$3,107.46	$22,304.35
8> Public Administration	$7,213.01	$1,308.54	$176.94	$5,727.53
9> Soc Sci General	$15,296.11	$2,690.20	$631.19	$11,974.72
0> Sociology	$21,853.51	$13,524.67	$0.00	$8,328.84
TOTAL	$226,965.31	$75,603.31	$14,632.45	$136,729.55

```
To see more detail about a particular line key its number
        A > To scroll AHEAD
        G > To GRAPH this data
        U > To use UNENCUMBERED balance in displays
        M > To see MORE options
        R > To RETURN to last level
        Q > To QUIT management report
     Choose one (1-9,A,G,U,M,R,Q)
```

ACQUISITIONS OF SERIALS AND MONOGRAPHS

A primary concern with the establishment of the system for serials acquisitions was the loss of historical payment information for renewals and standing orders. Over a period of years, the manual system had created a very visible and accurate payment history which was placed adjacent to the check-in record in the Kardex file. It became apparent that, short of reentering data from previous years, it would take at least one year before any sort of relevant payment history would become available in INNOVACQ. Since it had formerly been the practice to notify collection development selectors of price increases of more than 25%, it was necessary to compare manual records when creating new payment records in the system. After the first year, the manual records could be retained, but would not need to be frequently referred to for comparing information.

Every currently received title needed to have an order record and a check-in record connected to a bibliographic record (the basic record to which other records are attached). Additional personnel were hired on temporary contracts to assist the permanent staff in entering and establishing order and check-in records. It was anticipated that the first year would be the most difficult for the new system but that in the future, once the database was established, procedures would be quicker and more efficient than with the previous batch system. Volunteers from other departments of the General Library also worked on record creation. Data accuracy was considered critical in all aspects of the new system: location, call numbers, fund designations, vendor information, etc.

Because the system initially provided space in the name/address vendor file for only 750 vendors, acquisitions and serials staff decided to use the vendor directory codes only for those vendors to whom at least 10 payments had been made in the last fiscal year. Vendors not meeting this cutoff point were given a "none" status and the complete name and address placed in a "vendor" field coded "Q" within the order record. Thanks to the list making capabilities of the system, a list of the "none" vendors was compiled in alphabetical order on a regular basis. The list gave not only the vendor's complete name and address, but payment information could also be included, making the checking of statements quite simple, and providing a vendor "directory" which could be consulted as needed. At the end of each fiscal year, any vendors who received 10 or more payments would be considered for inclusion in the indexed vendor file.

The processing of invoices caused some trauma for serials and acquisitions staff members. While in the actual function of processing invoices, changes could be made quite easily and notes added (for example, serials notes always include the period and/or volumes covered by the payment and the initials of the person processing the invoice). Once an invoice was processed, the total entered by the payer had to correspond to the sum of all individual items on the invoice, including additions for postage and handling, and deductions for discounts. The invoice function would not process an invoice until the totals matched. This function also provided for automatic currency conversion using foreign currency rates that were updated each week by an acquisitions staff member. Currency conversion saved at least one full day of invoice processing time. Once processed, the payment line could not be changed. Changes had to be made through crediting and debiting on subsequent payment lines. While this was absolutely necessary for auditing purposes, some of the staff were concerned that they could not make corrections, even in the note area, after the fact. All personnel were encouraged to look over invoices very carefully before entering the invoice processing function to minimize the necessity to correct errors through the credit or debit functions. Frequent errors became very visible and staff became very error conscious.

After invoice processing was completed, a high level staff member performed the posting function which encumbered and expended to funds and which prepared invoice registers and summaries. The registers and summaries were sent with the invoices to the General Library fiscal services section which prepared the invoices for payment. The payment requests were then sent to the University fiscal services division where checks were prepared and mailed out.

INTERFACES WITH OTHER VENDORS

Payment of invoices for renewals and standing orders proved to be much faster and more efficient with the new system. Since the major domestic vendor used, Faxon, had been sending the annual renewal invoice on magnetic tapes for the past five years, it was evident that the initial task of establishing order records for the Faxon titles would be time consuming and yet had to be a high priority in order to facilitate the receipt of future invoices on a tape cartridge which could be loaded and processed automatically by INNOVACQ. At least one other vendor, Blackwell's Periodicals Division, expressed interest in establishing the capability of providing renewal invoices on tape cartridge for loading into the system.

IMPACT ON OTHER AREAS OF THE LIBRARY

The reference department initially installed two terminals, one at the main reference desk and one at the periodicals index reference desk. Both quickly became invaluable. As the serials check-in records were moved over to the system, a reference librarian could tell at a glance when the latest issue of a serial or newspaper had arrived. The ability to truncate search terms was far superior to searching the old serials fiche, which offered only title access with far too few cross-references. In the public access mode, INNOVACQ searched author, title, subject, and call number. The availability of order and in-process records for monographs proved to be useful also, as it eliminated the need to use the "book history" fiche, a product of the discarded batch system, and offered a more up-to-date tool for checking on ordered titles.

The impact on the cataloging operations was minimal, consisting of a loss of several multiple-copy forms that had been used in various routines to check book marking and OCLC card receipt. A few manual files were discarded, with the net effect of reducing the processing overhead of manually filling out slips of paper that weren't needed.

THE FUTURE

In the future, the possibilities inherent in the system may indicate some organizational changes such as cataloging all monographic titles with Library of Congress copy at point of receipt, or decentralization of some functions such as the physical separation of serials cataloging from the check-in files. The issue of decentralization of monographs and serials acquisitions will be given much more scrutiny. Pam Cenzer[6] in a thought provoking article a few years ago, points out that there are trade-offs. The major consideration for UNM would be that the coordination needed in a decentralized environment would add a layer to management that has cost implications not yet fully identified or considered. These issues, and others, will be evaluated in the coming months.

By fall, 1988 the University's computing center newsletter will have announced the system's availability to the entire campus community for searching orders and current serials. Although, strictly speaking, the INNOVACQ screens are readable using most kinds of terminals and PC communications software, those devices which emulate Televideo 925 terminals produce far superior results. Soft-Term and ProComm are among the less-expensive terminal emulator programs that meet that specification.

At present there is no direct, electronic, interface with the University fiscal operation or with accounts payable, but future plans include a link. The INNOVACQ system already provides a field into which vendor account numbers assigned by the vendor can be entered, and that in itself will provide an important access point for vendor and invoice information. It will also expedite payments to vendors, which should make them extremely happy.

REFERENCES

1. Sara C. Heitshu, "Changing Acquisitions Systems: An Evolutionary Process," *Technicalities* 4, no.4:3-7 (April 1984).
2. Shirley W. Leung, "The INNOVACQ 100 System: Experience of a Pilot User," *Library Acquisitions: Practice and Theory*, 7:127-138 (1983).
3. Roger L. Presley and Carolyn L. Robinson, "Changing Roles of Support Staff in an Online Environment," *Technical Services Quarterly* 4, no.1:25-39 (Fall 1986).
4. Peggy Johnson, "Implementing Technological Change," *College & Research Libraries* 49, no.1:38-46 (January 1988).
5. Ibid., p.44.
6. Pamela S. Cenzer, "Decentralized Acquisitions: A Future Trend?" *Library Acquisitions: Practice and Theory*, 9:37-40 (1985).

APPENDIX A
Evaluation Criteria — Acquisitions

POINTS	PERCENTAGE	CRITERIA
15	7.5	1. General system Requirements: Response time, reliability and serviceability of hardware and software, system uptime, maintenance, physical and environmental requirements, hardware interface with university mainframe.
15	7.5	2. Security: Password/terminal controls for all system components.
20	10	3. General Considerations: User friendly, ease of use by staff, training, interface capabilities, word processing capabilities, references, past performance on projects of similar scope, size, and application, transfer of date from current to new system, vendor commitment to timely installation, and implementation.
30	15	4. Order function: Provision for maximum number of data elements, defaults, claim functions, flexibility in searching and retrieving of order data, automatic transfer of bibliographic data.
20	10	5. Invoice Function: Provision for maximum number of data elements, mathematical calculations, access to outstanding invoices, reports on vendor performance.

POINTS	PERCENTAGE	CRITERIA
20	10	6. Vendor Function: Name-address directory, each library's ability to manipulate vendor information, adequate field lengths, capability with university vendor file.
20	10	7. Fund Accounting: complete fund information online, mathematical calculations, hierarchical structuring, ability to combine several data elements for selector reports.
5	2.5	8. Audit Trails: Compliance with accepted accounting principles and practices.
30	15	9. Searching: Variety of search strategies, qualifiers, browse capabilities, arrangement of displays.
20	10	10. Management Reports and Statistics: Flexibility to accumulate statistics and create a variety of reports from any keyed elements specified.
5	2.5	11. Miscellaneous: Desiderata, negative decisions, approval forms, selector/fund/faculty liaison table, price.

APPENDIX B
Augmenting a Turnkey System

One acknowledged shortcoming of a turnkey system when compared to one developed in-house is its inflexibility of adaptation to an individual customer's needs. Although system designers may build into their product as much flexibility as they expect the market to demand, excessive customizing negates the goal of simplicity through standardization. Even extremely routine and labor-intensive operations in a library might not be accommodated by a turnkey system if they are unique to a few sites or if the system was under-designed.

Despite INNOVACQ's rather sophisticated communications links and report generation facilities the University of New Mexico General Library has several needs that INNOVACQ does not meet. In three instances a general-purpose microcomputer has been interfaced to INNOVACQ to perform the needed processing.

Transferring Serials Records

Some years ago the General Library loaded OCLC records for most of its serial titles into the (then DataPhase) LS/2 circulation system database in preparation for an on-line catalog. Since then the staff have made hundreds of changes to those records. In order for INNOVACQ to replace both the current manual check-in system and microfiche holdings list it was desirable to transfer the full cataloging records for those titles mechanically into the new system. But INNOVACQ's communications links do not include an LS/2 transfer facility. Consequently, the Systems Librarian wrote a program (in the BASIC language) for an IBM-compatible microcomputer. The software functions as follows.

1. The program is started, the Input option is selected and either OCLC or LS/2 Bibliographic Record Numbers are keyed into a disk file. (Because the Library had access to a machine readable list of OCLC numbers it was able to transfer 6,600 serials records from LS/2 to INNOVACQ in the summer of 1987 without keying a single record number.)

2. The PC is connected to a standard LS/2 port and the Download option is selected. The operator specifies (a) the name(s) of the

file(s) containing the record numbers, (b) the INNOVACQ command string (which that system later uses to process incoming records), and (c) a quitting time or number of records to download (since the process runs unattended but must stop if LS/2 is taken down that night for file backup).

The PC then simulates an operator's session at a LS/2 terminal. It logs off any previous session, logs on with a password and ID and enters the Bibliographic Maintenance function. It reads each record number from disk and issues a "V" or "B" inquiry. It then analyzes the response, bypassing all problem inquiries.

When the first data screen is received the program prints the command string to disk, reconstructs the OCLC number and fixed field names and data and prints that information to disk. Then it prints the bibliographic tags and their contents to disk, in the exact format of an OCLC screen. The program prompts for additional screens until all have been received, then exits to the Inquiry screen for the next record.

All operator specifications and program activities are logged to a parallel printer attached to the PC. The data include the time of receipt, sequential number of the record, its OCLC or LS/2 number, and an explanation if a record could not be downloaded. With good response time from LS/2 a full cataloging record is retrieved, received at 9600 baud, reformatted and stored on disk in the OCLC screen format in about 20 seconds. Upon completion the program logs itself off the LS/2 system.

3. The PC is connected to an INNOVACQ OCLC port. (RS-232 switch boxes to LS/2 and INNOVACQ and dual COM ports on the PC facilitate daily operation of the transfer program.) The operator selects the Upload option and specifies the number of records to be uploaded and an optional quitting time.

This process also runs unattended. The program reads the command string for each record from disk and transmits it, then transmits the OCLC screen image of the record. It logs the activity to its printer and then waits for INNOVACQ's response. It logs that response to the printer (instead of to INNOVACQ's logging printer) and repeats the process. With good INNOVACQ response time the OCLC screen image of a full record is retrieved from disk, transmitted at 1200 baud and accepted in about 30 seconds.

About 7,000 records have been transferred between the two systems in this manner, and plans are to transfer perhaps another 10,000 records. As can be imagined, the savings in staff time and the accuracy is very substantial and definitely justified the development effort.

Monthly Invoice Listing

One requirement of the auditors at UNM is for a monthly reconciliation between the invoices processed by INNOVACQ and the University's Accounts Payable System which writes the checks. While INNOVACQ is capable of producing a variety of accounting reports based on funds it is less versatile in preparing vendor-oriented reports.

To obtain that reconciliation report a file is created in INNOVACQ which contains all orders for which one or more payments was made in a specified month. It is then sorted in vendor order, although seldom-used vendors are grouped separately from frequently used ones.

A program was written for a PC which receives that file as it is "printed" through an auxiliary port attached to an INNOVACQ terminal. The program discards duplicate occurrences of the vendor name, field headings and form feed characters, and it also disregards payments which were not made in the specified month. It prints a combined list of payments under each vendor's name, a total for the vendor, and a grand total at the end of the report.

Response Time Monitor

In a slightly different application from the previous two (where the PC either simulated an OCLC terminal attached to an INNOVACQ port, or else passively captured output data from the system) the General Library is testing a program wherein the PC simulates an operator session at an INNOVACQ terminal.

The PC is attached to a standard INNOVACQ port. At specified intervals throughout the day the program issues a command to INNOVACQ to display the list of users, and then begins timing the response. When the next screen is fully displayed the program writes to disk the time of day and elapsed time for the response, along with the user list.

Very detailed statistical reports can be prepared from the data gathered, and the users lists captured on disk will be helpful in verifying that the system meets the response time provisions of the contract.

The Library is considering several other applications which employ a microcomputer to enhance INNOVACQ. Key factors in those decisions are (a) the importance of the application to library operations, and (b) the time needed for program design and development. If too many programs are written the library will have, in practice, overturned its earlier decision to avoid in-house development in favor of the turnkey approach. But by judicious augmentation of the turnkey system with a microcomputer interface the best features of both design philosophies will be realized.

In-Process Control of Order Requests for "Out of Print" and "Not Yet Published" Materials Using the INNOVACQ Acquisitions System

Stephen Bosch

SUMMARY. The processing of orders for materials that are not currently available because they are either out of print or not yet published is problematic. A large number of books are going out of print in short periods of time. Too many orders are returned to libraries after a vendor discovers the title is indefinitely out of stock or out of print. Publishers announce books well in advance of the expected publication date whetting the appetite of library patrons and frustrating the acquisitions department that tries to purchase the items. In manual operations these requests must be reshuffled, and reprocessed until the item is either in the library or the request falls into that certain limbo that awaits any order that gets shuffled one too many times. This paper will describe how the INNOVACQ acquisitions system can be used to process order requests for out of print and not yet published materials in an effective and expeditious manner.

INTRODUCTION

Acquisitions departments have a love/hate relationship with the paper they must process. Even in departments that use sophisticated automated systems the amount of paper shuffling is astronomical.

Stephen Bosch is Acquisitions Librarian, University of Arizona Library, 1510 University Blvd., Tucson, AZ 85721.

© 1989 by The Haworth Press, Inc. All rights reserved.

Incoming order requests and publishers' catalogs and advertisements load the front end while invoices and correspondence with vendors load the back end. Anything that can be done to organize and reduce the handling of paper is a welcome relief in any organization. One particular problem and one of the most frustrating aspects of the acquisitions process in a library (especially academic libraries) is a frequent inability to purchase requested materials in a timely fashion due to the fact that these items are either out of print (OP) nor not yet published (NYP). The processing of NYP and OP order requests has always been a labor intensive activity requiring a disproportionate amount of time and resources when compared to other operations in an acquisitions department.

THE OP/NYP PROBLEM

Requests for out of print materials create processing problems for most acquisitions departments. Smaller press runs and the inability of publishers to warehouse extensive stocks of their backlists force an increasing number of titles out of print in short periods of time. Library collections are aging and the number of titles that require replacement seems to be escalating in nearly geometric terms. Despite the best efforts of library security systems hundreds of books turn up missing. A large proportion of these missing items are no longer in print but are still in demand by the public. Patron requests for OP materials that support teaching and research in academic institutions can't be ignored since libraries are service organizations and should make every attempt to acquire those materials that are requested by their patrons.

Once an item has been identified as being OP or out of stock an acquisitions department has two options. They may pursue the items in the OP/remainder/secondhand market or they can inform the patron that the item is no longer available and drop the matter. The later solution is generally unacceptable and is detrimental to the library's public image. It seems that to have at least tried and failed to locate an item makes the patron feel that the library has fulfilled its service role. A third option does exist if the title is known to be out of copyright. The book may be borrowed through interlibrary loan and copied. Copying is not cheap nor is it aesthetically pleasing but it does gain access to the requested information as long as the title is not protected by copyright laws. The processing of out of print requests has always been labor intensive. Beyond the searching that must be done to verify that the item is not available in alternative formats the item must either be advertised in OP trade journals or forwarded to search services or OP/secondhand bookstores. Sometimes both methods are required before a request is filled.

Order requests for not yet published titles pose a similar problem. Frequently library patrons will submit selections for materials that won't be published for a substantial period of time. The practice of advance advertisement of soon-to-be-published books is well entrenched in the publishing world and most publishers are not about to change this practice to help libraries avoid the problems that NYP materials can cause. After a title has been identified as being not yet in print an acquisitions department does have the option of ordering the item as if it were a regular book. This solution is not universally acceptable. Some vendors will cancel NYP orders in which case further correspondence is required to reinstate the order. A large number of NYP orders in a vendor's file increases their workload and could decrease their statistical average for time until fulfillment. Some libraries have problems with large unproductive encumbrances especially if their local laws do not allow a carry over of encumbrances at year's end. If a library has approval plans and its vendors do not discount firm orders in lieu of expected materials at the approval rate, there could be a significant loss of discount.

Not placing the order can be equally as problematic as the request must then be filed and rechecked at a later date to determine if the item has been released. This process can generate multiple searches of the order as expected dates of publication change, not to mention title changes and outright cancellations of publication. The patron frequently checks back to locate their request and retrieval becomes difficult as a manual NYP file will probably be arranged by expected date of publication to ease processing.

THE INNOVACQ SYSTEM

It matters little how the problem of out of print or not yet published orders arise, these orders have never moved smoothly through an acquisitions department. In the past, bulky paper files were processed over and over again in hope that either the item has finally appeared in print or appeared on the shelf of some book store. The advent of automated systems, in general, and the IN-NOVACQ system, in particular, have helped acquisitions departments organize and process these orders, saving the organization a large amount of time and labor. The INNOVACQ system design is such that its flexibility lends itself to dealing with these problems. The paper files of OPs, NYPs, and other such desiderata may be discarded and the information made easily accessible and manageable by the system. Different libraries have differing needs and procedures, consequently what we do at the University of Arizona Library may not be entirely pertinent to your operation but this presentation will discuss how the INNOVACQ system is used to process non-order records prior to actually generating a true order.

The INNOVACQ acquisitions system is manufactured and marketed by Innovative Interfaces Incorporated of Berkeley, California. The overall design and functions of the system will not be reported here except as they relate to the processing of NYP and OP orders. The INNOVACQ system has been discussed widely in library literature so it would be redundant to provide general information in this context. The system enables the user to create records that INNOVACQ recognizes as being on hold or pending orders. These records do not encumber the accounting system yet have all the same access points as regular orders. Also the system allows for the attachment of particular codes to NYP and OP records which facilitates the retrieval of this information. The procedures described here may be of value to users of different systems if their systems have the capability of treating requests without encumbering the accounting system combined with the ability to flag and retrieve particular types of records.

Processing the Requests

Before an order request is declared OP or NYP all available resources are thoroughly checked to avoid mistaking a viable order. At the University of Arizona Library preorder searching is centralized in Acquisitions. Four librarians coordinate collection development activities and initiate all orders. Faculty and library staff are extremely active in selecting library materials consequently many selectors lack intimate knowledge of the book trade that would enable them to recognize NYP or probable OP requests before they are forwarded to Acquisitions for processing. Before a selection is treated as OP all appropriate trade bibliographies, publishers' catalogs, and resources like *Books On Demand,* and *Guide to Microforms in Print* are checked to see if the item is available in the requested format or in a reprint, newer edition, microform or any other alternative format. NYP orders are usually identified by a Library of Congress CIP record that lacks any holdings during the preorder search. Again, we will make every effort to be sure that the item is still unavailable before treating the request as not yet published. As we have extensive approval plans we will also try to ascertain if a vendor has treated the item before we process the request. Cancelled orders that are returned to the department from vendors because the items are OP or NYP will be updated on the INNOVACQ system and have their order type and status changed to reflect the disposition of the order. We have assigned each type of cancellation its own order type code to provide management reports on this activity and to prevent future attempts at repeating the order. After notification that an order has been identified as OP and the vendor is searching for the item we assign a new order type code which would indicate the book is out of print but the vendor is searching. This enables us to exclude these records when compiling vendor statistics as OP search orders would have a detrimental impact on the rate and speed of fulfillment.

After an order request has been identified as being OP or NYP the request is returned to the acquisitions librarian who initiated the original order. When the librarian receives the returned orders from either the preorder search section or as a report from a vendor they will determine if a patron needs to be notified concerning the current status of the order. In the case of OP requests this is important as the patron may wish to acquire the item through interlibrary loan and further pursuit by the acquisitions department may be unnecessary. Once a decision has been made concerning notification the acquisitions librarian would then determine if the item was worth further attempts to acquire. If acquisition of the item is desired it would then be processed on INNOVACQ.

Entering the Records on INNOVACQ

As the items are entered on the system the orders are assigned a status of "1" (on hold, under consideration, etc.). The status field in the INNOVACQ system relates the order to the accounting system. Status 1 records do not encumber. Order type codes are assigned that indicate whether the item is NYP or OP. It is possible for the user to define order type code within the system's parameters. The code is a single character and there is a limited amount (36) that may be assigned. The record is entered on the system including all normal bibliographic and order processing information as if the item was a regular order. There are exceptions. The expected date of publication is included as an internal note for NYP records and orders for U.S. imprints will not be assigned vendors. This applies only to U.S. imprints. All OP requests for books published outside the U.S. are assigned a vendor from a preselected list of jobbers that do out of print searches for materials published in a particular locale. This procedure permits the department to produce special OP lists for foreign materials. Vendors will be assigned for U.S. materials only when an actual order is placed. Vendors are not assigned to U.S. OP records as totally "clean" out of print lists are not produced for all searches. Not knowing the exact effect of Status 1 records on vendor reports, statistical and other management reports, all Status 1 records are excluded during Boolean searches concerning regular materials.

Retrieval of OP/NYP Lists

When processing lists of not yet published materials from INNOVACQ, the information is retrieved using status and/or order type as the Boolean operator. The list is sorted by order date (the date the request was originally input) and by publisher. A Boolean review file can be sorted by various fields before the list is printed. This procedure groups the records in a way that quickly isolates the oldest and organizes these by publisher. This facilitates inquiries concerning the status of a publication. Lists are created and printed from the system every six weeks. (This time period was selected entirely at random.) A list is searched again on OCLC or in trade bibliographies (BIP etc.) to determine which titles have been published. It is also checked against our approval vendor's list of titles treated by their plan to determine if any items have been picked up by the approval plan. The items that have yet to be published can be left in the system for searching at a later date. If the expected date of publication has passed, an inquiry could be sent to the publisher to determine the status of the title. Checking with publishers is practically the only means of identifying cancelled publications which need to be purged from the system.

Fortunately, Status 1 records are very simple to delete because they are not involved with the accounting system. As the lists are processed, items that are determined to have been published are assigned vendors, the status changed, and an order generated. We see about a 20% turn around of NYPs that have been published on each list. This statistic does not include the materials that are received from other sources (approval plans, blanket orders, etc.) that fulfill a NYP record on the system. It indicates that one out of five titles on each printed list has now come into print, has not been received in the library and may now be treated as a regular order.

Out of print lists are retrieved from the system using the order type code as the primary Boolean operator. Before a review file is printed from the INNOVACQ system OP lists are sorted by vendor and, in some situations, by subject. Also, the format of the printed list is selected to include only the author, title, publisher, and edition information. After printing, the lists are forwarded to a preselected vendor if they consist of foreign materials. For U.S. imprints the lists are manually divided and sent to booksellers, search services, etc. We are using this procedure to study vendor response to OP searches. Lists are being generated and sent to different types of book dealers based upon the materials being searched. Some are sent to major secondhand operations that keep large stocks like the Strand Book Store in New York. Lists are also sent to specialized academic search services like International Book Finders and to smaller independent OP dealers. Fresh lists will also be produced at some time in the future and advertised in AB Bookmans or other OP trade journals. Hopefully this analysis will produce some indication as to the most cost effective and or the most successful means of acquiring OP materials for our Library. If no pattern emerges we have at least covered all possible sources in pursuit of an item.

Resolving Duplication Problems

In the event that a title being received in the acquisitions department matches a Status 1 NYP or OP record already on INNOVACQ, the received item will always be accepted and the Status 1 record updated to indicate a fulfilled order. Duplication of NYP records by incoming approval books occurs with great frequency since weekly four to five new U.S. approval books will match records in the system. Gifts received by the library sometimes match OP requests. Also, selections from antiquarian catalogs sometimes match requests in the system. In the case of approval materials that are received all necessary information (requestor, branch location etc.) will be transferred from the Status 1 record to the new record if the approval record has been electronically transmitted from a vendor.

The INNOVACQ system accepts the electronic transmittal of bibliographic records and invoice information for received approval books. The bibliographic records are linked to the invoices, consequently it is easier to transfer information from the Status 1 to the new record and process the new one than vice versa. In this case the original record would then be deleted. When a new order request duplicates a NYP record the new request is checked to make sure that the desired item has been published. If the item is available the original record is updated and an order generated. If the item is unavailable, all necessary information is transferred from the duplicate and added to the record on the system. If new requests are duplicates of records for cancelled orders, these requests are returned to the acquisitions librarian that initiated them and the items processed according to his or her instructions. If necessary, the requestor is notified. When a new edition is received that supersedes an item on an OP list, the new edition is accepted and a librarian consulted to determine if we should continue the search for the old title.

Expensive Purchases

The acquisitions department is using similar procedures to track deferred expensive purchases and to track the Center for Research Libraries' purchase decisions concerning major serial and microform collections. These items are entered as Status 1 records and our decisions regarding the priority of purchase are entered as an internal note. Multiple internal notes that can contain a great deal of textual information may be entered on individual order records. In the case of items considered by CRL for addition to their collections the outcome of that purchase decision and the library's response is recorded as an internal note. This procedure enables us to avoid rethinking major purchases once a firm decision concerning acquisition has been made.

Major purchases may not be necessary if the item is soon to be available from the Center for Research Libraries. If a new request for an item in this category is received we can quickly report back to the requestor that the item is under consideration but has been deferred, or that the item will not be purchased locally but is available from CRL. Management reports can also be created by the system indicating the projected costs of these expensive items and the fund areas in which the expenditures would be made.

Benefits and Liabilities

Our use of the INNOVACQ system for in-process control of out of print and not yet published order requests has many benefits. Once a request has been identified as not being readily available the item is stored online. We process the original paper request one time. Searching the system is an integral part of our preorder search and repeat items are quickly identified and dispatched. The information contained in the system is organized according to our specific needs and easily retrieved. Information concerning requestor, branch location, or special processing instructions can be attached to newly received materials that duplicate items in the system. We can input patron requests for NYP materials allowing the materials to arrive on the approval plan. This maintains our rate of discount and matches the patron to the newly arrived title expediting notification of the requestor and the cataloging of the item. We are able to respond to patron inquiries concerning the status of their order and inform them of the exact state of their request. The out of print list is integrated in our in-process file in real time. Incoming gifts and OP catalog selections immediately update the file. We maintain records of out of print and out of stock orders that were cancelled avoiding repeat attempts at purchase. The lists produced by the system are organized to our specifications making processing a simple matter. The labor intensive paper shuffling associated with out of print files and searches is now over. We can send clean lists to booksellers for searching or we can have a title searched by multiple services. The system provides a wide variety of management reports including expenditures for OP materials arranged by subject areas and the cost of book replacements. The use of the INNOVACQ system for the processing of OP and NYP requests has decreased the amount of paperwork and manual files, improved access to information relating to the request, and streamlined our methods of processing these materials.

The major drawback we have encountered with these procedures involves public access to our in-process files. INNOVACQ terminals have been installed in public areas and patrons are encouraged to search the database to locate newly received items and to determine if an item is on order before requesting purchase. The University of Arizona Library is also in the process of bringing up INNOPAC, the online public access catalog designed by Innovative Interfaces Inc. The two systems interface and in-process records located in the INNOVACQ system display in the online catalog. The various codes, status levels, etc. make perfect sense to people that use the system frequently. Infrequent users are easily confused by the meaning of what they see in the system and assume that on hold records are true orders. All public service units that use INNOVACQ have been trained to recognize Status 1 records as requests that are not active. They explain to patrons that these records are pending orders that won't be accessible in the near future and we regret any inconvenience.

Another possible drawback may be the amount of system storage utilized by these procedures. At this time all OP, NYP, and Expensive Item Status 1 records amount to only about 800 bibliographic and order records. This level of utilization does not represent a large portion of our system's capacity. The amount of space occupied when compared to the convenience offered is well worth the sacrifice. The ease of processing OP and NYP records on the INNOVACQ system and our ability to report to patrons the status of their problem requests at a moment's notice are well worth the effort of establishing these procedures and the expenditure of the resources.

GEAC

The INNOVACQ and Geac Acquisitions Systems Compared: A Large Academic Library Perspective

Carol Pitts Hawks

SUMMARY. The INNOVACQ and Geac Acquisitions Systems have been successfully implemented in several large academic libraries. All basic requirements for a full-scale acquisitions system have been met by both systems. Size, as measured by number of orders placed or number of subscriptions maintained, magnifies the problems, deficiencies, and difficulties of any system. This paper focuses on significant differences between the two systems, particularly as they relate to large academic libraries. These areas include capacity, in-house control and environmental concerns, backup procedures and printing, command structure, record structure, integration versus interfacing, password security, serials control, invoicing and fund accounting, and management reports.

INTRODUCTION

Acquisitions represents a "last bastion of manual operations in an increasingly automated library environment."[1] The acquisitions

---

Carol Pitts Hawks is Head, Acquisition Department for the Ohio State University Libraries, 1858 Neil Avenue Mall, Columbus, OH 43210-1286. She was Head of Acquisitions at the University of Houston Libraries from 1982-1987.

© 1989 by The Haworth Press, Inc. All rights reserved.

process includes many exceptions, intricacies, and subroutines which vary substantially from one library to another. Typically a library's local requirements for acquisitions are much more individualized than for cataloging or circulation. The increased uniformity in cataloging results from universally accepted national standards such as MARC and their use in common databases, such as those maintained by RLIN and OCLC. In the area of Circulation there has been a similar convergence of approaches over the years. However, acquisitions is subject to local policies and procedures governing purchasing and financial transactions that are usually mandated by another department in the library's parent organization. This stymied most attempts to adopt a more standardized approach to acquisition processes. By early 1982, most automated systems had overcome this difficulty by offering a range of purchase order and financial report formats.[2] Nevertheless, each library's specific procedures and policies will determine how well any system meets the needs and expectations of that individual library.

Early automated systems were supported by expensive, full-size computers. Few libraries could afford to obtain their own computer; most had to rely on sharing available hardware. The 1970s and 1980s have seen dramatic developments in hardware, enabling almost any library to consider an online system.[3] Although computers are often divided into three basic kinds—microcomputers, minicomputers, and mainframes—the differences between them are rarely that distinct. The power of computers at the lower end of the spectrum is rapidly eroding the differences.

> Traditional distinguishing characteristics have included the number of terminals which may be supported, the number of simultaneous tasks which may be carried out, hardware capabilities (for example, the size of the memory), the kinds of storage devices supported, and the price.[4]

However, the best approach is to evaluate the system based upon its ability to meet the library's requirements. The limitations of particular systems, whether hardware-or software-based, will become apparent when a thorough analysis is undertaken. This paper will analyze and compare the INNOVACQ and Geac Acquisitions Systems as they relate to large academic libraries.

BACKGROUND—GEAC COMPUTERS, LTD.

Geac was founded in 1971 with its first product being an inventory control system for municipal school boards. The company made a significant move into the retail banking world in 1974. From a computing point of view, the similarities between banking and library applications, primarily the shared need for large databases and high transaction processing levels, made the move into library applications a natural step. Geac's integrated library system was developed in a piecemeal fashion, beginning in 1977 with the development of an online circulation system for the Universities of Guelph and Waterloo.

A circulation system is, by definition, a form of an online catalog so the logical next step was the introduction of public access capabilities. Geac's cataloging package, known as the MARC Records Management System (MRMS), provides the data upon which the catalog is based. Acquisitions was the third of the major packages which was created in the early 1980s as a direct response to customer demands for a totally integrated system.[5] The entire Geac system was purchased by the University of Houston Libraries (UH) in 1982. The online catalog was given first priority in implementation, followed closely by circulation and MRMS. The Acquisitions module was implemented in September 1984. At that time, UH was one of the largest and earliest implementations of the system in a large academic library which included the University of Waterloo and Princeton University.

BACKGROUND—INNOVATIVE INTERFACES, INC.

The Innovative Interfaces' INNOVACQ System varies in one very significant way from the Geac system—it was developed from the ground up to deal specifically with library acquisitions tasks. Innovative Interfaces, Inc. (III) was founded in 1978 by Steve Silberstein and Jerry Kline. Both Kline and Silberstein had been instrumental in the development and implementation of a batch acquisitions system at the University of California at Berkeley. This previous experience and their own vision of what an ideal system should be formed the basis of the INNOVACQ system. III began its development with five overall goals:

1. Replacement of all manual functions;
2. Increased services such as reporting and analysis of data;
3. Ease of use;
4. Full integration both internal and external;
5. Flexibility.

INNOVACQ was initially developed in 1981 to meet the specifications of the University of California at Riverside and California State University at Long Beach. The serials check-in component was first implemented in 1983 at the University of California Boalt School of Law.[6] INNOVACQ was purchased by the Ohio State University Libraries (OSUL) in 1984. Implementation of the basic system began immediately and has been operational since then. The serials check-in component was implemented following introduction of an interface with the Libraries' online catalog, LCS, to load on order records into the catalog. Although the University of Michigan Library was one of the earliest and largest academic libraries to use INNOVACQ, OSUL still represents one of the largest ongoing implementations of INNOVACQ.

SYSTEM COMPARISONS

Marlene Clayton[7] and Richard Boss[8] have developed extensive checklists for evaluating online systems. Boss also conducted a survey in which he evaluated twenty acquisitions systems against over 190 criteria.[9] A thorough analysis of the responses made by Geac and Innovative Interfaces to his survey reveals that all basic requirements for a full-scale acquisition system have been met by both systems. Therefore, this paper will focus on a few significant differences between the two systems, particularly as they relate to large academic libraries.

Size, as measured by number of orders place or number of subscriptions maintained, magnifies the problems, deficiencies, and difficulties of any system. What is a minor inconvenience in system design for a library with 2,000 subscriptions may become a major system flaw for a library with 24,000 subscriptions. For example, in an earlier version of the Geac system, a new bibliographic record had to be entered every time that a title was redirected to another vendor. This is a minor inconvenience to a small library or even to a larger organization which orders directly from the publisher. However, it becomes a significant problem for a library like UH which must, due to contractual obligations, order all in-print domestic titles from a single vendor. However, those titles can be redirected to another vendor as early as 90 days after placement of the original order. Geac eventually enhanced the system to provide this option, but the interim inconvenience was not inconsequential. Therefore, the requirements for any system are very susceptible to local custom and practice

Capacity

Size is also a factor in the hardware on which a system runs. Although Geac operates on a minicomputer as opposed to the INNOVACQ microcomputer system, both systems employ a multiprocesser machine. The assumption is often made that a micro system lacks the power and expandability of a minicomputer. The particular configuration selected by III negates this assumption. Sandra Weaver, Vice President of Library Services (III), cites one such example. "For instance, the system . . . installed at the University of Michigan has 3/4 of a megabyte of main memory. This is approximately four times the main memory found in the average minicomputer in use today."[10] However, III has structured the INNOVACQ system in such a way that some files are universally limited in size. For example, the vendor and fund files were only recently expanded from 750 to 1,200 entries. For large libraries with significant gift and exchange programs, such as OSUL, these numbers are still not sufficient. In contrast, the Geac system is limited only by the space occupied by other files. For example, if a library needs to create files for 500 funds and 2,000 vendors, file size can be adjusted locally to accommodate these differences. Nevertheless, the architecture of both systems is such that few compromises in power, reliability and expandability are needed.

In-House Control and Environmental Concerns

Geac and INNOVACQ vary significantly in the area of in-house control and environmental concerns. INNOVACQ was developed as a stand-alone acquisitions and serials control system, and only recently added an online access catalog (INNOPAC). The system is usually installed in a normal office environment and requires about the same space as a desk. Because the Winchester disk drive is totally enclosed and less susceptible to dust, smoke, and other environmental hazards, the system does not require a specially designed, climate-controlled environment. This is a definite bonus for any library where space is at a premium. On the other hand, system maintenance activities such as tape loading and backups must often be handled by existing staff because no systems staff is available. An additional advantage is that this stand-alone system can insulate the acquisitions process from having to compete for priority or service with other subsystems.

Although the Geac Acquisitions System can be run on the Geac System 6000 hardware which requires no special environmental control, it is most often purchased as part of the Geac Integrated Library System which runs on System 8000 or 9000 hardware. These larger systems do require environmental protection such as climate-controlled temperature and humidity, dust-free air, and often supplemental or independent air conditioning. In addition, the load-bearing capacity of the floor cannot be overlooked.[11] In the typical integrated system, such as Geac, systems staff are required to maintain the hardware thus relieving Acquisitions staff of this responsibility.

Backup Procedures and Printing

Any automated system requires the precaution of backing up the system on a periodic basis to protect the software and database against system or power failures. These backups must be done frequently enough (usually daily) so that in the event of a failure, the system can be restored with the loss of as little data as feasible.

Geac and INNOVACQ are fundamentally different in their approach to backup procedures and the generation of reports. The Geac Acquisitions system must be brought offline each night in order to perform backup procedures and to run the overnight programs. Once the backups are completed, the overnight programs can be initiated and will usually run unmonitored throughout the night. These overnight programs extract data from the system, format reports, and automatically reset statuses within the system. For example, the purchase order program will run through the entire database and extract titles which have been authorized for purchase during the day. The online status of each of these records is changed from "on order" to "on order-printed" to indicate that not only has the order been initiated online but that an actual purchase order has been printed. The next morning the online system can be brought up for staff use and the actual printing can be performed with the online system up. Programs which change information in the system must be run with the online down. Simple extract programs which only report information from the system can be run with the online up, but response time will be somewhat degraded. As the size of a database increases, the time required to perform these routine operations increases. Additional tasks such as rebuilding indexes on a weekly basis will require substantial time blocks for any system supporting a large library.

The implementation of the serials check-in module at UH introduced an entirely new factor into this equation. Prior to this implementation, the system had been brought down at 8:00 p.m. when all Acquisitions staff left for the day. With the implementation of the online serials check-in paper records were eliminated and the online system provided the only access to issue-specific receipt data. Previously, public service staff had routinely consulted the paper records after normal working hours to assist patrons; therefore, it became apparent that the Geac system would have to be available almost all of the open library hours. Since the library closed at midnight and reopened again at 7:00 a.m., the number of hours available for both circulation and acquisition backups and overnight programs was seriously reduced. As a result, more compromises were made regarding which programs would be run overnight and additional programs were run during the day or over the weekend.

Conversely, INNOVACQ can be run on a 24-hour schedule if so desired. All purchase orders, claims, cancellations, accounting and financial reports, and management reports, with few exceptions, can be run or printed at anytime. Backups can also be performed with the system up. The INNOVACQ maintenance and overnight programs are not nearly as extensive as Geac's. However, this also has consequences. Response time is degraded to varying degrees by each of these activities. As a result, OSUL staff have organized themselves in much the same way that Geac dictates the organizational structure. For example, backups are done late in the day and index builds are done on Saturdays. The implementation of serials check-in has also decreased terminal availability. As a result, consideration is being given to batch production of management reports at night or on weekends. Nevertheless, the flexibility gained by having this option available is important.

Command Structure

Geac and INNOVACQ vary substantially in their command structures. One of INNOVACQ's goals, as mentioned earlier, was ease of use. This goal resulted in the selection of a menu-driven approach. Menu-driven systems are easy to learn and usually self-instructive. They are also considered user friendly because all available options are presented at any point in time. Such an approach is also conducive to self-training. Staff members can be expected to work independently and learn aspects of the system through simple exposure and access to documentation.[12] INNOVACQ also uses its menu-driven system to prompt the operator through the process of creating reports or entering orders.

Geac is generally command-driven using three-letter mnemonics, although there is an initial menu. In addition, function keys can be programmed to replace command codes and templates are available to label these keys. One deviation from the command structure is the automatic prompts for order entry. Although this can be overridden at any point, generally the prompts will carry the operator through the screens needed for order initiation. Help screens are available throughout the system, but they are rarely comprehensive and have not always been updated when software changed. However, Geac currently has an excellent users's manual which contains a command summary sorted by module. In addition, Geac's three-letter mnemonics are consistent across its subsystems. For example, the command mnemonic for display—DSP—is used in circulation, MRMS and the online catalog.

In a 1986 article in *The Electronic Library*, Peter Leggate delineates the pros and cons of command-driven versus menu-driven systems.

> Although the distinction is not absolute, generally a command driven approach is likely to be preferred by experienced users and for frequently used functions. Conversely, a menu-driven system will be preferred by new users and for infrequently-used modules. The main objectives being speed for the experienced user and clarity which may be given at the expense of speed for novice or infrequent users.[13]

INNOVACQ has circumvented this speed issue by allowing the operator to key ahead. In other words, a user familiar with the next options can, in effect, answer them in advance. However, one word of caution should be noted here. An operator can key through a series of menus without seeing the effect of those responses or the resulting changes which may not be desirable. Nevertheless, selection of a command-driven or menu-driven system is a factor of personal preference or circumstances.

Record Structure

The acquisitions process varies considerably from library to library. For a system to be profitable enough for its developer, it must be flexible enough to serve many different libraries but also general enough to protect the vendor from being asked for countless individual variations. The Geac system is initially customized for the specific library based upon the library's response to a large questionnaire known as the Policy Parameters. These parameters are supported by tables which identify such things as locations. In addition, conditional compile options (CCPs) allow each program to have several variables. Each program will behave in slightly different ways based upon how the options are answered. Unfortunately, the policy parameters and CCPs must be answered in the initial setting up period before a thorough understanding of the implications can be gained. Tables can support ongoing additions, but parameters and CCPs must be seen as more or less fixed because they usually cannot be recompiled without the assistance of a Geac programmer.[14] An example of a CCP follows:

> Do funds apply as a percentage or by number of copies? Academic sites tend to wish to divide the costs of orders by a percentage figure between different accounts whereas public libraries tend to wish to apply the costs of so many copies to each account. This CCP allows a site to choose one or other method as a standard.[15]

The fixed and variable fields in Geac records are fairly comprehensive, but standard. A basic MARC format is supported. Few fields can be eliminated but must simply be skipped if a library does not wish to use them. Some fields cause a specific action by the system and must be used consistently. Other fields such as status codes like "vendor delay notice" cause no action in the system and can be interpreted by the individual library. The wording cannot be changed but its meaning from library to library will vary.

In contrast, INNOVACQ has a very flexible record structure. Each installation of the system may be customized to library needs. The library designs its own record structure and determines which fields will be stored and which will be indexed. The INNOVACQ records have predefined fixed variable length fields but also support additional library-defined fields. In addition, the library determines its own values for codes and its own names and codes for variable-length fields. Therefore, if a library has unique requirements it is a simple process to add that feature to the system and have the field indexed and searchable. Within this structure, a library can add a code as the need arises. For example, OSUL undertook in 1987 a very limited serial cancellation project focusing on duplicate subscriptions. This would have been an impossible task if the Continuations Acquisition Division had not first coded the original or first copy and the duplicate copies. Printouts could be constructed from this code and used for review. In contrast, Geac would not have been able to accommodate this very specific requirement within the limited time constraints.

Integration versus Interfacing

Historically, the issue of integration versus interfacing has been debated widely. The two systems under discussion have taken radically different stands on the issue. The Geac Acquisitions System is a fully integrated module of the Geac Integrated Library System and usually operates in association with the other modules. Although some libraries have purchased the Geac Acquisitions System as a stand-alone option, Geac does not support interfaces with other automated systems. Geac can support interfaces with materials vendors, such as Blackwell North America and bibliographic utilities such as OCLC, but not its own competitors. In other words, a library cannot purchase a NOTIS online catalog and interface the Geac Acquisitions Systems with it. This is not an uncommon position for a vendor who can provide an entire integrated system.

Internally, Geac is fully integrated. Data in the Acquisitions system is available to users of the other Geac databases and vice versa, at the discretion of the library, and this access can be achieved from a single terminal. For example, a new order can be created for an item that already exists in circulation or the online catalog. With a single command within Acquisitions, the bibliographic information can be transferred into the Acquisitions database. This establishes a link with the other record which can be used to transfer receipt information back to the online catalog. Transfer of information from Acquisitions to the online catalog to form the basis of on order records is also possible.

By its very name, Innovative Interfaces, Inc. has indicated its commitment to interfacing. One of the early III goals was to be fully integrated both internally and externally. Externally, the system is expected to interface with all other automated systems used by the library including bibliographic utilities, circulation systems, online catalogs, and vendors, as well as accounting systems used by the library's parent organization.[16] However, it is important to remember that each unique interface may incur programming costs for the library. In addition, the INNOVACQ system provides one-step processing with no repetition of keying. Any process that was initiated at one terminal is automatically transferred throughout the linked system. For example, at OSUL when titles are received on INNOVACQ the status in LCS is automatically discharged from an on order status to a status representing the Cataloging Department.

This ability to interface is often the ultimate selling point for the INNOVACQ system. At OSUL the Library Control System (LCS) was locally developed and the willingness of INNOVACQ to design an interface for LCS which would have virtually no other application was a primary factor in its selection. Gay Dannelly, Collection Development Officer and former Head of Acquisitions at OSUL, has been quoted in INNOVACQ publicity as follows.

> The system's ability to communicate with our internal online catalog/in-process record file, as well as its potential communication with our university accounting system, were factors in our decision to choose INNOVACQ as our acquisition system.[17]

The ability to link an independent system to other automated systems permits more flexibility and wider appeal of that system.[18] Nonetheless, this issue of integration versus interfacing is dictated by the individual library's environment, goals, and existing systems.

Password Security

The use of passwords is the most common form of security employed by automated systems and is, therefore, an important consideration in the selection of any system. The scheme of password authorization built into a system protects the database, guarantees file integrity, and prevents unauthorized actions. The various operational functions of the system are regulated by the passwords governing the extent of any individual's access. Security is of particular significance in a system which authorizes the expenditure of funds.

Geac's history of software development for the banking environment has translated itself into the security systems developed for the Acquisitions module. There are three levels of system security. There is no access to any function of the system without first signing on with both one's personal name and a unique system-assigned password (or by wanding a barcode). It is not possible to use the online software to discover this password. At the second level, each staff member's record contains a security level between 1 and 7. Higher security levels permit the performance of certain functions, such as authorization of invoices for payment, which are not available at lower levels. The third level is the most detailed. Each staff record includes 28 privilege bits which are set to precisely define the scope of each person's responsibilities. For example, a staff member can be authorized to enter and update requests but would lack the authority to assign funds or print orders. In the same vein, specific fields in an order record such as order date and receipt date are automatically assigned by the system and are not updatable. This third level also defines the specific accounts accessible to each person. This technique would enable selectors to enter their requests directly into Geac but leaves the placement of the order to Acquisition staff at a higher security level.

Geac also provides an internal signature for critical transactions such as fund transfers. Because no access is permitted without signing on, the system can record the name of the person performing the activity. Therefore, each time a sensitive transaction such as manipulation of funds is performed, the name of the individual is attached to the transaction. This is particularly valuable for maintaining audit integrity and has the additional benefit of being able to track errors. For example when an error is consistently repeated it can often be tracked to a specific staff member who may require additional training. Terminals themselves can be restricted in the access they permit but this is rarely a useful feature in an Acquisitions Department. The single greatest flaw in Geac's passwording involves the case where the security of a password has been compromised. An entirely new staff record must be entered, or *all* staff passwords must be reissued by an overnight program.

The INNOVACQ system takes a somewhat less rigid approach to the password security issue. The Data Retrieval System is accessible without any sign on or password authorization. This is a useful feature if the system is used for public access, but the majority of the system functions such as creation of records, invoice processing, and update of records are password protected. INNOVACQ passwords consist of three letters for the person's initials and three letters for the password selected by the person. Once set, individual passwords can be changed at any time with no impact on the authority level for specific functions to be performed. Since INNOVACQ does not support an internal signature, OSUL staff often add their initials to the end of a field so that later questions may be referred to them. INNOVACQ passwords allow twelve specific activities with four additional passwords which permit a library to authorize normally unauthorized functions. These twelve passwords are broader in scope than Geac's and include backup and system maintenance which are not controlled in the Geac Acquisitions System. This broad scope has created problems for OSUL in an internal audit conducted in 1987. OSUL has requested refinements of password security to meet internal audit recommendations.

Serials Control

The very nature of serials creates control problems for a library. Despite the magnitude of the control problem for large academic libraries, these difficulties can be surmounted by a good automated system. Although OSUL did not initially purchase the space to implement serials check-in, there was little doubt that INNOVACQ would be the system of choice when funds became available. The INNOVACQ Serials Control Module is one of the greatest assets of the entire system. The basic manual method of controlling serials — the Kardex file — has been replicated in INNOVACQ. Its format resembles the familiar Kardex record and is easier to read than many other systems which use lines only. When the publication follows a predictable pattern, receipt dates are projected not only for the next issue but subsequent issues as well. Supplemental issues can be inserted in the pattern; issues which will not be published can be deleted. INNOVACQ's repeatable, variable fields such as title also allow for extensive cross references. This allows an operator to locate a record faster and more efficiently. INNOVACQ also permits multiple check-in cards to be attached to a single record with an "identifier" to assist the operator in selecting the appropriate card. For example, multiple copies and formats of the journal *Nature* are received at OSUL. A title search for *Nature* retrieves a single record with five check-in records attached. The first four records are paper copies received by four different departmental libraries. These records are entered in priority order in case all four copies are not received simultaneously. The fifth record is a microfilm copy and is so designated in the identifier field.

INNOVACQ also supports the production of routing lists within the serials check-in module. The routing module permits up to 750 names, and each individual copy may be routed to up to fifty people. Routing labels are automatically printed upon receipt of the title and may be printed in priority order. Lists by journal title or recipient can be printed on demand.[19]

The Geac serials subsystem has often taken a back seat to other development priorities within Geac. As a result, the system provides all of the basics but has not been significantly developed beyond those basics. For example, no routing capability exists. The prediction algorithms are complex and permit display of only the next expected issue. The prediction can be tested through programs run at the main computer console, but this is labor intensive and time consuming. Geac does support seven levels of holdings enumeration which Richard Boss has identified as one of the requirements for serials systems.[20]

However, the Geac serials component is superior is one very critical feature—the historical price analysis of journal titles. Certainly, INNOVACQ provides a detailed fund accounting record of each title's historical prices, but analysis on price trends and projections of future expenditures must be done manually. At OSUL an annual year-end project is undertaken to analyze the payment history for each title and to encumber an estimated price based on that analysis for the coming year.

The Geac programs function from a review date entered in each record. This date reflects the date that the title is to be encumbered again. UH elected to perform this renewal once a year at the beginning of the fiscal year. Review reports are generated which include the invoice history and projected price of the item for the next subscription period. The complex algorithm used by the system assigns the highest weight to the most current payments, factors in subscription periods, and adds a library specified inflation rate. This algorithm has been refined by Geac and continues to improve in accuracy. This report can be run as often as desired until the specified set of titles is identified and projected. Although this information is now available from subscription vendors such as Faxon, only the titles on order with that vendor can be provided. An in-house system will provide access to all of a library's subscriptions. Once refined, the report is run in an update mode. Titles are encumbered at the new estimated price and the review date is advanced for the length of one subscription period. However, it cannot be overlooked that the quality of this process is highly dependent upon the information entered at the time of invoicing particularly for the subscription period.

> For projection purposes, what is important is consistency. Not whether an invoice is paid in July or November, but whether it is paid on the same basis each year. Successful projection also depends on a large enough statistical pool to blur inconsistencies, or a small enough pool to do an item by item check.[21]

Invoicing and Fund Accounting

Both Geac and INNOVACQ have fiscal routines which are detailed and provide complete audit trails. It is in the implementation of these routines that differences emerge. The INNOVACQ invoice processing procedure requires the input of complete invoices in a single session. The operator keys in the purchase order number for each line item on the invoice as well as the amount. The total dollar amount plus shipping, service charges, and discounts are also entered. The system verifies each entry and prorates the charges to each line. Although payment history is posted to each order record, the invoice itself cannot be displayed, corrected, or held for additional information. At the end of an invoice processing session, the invoices are posted and order records are updated with payment data.

In contrast, Geac invoices are entered on templates much like order records. Each line is linked to its order record and payment data is visible on the order records. However, it is not necessary to complete the verification and authorization of each invoice in one session. For example, if the operator encounters a problem, all prior work can be saved online until the problem is resolved. This ability to enter invoices as soon as they are received without having to pay them immediately allows the library to keep track of outstanding invoices online. In this scenario, the library is prompted if the invoice is not paid within a library-specified period of time. This process is an essential one for UH serials payments. State regulations prohibit the payment of subscriptions more than six weeks in advance of the start of the subscription. To control this workflow, invoices are entered upon receipt and authorized for payment with an action date set to the first date that the invoice can be paid. The system automatically retrieves the invoice on the specified date and produces the voucher. In fact, Geac's ability to automatically print these University-specific vouchers saved UH .5 FTE in staff support.

Computers are particularly valuable in fund accounting. They provide far more detailed fund breakdowns than it is usually possible to maintain manually. INNOVACQ funds can be up to five letters or numbers. The funds themselves represent no hierarchy but can be combined at will to create customized fiscal reports for each selector. Once these customized reports are created they can be stored for automatic production on a monthly or on-demand schedule. Geac's funds are fourteen digits long and are hierarchical in nature. Subsets within the account may repeat from fund to fund to establish the hierarchy. This repetition keeps the length of the number from being cumbersome. In addition, funds are also accessible by a long name and a short code. However, it is the hierarchical number which serves as the sort for most reports. Therefore, the initial time invested in understanding and constructing the fund numbers is critical to the success of the financial reports. INNOVACQ's funds can be graphed online or in printed form. This graphic capability provides an accurate, visual representation of a fund's financial status.

The journal entry function permits and records the receipt of new money into the system, the distribution of funds to various accounts, and the movement of money between accounts. Geac maintains an online record of each such transaction including date, amount, explanation of transaction, and internal signature. This transaction log not only provides an exceptional audit trail but also provides the department with an online record of how the existing balance came to be. Unfortunately, there is no such transaction log in the INNOVACQ system. In the absence of such a log OSUL has continued to maintain this log manually. Of course, the transactions are performed on the system but no record except the resulting fund allocation exists to document the transaction.

Management Reports

The flexibility of the management report module is one of IN-NOVACQ's strengths. All fixed-length and variable-length fields are searchable using Boolean logic. In addition, keyword searching on up to fifteen characters within variable-length fields is supported. With this keyword capability, individual text within fields such as internal notes is retrievable. Records extracted by Boolean search can be sorted by up to ten fields. Results can be reviewed online or printed specifying the data elements to be included and in what order. Statistical packages can also be applied to the results of any Boolean search. Unfortunately, only one terminal can use the sort function or the statistical package at any one time. A good example of the specificity of Boolean searches follows:

> For instance, a report can be produced which shows the unpaid science standing order titles placed with Blackwell by searching on "acquisitions type 's', requester science, vendor Blackwell" and "fund range 7400B10 to 7400Z00 negative." By adding "Status B" (continuing order) to the search argument any cancellations or brand new orders can be eliminated.[22]

When the Illinois State University Library first installed INNOVACQ, they considered the Boolean capability as a fringe benefit. It quickly became an essential component, often used daily for both technical and public services applications.[23]

Because of the structure of the Geac system, most reports are generated in the overnight programs. Offline programs read through the entire database, extract information requested, and format the reports. The batches which produce these reports have compile options which allow individual libraries some flexibility in design. For example, the vendor discount statistics can be produced in either summary or detailed versions. The detailed version reports every invoice which contributed to the computation of the average discount. The summary report reflects only the total amount invoiced, discount totals, and discount percentages. Although Geac provided over sixty possible reports and notices, there had been no equivalent to the INNOVACQ Boolean package. In the 1987 software release, Geac issued its first report generator software for Acquisitions. Report generator software allows an operator to select a subset of predefined fields or conditions to extract. Flexibility is provided in the sorting options and the program can produce either raw figures or a list of entries that satisfy the criteria listed. However, the criteria available through the report generator is by no means comprehensive in the way INNOVACQ's is. On the other hand, what one loses in comprehensiveness is countered by the polished format of most reports.

CONCLUSION

Automated acquisitions systems must be evaluated in light of a library's procedural and policy environment. It makes no sense to select a system based upon excellent performance for functions that are not important for the library. A library administration's decision to purchase an integrated system may eliminate some excellent systems from consideration, or the existence of in-house systems may limit options to systems which can be interfaced.

> The point is that the requirements of each library are unique and the successful selection of an automated . . . system can only be achieved after careful definition of the needs of the individual library, followed by evaluation of the capabilities of the candidate systems.[24]

REFERENCES

1. Judy McQueen, "Serials Control in Libraries: An Update of Automation Options," *Library Technology Reports* 21 (May/June 1985): 238.
2. Richard W. Boss, *Automating Library Acquisitions: Issues and Outlook*. (White Plains, NY: Knowledge Industry Publications, 1982).
3. *Ibid.*, 3-4,

4. Marlene Clayton, *Managing Library Automation* (Aldershot, Hants, England: Gower, 1987).
5. Duncan R. Westlake & John E. Clarke, *Geac: A Guide for Librarians and Systems Managers* (Aldershot, Hants, England: Gower, 1987).
6. Sandra Weaver, "Developing an Automated Acquisitions Package," *Library Acquisitions: Practice and Theory* 7 (1983): 189-194.
7. Marlene Clayton, *Managing Library Automation*, 28-30.
8. Richard W. Boss, *Automating Library Acquisitions*, 43-44.
9. Richard W. Boss, "Automating Acquisitions," *Library Technology Reports* 22 (Sept./Oct. 1986): 547-604.
10. Sandra Weaver, "Developing an Automated Acquisitions Package," 191.
11. Westlake & Clarke, *Geac*, 24-26.
12. Douglas A. DeLong, "Implementation of the INNOVACQ Acquisition System," *Illinois Libraries* 67 (May 1985): 480.
13. Peter Leggate, "The Microcomputer in the Library: IV. Cataloging and Acquisitions Software," *The Electronic Library* 4 (June 1986): 165.
14. Westlake & Clarke, *Geac*, 58-62.
15. *Ibid.*, 223.
16. Sandra Weaver, "Developing an Automated Acquisitions Package," 190.
17. INNOVACQ publicity brochure.
18. Janet Padway, "Serials Automation: Examining the Problems," *The Serials Librarian* 11 (Dec 86/Jan 87): 36.
19. Laura Peritore, "INNOVACQ and Serials Automation at Hastings Law Library," *The Serials Librarian* 11 (October 1986): 72.
20. Richard W. Boss, "Developing Requirements for Automated Serials Control Systems," *The Serials Librarian* 11 (Dec. 86/Jan. 87): 51.
21. Houghton, Jean, "Automating Serials Payments: The Right Tool for the Job," *The Serials Librarian* 12 (1987): 108.
22. *Ibid.*, 107.
23. Douglas A. DeLong, "Implementation of the INNOVACQ Acquisition System," 479.
24. Richard W. Boss, "Developing Requirements," 39.

Ideal and Reality: Automating Acquisitions in a Time of Austerity

Heather S. Miller

SUMMARY. Administrators may hope to save money by reducing staff when the acquisitions process is automated. Some employees may dream of the ergonomic office. In times of limited funding reality approaches neither goal. It means instead a long, difficult transition period, increased work loads, backlogs and limited goals, the attainment of which seems to move ever farther into the future. Nearly two years and less than half way toward ultimate goals, an acquisitions librarian can pause to evaluate where we are, how we got there, what lies ahead and what we wish we had known when we started.

IDEAL: AUTOMATION AS A MEANS OF SAVING MONEY

It seems that hopes of saving money have been with us as long as we have wrestled with automation. Libraries, traditionally underappreciated and underfunded, seem to be tempted to grasp at automation as a means of better utilizing meager budgets. Indeed, Martin M. Cummings states "Automation remains a most logical approach to improving library services while seeking cost reduction."[1] This is usually seen in terms of staff reduction and consequent salary savings.

That this is a widespread and persistent if not clearly articulated ideal is evidenced by frequent recent references in the literature to

---

Heather S. Miller is Head, Acquisitions Department, University Libraries, University at Albany, State University of New York, 1400 Washington Ave., Albany, NY 12222.

its fallacy. Were such a belief not persistent there would be no need to refute it, yet one repeatedly reads cautionary statements such as

> All libraries would like to justify automation on the grounds that it will immediately lower operating costs. There certainly are cases where cost savings have been realized through automation, but the overall evidence suggests that the financial benefits of automation are not as sweeping as once anticipated.[2]

and

> There are two ways you can justify an automation project. One is to say that it will result in savings of staff and/or money, which in the library world is almost never true. The second is to say that it will allow you to do more of what you were doing, or allow you to do it better, which is often true, even though it will cost more.[3]

Similar hopes have been expressed locally, although they are difficult to find in written form. Most such hopes focused on automation as a whole, not specifically the automation of acquisitions. However, in 1985, a recommendation for the implementation of an acquisitions system at the University at Albany library did project a savings of three full-time positions once monographs, serials and fund accounting were fully automated.

Moreover, prior to the purchase of the present circulation system, the existing circulation system was very expensive to maintain in terms of monthly service bureau costs and staff programming costs. It needed a major upgrading to meet our needs. It was not difficult, under these circumstances, for a turnkey system to appear to be a means of cutting costs. Not included in the equation was the fact that we would expand our demands on the new system, add new functions, and require more equipment as time passed, and the system would inevitably become obsolete and require replacement itself.

IDEAL OF A FEW: THE ERGONOMIC OFFICE

Meanwhile staff members anticipated the automating of acquisitions in their own ways. Some were apprehensive to the point of stating that they would not use the computer. Others found advertisements in computer and office management magazines showing hi-tech furniture, kind to one's back, easy on one's eyes and sleek and beautiful to look at. They dropped these pictures on my desk asking, somewhat tongue-in-cheek, if that image would become ours. For a few, automation couldn't come fast enough. These staff members looked forward to learning new skills both as a means of adding interest to their jobs and as a means of enhancing their abilities, possibly leading to other jobs in the future. In addition, they dreamed of more pleasant, comfortable working conditions.

IDEAL: THE MIDDLE MANAGER'S VIEW

As Head of Acquisitions, my goals were related to efficiency and accuracy of processing and to obtaining accurate, current, detailed and manipulatable data relating to orders, receipts and claims as well as financial transactions. The prospect of automating acquisitions impinging as it would on other areas of the library gave rise to hopes among other departments. Better service to the public through the increased accessibility of order records became an important goal. Collection Development hoped not only for fuller, more accessible and more manipulatable financial data but also for the more accurate and more efficient creation of order records. It was also hoped that an automated system would permit more timely and informative feedback to faculty and students regarding orders.

As for the Acquisitions Department, having previously suffered staff reductions, we had to find ways of doing our tasks more efficiently because the numbers of orders and receipts did not decline along with numbers of staff. We were unable to maintain regular claiming for either serials or monographic orders. Outstanding orders were represented by one slip in the card catalog, which we considered inadequate even though this itself was more information than many libraries of our size provided to patrons about items on order. Monthly statistics on orders and receipts were laboriously compiled manually.

It seemed that an automated system offered hope of improvement on all these fronts. Not only would it help us do what we were already doing or supposed to be doing in a more efficient way, but the capabilities of an automated system promised to do more than we had ever attempted. For example, the flimsy on-order slip could be easily misfiled, mutilated, lost or overlooked. The automated system offered instant availability of any input record through at least two access points, author and title.

REALITY:
PREPARATION FOR AUTOMATING ACQUISITIONS

The State University of New York, University at Albany

The University at Albany is one of four university centers of the State University of New York (SUNY) system, which was established in 1948. The University at Albany has nine degree granting colleges and schools; approximately 16,000 students including 4,400 graduate students are currently enrolled.[4] The library's collection numbers well over one million volumes. Approximately 20,000 monographs are added each year. Continuations number approximately 16,000 titles excluding U.S. documents. Decisions as to the titles that will be added to the collection rest with the Collection Development Department. The Acquisitions Department manages the mechanics of ordering, receiving and paying for items selected by Collection Development. The Acquisitions Department consists of three units: Serials, Documents (state and international) and Monographs.

Being a state agency, we are subject to numerous regulations. We dream of controlling our own expenditures including writing our own checks, but as it is, we must produce acceptable paperwork to accompany invoices we want paid. University Accounting pays invoices totalling less than $250.00. Invoices for $250.00 or more pass through University Accounting to be paid by the State Department of Audit and Control. Payments in excess of $1,500.00 required justifications (which may be returned for further "justification") and, in some cases, bid proposals. Prepayment is a concept not recognized by the state. Delays are possible at more than one point.

Moreover, in 1984, the state enacted prompt payment legislation which requires payment to be made within 45 days of the receipt of material purchased by state agencies. Failure to meet this deadline results in interest payments to the vendor. These payments are supposed to come from the offending agency's funds. It is unclear how it is determined where a delay occurs since an invoice makes numerous stops on its way to payment. This legislation was aimed at other than library vendors, but has added to our burden. Most large library vendors are tolerant of somewhat slow payment. They want to sell books, not simply collect funds that will reduce our ability to buy more books.

Automation Prior to Acquisitions

The University at Albany began its current phase of automation with the purchase of Geac for circulation control in 1983. Geac was chosen because, of those system that bid, it most closely met our criteria for a circulation system. One major criterion was the ability to interface with acquisitions and an online catalog. In short, it was required to provide the basis of an integrated system. Prior to this Circulation had used LCS, an automated system in use since 1974. By June of 1984 MRMS (the Geac MARC Records Management System) had been installed and database conversion had begun. Actual use of MRMS began in September 1984. Early in that year barcoding of books began. During the fall, linking of barcodes and bibliographic records assumed highest priority.

Preparation for Automating Acquisitions

When the circulation system was purchased, acquisitions software was available for a nominal additional fee. This appeared to be advantageous so the acquisitions software was acquired at that time even though this was expected to be the last area of Technical Services to be automated.

When I interviewed for the position of Head of Acquisitions in

1985, I was asked whether I considered myself competent to select an acquisitions system. However, it was apparent even at that time that there would be little likelihood of having to choose a system. We owned Geac software. It appeared to serve our purposes. It was compatible with our Geac circulation system and our proposed online catalog.

The automation of circulation with the attendant creation of the MRMS database had been accomplished with insufficient staff, too few terminals, and by funding unexpected cost overruns (due to maintaining dual circulation systems) from the acquisitions budget. Given these circumstances, there was little prospect of purchasing a different acquisitions system when we already owned one that seemed adequate.

Nevertheless, Geac was not accepted blindly. In 1983 a Task Force on Automation Planning for Acquisitions and Fund Accounting had evaluated six automated systems and recommended the purchase of a turnkey system that would permit integration with online catalog and circulation systems. The report did not recommend that a specific system be purchased and cautioned that its recommendations would become quickly outdated as systems continued to evolve. In 1985, a thorough evaluation of the Geac system was made by the Assistant Director for Technical Services based on information from the vendor, other users of the system, our systems personnel and demonstrations of the system. The system appeared well suited to our needs, but it was known that it would not be perfect and that "no system except, perhaps, one developed locally would replicate the current procedures and meet every requirement."[5]

During 1985, the Assistant Director for Technical Services began a push to get Acquisitions started, fearing that nothing would get done if we didn't at least make a beginning. Her dealings with the Director resulted in the go ahead with the aim of switching to the new system at the start of FY 1986/87 on April 1, 1986.

The Acquisitions and Collection Development Departments began to plan for the changeover. A timetable was drawn up that called for software installation in August 1985, staff training in late August, monograph order production to begin in January 1986 and testing of the serials check-in system in the spring of 1986. For this we projected a need for three terminals at the outset for ordering, receiving and fund accounting for *monographs* only.

Due to delays by us and the vendor, this timetable became compressed so that training did not begin until the last week in October. In September the Head of Collection Development, Head of Systems, Assistant Director for Technical Services and myself met several times to prepare "policy parameters." This was not an easy task given the nature of some of the questions asked and our unfamiliarity with the system. In many instances, the consequences of policy parameter decisions were not fully known.

In some cases, acquisitions parameters related to the configuration of the circulation system that was already operational. In other cases we simply did not know what the questions meant. There is no way these parameters could have been set without the involvement of a knowledgeable systems person. There were more than fifty questions called compile options, complex and significant choices through which the basic software package would be set for our library. Clearly the answers were not to be given lightly. The vendor made a genuine effort to explain and make clear what was meant, but we simply could not foresee all that was involved.

Along with this was a group of terms called order types that we had to define. Subject-based funds were also established. The configuration of both of these items is variable within an established framework. Together they determine how information will be provided in various off-line reports. Therefore, it was critical that we understand and correctly set up both order types and funds in order to obtain the information we required from the system. This task became the responsibility of the Head of Collection Development who worked closely with the Head of Library Systems and with Technical Services.

Each order record carries a two word term that describes its "type" as defined by the library. Ours are a combination of an indication of physical formats and fund category. For example, discretionary/monograph, standing ord/serial, approval/monograph. There are two lists—primary and secondary, there can be no more than 36 in all, and none can be longer than 12 characters. This last requirement meant that we are committed to misspelling discretionary forever. To obtain 12 characters we dropped the a.

Even more critical was the design of fund numbers. We already had a system of subject-related fund codes and were using an automated fund accounting system that served our own purposes as well as those of the University Accounting office. We had to convert our current system to the new one, conforming to its limitations, our needs, and state requirements. Designing these features was one of the most complex and frustrating parts of the preparatory phase. Our library very carefully keeps track of the condition of its money, attempting to account for each cent spent and regularly making predictions for future expenditures. A monthly report is issued showing allocations and expenditures for all accounts. We did not want to lose any information available to us under the old system. Indeed, we hoped to gain both data and flexibility.

Our existing fund codes consisted of three digits indicative of subject, for example, 017 Italian, 010 Asian Studies and a few indicative of status such as 103 for Reference. We now needed a system of up to 14 characters, divided by dashes into a maximum of six segments. The significance of the format of these numbers is that the way they are segmented determines where dollar amount totals are provided in certain off-line reports. To some extent we felt that we were groping in the dark, but eventually we settled on a configuration of fund numbers, believing that they would serve our purposes.

Order types and fund codes were of interest only to some of the library staff. We also had to continue to adhere to requirements relating to the paperwork that the system would generate to accompany invoices beyond the Library for payment. Lengthy meetings were held between Library Systems, Acquisitions and University Accounting personnel resulting in local programming being done to permit the system-produced paperwork to meet state requirements.

Meanwhile, meetings and discussions continued at frequent intervals. Order and claim form had been designed, ordered and tested. In the next few weeks software was installed using the parameters, order types and funds that had been established. Finally, during the week of October 28-November 1, 1985 a trainer conducted daily training sessions for eight supervisory and professional staff members including several from Collection Development. These people in turn would train the clerical staff. It was an exciting time, which provided the first hands-on use of the system and permitted a real view of its capabilities.

In 1985 two terminals (all that we could afford of the three originally requested) were installed in the Acquisitions Department and were scheduled from 8:00 a.m.-4:00 p.m., Monday-Friday. Training of clerical personnel began and everyone practiced daily. We created a small vendor file and used only a few funds, but the basic processes were learned and practiced. Problems were documented and reported to our systems office, which in turn dealt with the vendor.

In December the complete fund code list was input. On February 10, 1986, the practice database was brought down. Work began immediately on building permanent staff, currency and vendor files. These files must be built before the system is used. A vendor must be registered in the vendor file in order to be used on an order. Staff members must be in the staff file in order to sign on or be notified of a new book. Currencies must be entered in the currency file to permit using them on orders. We were in a practice, "make believe," mode no longer. We were busily working toward the day when we would go live at the start of a new fiscal year on April 1.

REALITY: HANDICAPPING THE RACE

From the preceding, one can glean certain warning signs of difficulties that lay ahead, primarily the fact that no RFP was ever issued for an acquisitions system. We were happy to have received an acquisitions system piggy-backed on the circulation system. While we did consider the possibility of going elsewhere for acquisitions, the fact that we already owned an apparently adequate and compatible means of automating acquisitions mitigated against purchasing another system. This meant that as we got into the intricacies of the system and found certain aspects of it wanting, we had no way to induce the vendor to make changes because we had never specified what we thought the system should do. This was to cause us some aggravation, but fortunately the system functioned well overall, and the vendor was generally responsive to our needs. Given our many requirements and need for continued rather sophisticated automated fund accounting, we still feel that the system we have is probably the best one for us at this time.

In reality, we were our own greatest handicap. We were preparing to plunge ahead into automation with insufficient staff, equipment and funding. In June 1980 Acquisitions had 19 personnel lines (one librarian, two library technical assistants, 16 clerks), and the materials budget amounted to $1,442,000. By June 1985 the staff had decreased to 14 lines, while the materials budget had risen to $1,957,780. The number of standing order book receipts went from 6,628 to 8,362. Monographic receipts similarly increased from 12,987 to 15,253. This meant that even in the months prior to actually automating, fewer Acquisitions Department people had more to do in terms of orders and claims to prepare and books to receive and process than had been the case several years before *while at the same time* learning and practicing the new automated procedures. Likewise, during the first year of automation these same people would have to work with both systems, would have to continue to create vendor records, convert old manual orders to the system for payment, train students in both systems while keeping daily work current. Fortunately, we could not foresee, in the fall of 1985 when all lines were filled, that the 1985/86 departmental annual report would begin with the words: "This year was memorable for time lost due to vacancies and illness." The equivalent of 66 weeks of one person's time were lost, most of it in more than one concurrent vacancy during the year in which we brought the system up.

Lack of equipment results from lack of money, a fact that has been with us since the early days of automation. The acquisitions budget which at one time had been untouchable for other than library materials purchases began to suffer inroads before we automated. We began paying for computer search service fees, OCLC and RLIN fees from the materials budget. Moreover, automating circulation had cut into the acquisitions budget. This was one way of finding funds needed at the moment. Now, in automating acquisitions itself, where were we to obtain funding?

Because we were simply adding a module that we already owned to run on a computer we already owned, costs were minimal. Nevertheless, we could not meet them fully. We needed terminals, printers and their attendant wiring requirements. We were to begin the changeover to automated acquisitions with only two terminals. Nevertheless, we not only decided to proceed but also to go beyond our original plan which called for monograph acquisitions only. We decided to check in online all monographic series on standing order and to process *all* invoices through the system in order to obtain a full financial picture.

Some of these handicaps were apparent at the beginning, some were not to appear until later, so we knew to some extent at least that we were attempting to automate under less than ideal conditions. We knew we could not contemplate automating serials for some time. We knew we would have no extra staff, nor would we be able to requisition any additional equipment. Nevertheless, we decided to proceed.

REALITY:
PROCEEDING, HANDICAPS NOTWITHSTANDING

On March 6, 1986, the last of the old order slips were filed in the public catalog. Detailed procedures had been written for entering and receiving all types of material on the system. The first system-generated orders were mailed March 21 in anticipation of the start of new fiscal year April 1.

Meanwhile, Collection Development had prepared its own procedures. They have one terminal where they input requests for items to be ordered. Overnight a "Search Request Form" is printed. Collection Development uses these forms to record searching information about the title. The RLIN record is printed and attached to this form. The record is updated, logged out and brought to Acquisitions. We check the records, assign vendors, make any corrections and authorize the orders. The orders are printed overnight, reviewed and mailed the next day.

Authorizing and mailing orders originally input by Collection Development is actually a simplification of the ordering process for clerical people in Acquisitions. Formerly, they typed multiples from hand or typewritten requests. However, this was only one of many tasks staff members now found themselves performing online. Some of the others are: processing English and foreign language approval books through the system (both manually input and tape-loaded records), approval returns, creating online records for serial and periodical payments, processing serial invoices for system input, creating online check-in records for monographic series on standing order, cancelling orders online, notifying vendors of system-generated order numbers for existing standing orders and subscriptions (a new form letter was designed for this purpose), placing new standing orders, placing firm orders (turning requests into orders), receiving firm orders, and last but by no means least, invoicing.

Only those who have already automated acquisitions can conceive of what it means to train staff to do such things in an automated environment. Most of these tasks relate to tasks formerly done manually, but *everything* we now do has changed to some degree. We achieve the same ends, but new procedures, some quite complex, have taken the place of old ones at the same time that the system itself had to be mastered by staff.

It may be revealing to describe just one innocuous sounding item from the above list: placing new standing orders. We decided to use the system to print order forms for these items even though check-in would remain in the kardex. In this way the system's capabilities are used, serial titles are available online and procedures remain uniform. However, once the order is printed a kardex must be made just as it always has. All special instructions contained in the online record must be transferred to the kardex so they will eventually accompany the material to Cataloging. The system order number must be displayed prominently on the kardex so that it will accompany the invoice for payment. An invoice for items lacking this order number (i.e., orders that predate use of the system) must travel a different route in order to have the number created. Errors here can result in the creation of two numbers for one title, not a happy situation. The variety of information required in the kardex comes from two sources: the order form and the search request form. This is amalgamated onto a kardex instruction form which is a revised version of one used in our wholly manual days. From this a kardex record is made. Such a transfer of information is awkward and provides opportunity for error. Were Serials wholly automated, the system would be the sole and unavoidable source for all pertinent information.

Given this dual manual/online method of handling serials one can imagine what happens to an invoice covering a variety of types of material, some with and some without Geac order numbers, some items to be checked in in the kardex, some monographic series which must be checked in online. Some of these latter may need series records created online before the clerk can check in the monograph itself, while some series records may already exist. The invoice stays with the books until all are checked in, one way or another. Then it goes on alone to have any remaining order numbers created before going to be input for payment. It can be a long road from receipt to payment for lengthy invoices!

REALITY: WHERE WE ARE NOW

In early 1988 we are nearing the end of our second year of automated acquisitions. In terms of monographs, we have settled in completely. Working online is the norm and present staff members have no qualms about it. Processing outgoing orders, claiming, receiving new books and recording vendor reports in the system are routine. We now have five terminals and the two original printers. The terminals are rarely idle, and we frequently encroach on the terminals in the Cataloging Department. Additional terminals for serials are to be funded by a U.S. Dept. of Education Grant and installed by mid-1988.

We have several approval plans, three of which provide us with tapes of items being shipped. One also provides a title and ISBN match report so we can identify some potential duplicates before the books arrive. Having the records in the system early prevents requests for these titles being input by Collection Development, as well as providing information for staff members or patrons who may be looking for one of these titles. Tape loading is wonderful, but not without its pitfalls, one of which is errors in the records. Nevertheless, we wouldn't part with it. Several small approval plans do not provide tape-loaded records. For these, a clerk in the Acquisitions Department creates the entire record online—a much easier, more accurate, more easily corrected and immediately visible method than typing multiples to be filed in the card catalog. All manual monograph orders have either been filled, cancelled or moved online. It is safe to say that no one misses multiples for approvals or any other kind of material.

In the Serials Unit, too, the online system has become a part of daily life although less so than in the Monographs Unit. With a larger staff than Monographs, people in Serials have varying needs to use the system as well as varying affinities for it. Nevertheless, the Serials clerks create orders, check the system for information, do claims and check in monographs in series using the system. Special projects such as creating system-generated order numbers for certain groups of materials have been undertaken by the Serials Library Technical Assistant.

Retirement has removed several of the less computer-oriented from the staff. They have been replaced by personnel who have had experience with computers or at the very least wish to acquire this experience. We expect this to continue over the next year or two so that eventually foot-dragging on the part of the staff will no longer be a problem. We have been fortunate in having a few people who were (and are) willing and able to increase their output and to take on new tasks and special projects.

We are putting a toe in the water regarding serial check-in online which had been put aside due to the shortage of terminals. The state documents kardex will be the first to be converted because it is the smallest and is in reasonably good order. The clerk in charge of this kardex has begun to build check-in records for these items. We see that the system works, that it is neat and efficient, and we feel our enthusiasm rising. Once again, we are proceeding despite deficiencies.

REALITY: WHAT WE WISH
WE HAD KNOWN BEFORE WE STARTED

Had we foreseen everything we would have to deal with, including resignations and retirements as well as backlogs and late payment of invoices, we might not have proceeded. However, knowing in advance some of what lay ahead in greater detail might have enabled us to avoid some of the difficulties. To a large extent our problems are of our own making in the sense that they result from decisions we made or from local conditions. Almost without exception, we failed to foresee their *full* consequences.

I wish we had known the difficulties we would face by going beyond our original plan of doing only monographs in the first year. At first glance, the addition of monographic series on standing order (they are monographs, aren't they?) seemed reasonable enough, but monograph check-in is and will remain more complex and time consuming online than it was manually, largely because much more information is recorded. Added to this was the initial creation of the series standing order record (called the Head record) which would be used for check-in of the individual monographs. The fact that vendors often group standing orders of several types on invoices further complicates the process: an invoice travels its lethargic way through various types of check-in with long delays at both Head record creation and monograph check-in, finally to emerge months later for payment long after the prompt-payment deadline.

I wish we had known the implications of processing all invoices through the system from the onset. We did not fully appreciate the fact that every order paid through the system required a system-generated order number. This meant that all monographic orders placed before we went online had to be input as "pseudo" orders simply to generate a number for use in invoice processing. It also meant that every existing subscription or standing order for which we received an invoice also had to have a "pseudo" order created for it. This is not a clerical job and it still consumes considerable time from Library Technical Assistants, although the first year, now behind us, definitely saw the greatest number of such orders. This meant that during the first year we created approximately 9,000 pseudo orders, not all for serials. Those that do represent serials must eventually be upgraded for check-in use. We did take some shortcuts such as paying all Faxon subscriptions on one order number, thereby losing fiscal data for individual titles.

Nevertheless, these two decisions were made because of expected benefits which did in fact occur. Monographic series check-in online provides immediate information searchable by series entry, monograph title and author throughout the library, assisting patrons and reference staff in locating material and helping to prevent the input of duplicate order requests. Processing all invoices through the system from the start of the fiscal year gave us complete financial information through the system's management reports.

I wish we had foreseen the tremendous amounts of time absorbed by tasks involved in maintaining online files. Creation of pseudo records was one. Moreover, each order must have a vendor and each vendor must have a vendor record with correct ordering and payment addresses as well as the Federal Identification Number (the latter, a New York State, not a system, requirement). Although creation of the vendor file began months before we went live, adding to and updating it took considerable time during the first months, more so than we anticipated. It now numbers over 1,000 entries. This, too, is an ongoing but no longer burdensome job. Accurate vendor records are crucial for correct payment of invoices as well as for the availability of data online and in management reports.

I wish we had realized that invoice processing itself is complex and rather slow also, but again we are gaining more complete information than we had before. We absorbed an account clerk from another department and made invoice input a full-time, rather than part-time, job. As of January 1, 1988, this clerk had processed 7,705 invoices representing 41,157 individual transactions since we went online.

I wish we had understood the full impact of staff resistance to automation. We felt that advance preparation, training, practice, and a generally upbeat attitude on the part of supervisors coupled with considerable individual attention and further training once we went live would engender acceptance if not enthusiasm among the clerical staff. This was not the case. In most instances, those who looked forward to this new experience did well, while those whose initial attitudes were negative never did well. As we near the end of the second year, attrition has removed most of the greatest resisters. Those that remain have reached a level where they can function on the system, but without adequate speed or comprehension and amid continual complaint.

I wish we had realized how our lack of equipment and personnel would impact all of the above. Burdens on staff and backlogs could have been considerably reduced if we had simply had more people and more terminals. However, had we waited for this bounty we would not be automated yet. We would prefer enough terminals so that one is available when needed much like a telephone, eliminating the need for scheduling and queuing.

I wish we had known the many complexities that would be added to our already complicated serial procedures. If someone had told us in advance what it was going to mean for lengthy mixed-type serial invoices (as described earlier) we might not have had the courage to proceed.

No doubt that is why it is best that we cannot foresee all that will happen. We would never get anywhere.

REALITY: WHAT HAPPENED TO THOSE IDEALS?

Saving Money

It is difficult to save money by reducing staff when the staff has already been reduced below an acceptable level. We were struggling to keep up prior to automation. The added burden of automating threatened to bury us under backlogs. At the present time, operating in a partly automated environment, we see no prospect of functioning with fewer staff members. We barely keep our heads above water now, cannot undertake various projects and studies that would be advantageous, and hope no one decides to take a long vacation.

As was indicated in the opening of this article, there is ample evidence for the fallacy of this ideal, but its tremendous appeal can be difficult to overcome, and we still occasionally hear hints of it from beyond our own department.

The Ergonomic Office

This, alas, remains a totally unattained and unattainable goal. It takes a long view and a willingness to expend substantial sums on a what can seem merely cosmetic to undertake revamping an office in this way. A vendor who recently redid the headquarters office, in trying to describe what it was like before, explained "You know, torn carpets, dirty chairs, old furniture. It was really awful — sort of like your place." So it will stay, despite the fact that this university's own Center for Women in Government has recommended that employers "develop an ergonomics implementation plan responsive to individual needs which includes employee participation and builds adjustability into workstations and work environments."[6]

The Middle Managers' View

My own goals of increased efficiency and accuracy in processing and obtaining accurate, current, detailed and manipulatable data relating to orders, receipts and claims as well as financial transactions have largely been met.

As the fiscal year draws to an end, I must carefully parcel out invoices using every penny by the deadline. I look daily at the bottom line of the budget on the terminal, watch the balance shrink and finally see it reach zero. Such is the neat, clean and accurate end to an automated fiscal year. One area where the system has not yet been of much help is in the compilation of monthly statistics. Although numerous reports are generated and vast quantities of data are available, they simply do not conform to the format in which we need to compile our figures. Other activities have not permitted pursuit of this so we continue our manual statistics collection. Similarly, the system-generated reports that Collection Development uses do not entirely meet our needs. Local programming could overcome these problems, but we do not have sufficient systems personnel to undertake it because of other priorities. We are reviewing programs done at other sites to determine whether any of them might be adaptable to our needs. The other goals originally sought by Collection Development have been better met.

REALITY: IMPLICATIONS FOR OTHER LIBRARIES

What is the import of all of this for other libraries? It is hoped that those who are considering automating acquisitions will find food for thought here, that their preparations may benefit from our experience and that they may approach the undertaking with a more realistic view of what it will take to accomplish it. It should also encourage libraries lacking ideal conditions under which to automate: it can be done despite handicaps.

Lack of equipment and personnel caused most of our difficulties. These are critical areas at all times, but especially so at the onset of a major automation project. We were forced by budgeting constraints to make minimal estimates of our requirements and finally forced by circumstances to accept even less than our estimates. In terms of personnel, we had no choice but to work with what we had. Perhaps others can avoid this situation.

Even when dealing with a turnkey system, our experience indicates the need for experienced systems personnel, who also understand library operations and speak both jargons. Careful advance planning, thorough investigation of the system's capabilities, flexibility or lack there-of, relevance to local needs, format and content of online displays and off-line reports cannot be overemphasized. It is not possible to ask too many questions. Make no assumptions. Does the system provide a vendor performance report? Good idea, sounds great, does it not? Maybe it is, but maybe it is not. What information is in it, how is it formatted and sorted, can the data be manipulated to produce specific reports such as a vendor's average price and length of delivery time for "rush" orders, orders for certain types of material, orders from specific publishers? What, *precisely*, does the library want in any report and what, *precisely*, does the system provide? Every aspect of the system must be scrutinized similarly.

Once a system has been chosen, considerable lead time will be needed to prepare staff and build files. Experience is the best teacher and clerical staff in particular may need many hours of practice before feeling comfortable with the system. Preparation for the maintenance of both manual and online systems, preferably by the use of additional staff, is necessary. It is possible to simply ask more of existing staff and ride out the difficult period of backlogs and overworked employees as we are doing, but it is not ideal. We were not entirely successful in overcoming staff resistance to automation, even though we thought we had approached this potential problem with care. It deserves considerable attention. Staff members who become unhappy because of automation can become troublesome in other ways, demand an inordinate amount of a supervisor's attention, undermine fellow employees' attempts to cope with the change and generally make a difficult period nearly intolerable.

It is wise to expect system bugs, down time, aspects of it that do not work as expected. We had minimal difficulty with the system itself, but there were some problems and in the early days of such a project even a small problem can loom large. It would be preferable to plan in such a way as to avoid backlog buildup. Try to determine where backlogs are likely and what can be done ahead of time in terms of reallocating staff time or changing procedures to prevent them. Of course, we all know what happens to the best-laid plans — sudden resignations, illness, lack of money, sudden receipt of a grant necessitating an avalanche of orders, the unannounced bankruptcy of a vendor — the possibilities are myriad, but plan we must, nevertheless. Plans may change and timetables may lengthen, but planning creates a structure around which the automation of acquisitions grows.

While immersed in the daily coping with the new system, one must remember who its users are. If they include other departments and the library's clientele, public relations forays into these other areas are in order. They must be shown the system, be taught how to use it and be given reason to relate to it.

These are some of the areas to which attention must be paid. The relation of our experiences in these pages may provide both encouragement and a cautionary note to others about to embark on a similar undertaking.

Automating in an age of austerity is possible. It is difficult. It is slow. It means asking more of one's staff. It means backlogs. It means some things will not be done when wanted. Perhaps they never will be. But it does not mean it is impossible or inadvisable to automate under these conditions.

IDEAL: ON-GOING GOAL

Ideals are still with us. Without them, generally termed "goals," we would lose all momentum, low though that may be. Our ultimate goal remains unchanged: a completely automated Acquisitions Department.

This means that much of our attention has shifted to serials. For the first time in two years, December 1987 saw the department fully staffed and optimism rose amid visions of reduced backlogs. By mid-January we were down one serials person again. The Monographs Unit has its three full-time employees and several students. Because our lack of acquisitions money has dramatically reduced the number of orders and receipts, it has been possible to put some of these people to work in Serials. We have determined to keep current in processing monographic series while continually chipping away at the creation of system-generated order numbers for all 16,614 standing orders and subscriptions, our most immediate goal being the creation of these numbers for certain items received from vendors with invoice tape-loading capabilities. Beyond this, full check-in records must be created. When additional terminals are received, we will proceed to build periodical check-in records and begin to check in online as the records are prepared. We will gain much from the experience of the Documents Clerk who is building check-in records for state documents. Obviously a project of this scope would best be done as a special project for which temporary help would be hired. We will have, at best, the staff we have now and we will be a long time converting. Everyone's work load will increase while both manual and online systems are maintained. Other projects must be pursued as well.

Although the acquisitions database can be accessed by the public and reference staff, its records are not in the Online Catalog per se. We need to test the Online Public Access Catalog pass through, determine which records should and should not transfer, establish methods for identifying and removing garbage, alter procedures and train staff. We may also consider a pass through of RLIN records, but at the present time costs are prohibitive. Nevertheless, we know that there is nothing to be gained by throwing up our hands and saying it cannot be done. Slow, even glacial, progress is better than no progress toward our goals and we have seen enough of the benefits of online records to know that the goal of automating serials is a worthy one.

I am reminded of the closing paragraph of E. B. White's classic children's book *Stuart Little*. Despite his diminutive size, Stuart is determined to function as a real person, and after many vicissitudes, he continues to search for his illusive avian friend, Margalo.

Stuart rose from the ditch, climbed into his car, and started up the road that led toward the north. The sun was just coming up over the hills on his right. As he peered ahead into the great land that stretched before him, the way seemed long. But the sky was bright, and he somehow felt he was headed in the right direction.[7]

We are a Stuart Little among research libraries: smaller than might be expected, but gritty and determined to reach our goals. And, like Stuart, I feel that we too are headed in the right direction.

REFERENCES

1. Martin M. Cummings, *The Economics of Research Libraries* (Washington, D.C.: Council on Library Resources, 1986), p.60.
2. Dennis Reynolds, *Library Automation: Issues and Applications* (New York: R.R. Bowker, 1985), p.208.
3. Christian M. Boissonnas, "What Cost, Automation?" *Library Acquisitions: Practice and Theory*, 10 (1986), p.107.
4. University at Albany, *Undergraduate Bulletin*, 1987-88, p.5.
5. "Office Automation: Center Survey Results," *News on Women in Government*, vol.11, no.1 (Winter 1988), p.4.
6. E.B. White, *Stuart Little* (New York: Harper & Row, 1973), p.131.

Going On-Line with the Geac Acquisitions System: Converting 1970's Clerical Procedures to 1980's Technology

Robert N. Thompson

SUMMARY. In December 1986, the Minneapolis Public Library Acquisitions Department began on-line operations using the Geac Library Information Systems Acquisitions module. Prior to this the Library had been using an IBM System 3 computer which provided a "semi-automated" batched operation. The major difficulties which the department needed to resolve were, (1) the shift of data entry responsibilities from EDP to Acquisitions, (2) the loss of traditional, hard-copy, files and reports and, (3) adjusting the work assignments of the Acquisitions Department staff. After one full year's operation the Geac System is seen to be well designed but inflexible. The benefits of improved vendor response time, increased budget control and the ability for any selector to do direct data entry outweigh our inability to manipulate the software.

THE SELECTION OF THE GEAC ACQUISITIONS SYSTEM AND ITS IMPLEMENTATION

Geac Computers, Inc. of Toronto, Canada, was selected to be the supplier of an on-line circulation system for the Minneapolis Public Library. The installation began in 1984 and will be completed in 1988. As a part of the purchase package Geac included its Acquisi-

---

Robert N. Thompson is Supervisor, Acquisitions Department, Minneapolis Public Library and Information Center, 300 Nicollet Mall, Minneapolis, MN 55401.

© 1989 by The Haworth Press, Inc. All rights reserved.

tion System software at no extra cost. If the library purchased the necessary hardware, which proved to be four Geac terminals, an additional disk drive and memory, and agreed to activate the Acquisition System within one year of purchase, Geac promised to provide support for the system through its Library Assistance Desk.

The library had been looking at automated acquisitions systems of all kinds for several years and we knew that some sort of system would need to be installed in the foreseeable future. This seemed like a golden opportunity to modernize our system with a minimal outlay of capital. The decision was made to make the necessary purchases and activate the Geac Acquisition System sometime before December 31, 1986.

The decision to go with the Geac system was made before I became the Supervisor of Acquisitions. One of my first tasks as supervisor was to review and analyze the various options Geac provided for local sites to customize their system. (In Geac terminology these are Conditional Compile Options, or CCPs.) This looked like an impossible task for a new supervisor but it proved to be manageable for several reasons:

- First, many of the decisions were technical and were decided upon by the Library's Electronic Data Processing Department, not by Acquisitions.
- Second, other Geac sites proved to very helpful when asked questions about the implications of a particular CCP.
- Third, a thorough analysis of our existing procedures gave me a good picture of the procedural elements we needed to retain and which could be altered or eliminated.
- Fourth, Geac assured us that the decisions about any CCP could be altered during training, or during testing, and that our decisions were not irrevocable.

After a good deal of study by the Chief of Technical Services, the Head of EDP and myself the final list of completed CCPs was sent to Geac on June 27, 1986.

Although a few CCPs were subsequently changed, the basic profile of our automated system was determined by two fundamental decisions which were made by the Chief of Technical Services and which have not changed as yet:

1. That on-line data from the ACQ system would not be transferred to the On-Line Catalog.
2. That the ACQ System would consist of one terminal port supporting four terminals and no printer.

Geac provided four days of training on site for five library workers which was our first "hands on" experience with the system. Up to this point we had only Geac's written documentation to work with and it was a relief to actually see the system which would become so central to our working lives.

This week of work with an expert to guide us was the key to developing a more holistic view of the system. For the first time we saw how the various ACQ functions worked and fit together.

With this knowledge we began a six month testing and training period. After Geac trained workers shared their new expertise with the rest of the Acquisitions Department we began a system of dual record keeping for selected book orders. Orders were placed using our existing system but were entered into the Geac System as if they were "live" as well. We were able to fine tune our new procedures quite quickly with this training method and I think we were actually ready to go live within a few weeks. Although we risked allowing the staff to go stale we decided to wait until December to activate the system because there were still some details to work out and the fund accounting would be cleaner if we changed systems with the annual budget changeover. This testing period revealed the impossibility of incorporating the Serials Subsystem at this time. We were daunted by the complexity of the task and the limitations of having only four terminals.

With administrative approval we informed Geac and our primary vendors that we would begin to place orders via our new system on December 14, 1986.

Our staff complement at this point in time consisted of eleven Full-Time-Equivalents: one Supervisor, one Continuations Clerk, two Clerk-Typists II, one Library Aide II, five full-time Library Aides I and two half-time Library Aides I.

The total materials budget in 1986 was $1,354,565, of which $927,389 was designated for non-serials. The 1987 budget allotment was to be $1,482,484 with $1,031,652 for non-serials.

THE 1972 ACQUISITIONS SYSTEM

Our existing system was a "semi-automated" IBM System 3 which was installed in the library in 1972. Its acquisitions functions included the creation of purchase order letters, claim forms, and order record forms and it performed some fund accounting. The programming and operation of the IBM computer was handled entirely by EDP personnel.

The IBM System 3 relied on key-punched item cards to record data and control operations. Over the years our computer system had been expanded and adapted almost continuously and the procedures files for both Acquisitions and EDP became enormous. But I believe that I can describe the old acquisitions system by describing the major steps involved in ordering and receiving a book which was new to the library.

Book order selections were made by the various Subject Department Heads and sent to Acquisitions. Although an order form existed for this purpose its use was not required and Acquisitions would process all forms of source material which were sent to us.

The selections were searched manually in a "New Received" file which held records, filed by author, for approximately two years. The search was performed by a Library Aide I. It was expected that the selector had already searched the catalog for titles older than two years.

After searching, a complex editing process was undertaken. Different bibliographic elements were indicated on the source material by means of different colored inks and/or a variety of symbols. This was necessary for many reasons, but primarily because the various forms of source materials we would see did not present the author/title/publisher/edition/date/language, etc. in an immediately recognizable way and the keypunch operators needed our assistance in identifying these elements.

In addition, the various fields which were to be key-punched had very narrow character limits. For example, the edition statement had to be compressed to two characters (PA for paperback, 02 for second edition, LB for library binding, etc.). The editing process standardized abbreviations of this sort and attempted to make other compressions of data comprehensible to the vendor. This editing was done by a Library Aide II and virtually every title ordered by the library passed over this aide's desk.

After the source material had been edited each piece was sent to EDP for keypunching. While in EDP a computer search was also conducted to identify titles missed by Acquisitions' manual search. In addition to author, EDP could search titles and ISBNs. This was extremely valuable of course, but quite limited because EDP could only store a few months data at any one time. The search in EDP was intended to catch items ordered but not received. All "New" titles ordered in the current year but not yet received were stored. Remaining file space was occupied by recent "Received" records.

Once a week EDP returned the source material and the newly created, punched item cards to Acquisitions. The department head of Acquisitions, or the assistant, would review the titles one by one, assign vendors, and apply an anticipated discount.

The punched item cards were bundled by vendor and returned to EDP for final processing.

On their return visit to EDP the vendor was keyed in and the anticipated discount data added as well. Purchase order letters and mail labels were printed, order record forms produced, and the Subject Department's budget was encumbered.

The time table for this work under ideal conditions would be:

— Search and edit: 2 days
— Item cards punched, computer search: 2 days
— Vendors assigned: 1/2 day
— Purchase order letters, etc., printed: 1 day

Thus, orders reaching Acquisitions on Monday could, under ideal circumstances, be listed on purchase orders mailed the following Monday. Needless to say the ideal was rarely achieved. Even under normal work flow conditions the entire process usually took two full weeks to complete and it was quite common for the procedure to stretch to four weeks during peak work loads or staff shortages.

1972 Shipment Check-in

When shipments were received and checked in a similarly elaborate routine was put into effect.

A Library Aide I would unpack the cartons and arrange the shipment on book trucks in invoice order (i.e., by author).

Another Aide I, working with an invoice copy, would extract the order record forms for that shipment and then pull the corresponding item cards linked to the order record form by a unique item number which the computer had assigned when the order record form was created.

The invoice was verified line by line by an Aide I who would match the bibliographic data on the order record form against the title page and the accounting data on the item card against the invoice. The accounting data corrections were a continuing problem area because our internal fund accounting crossed paths with the vendor's invoice only at this one place. The invoice was sent to the library's Accounting Office; the invoice amount disbursed from the library's materials budget and the invoice sent to the city's Comptroller's Office from where a check was issued.

The item cards were corrected manually and sent to EDP where the various department accounts were disbursed. The aide who checked in a shipment was expected to notice and indicate any changes from (1) the number of copies ordered, (2) the list price expected and/or, (3) the anticipated discount which was applied to the original list price. If the aide failed to notice a change, or if EDP mis-keyed the correction, Acquisitions' budget figures would vary from the Accounting Office's by the amount of the error and there was no hope of ever discovering the points at which we differed.

SOME CHANGES APPARENT BEFORE TRAINING

Obviously, the Geac Acquisitions System was going to affect every facet of our working lives. We knew that we could retain the most fundamental aspects of our old procedure but every element of the work flow would be changed dramatically and many of these changes were apparent even before we ever touched a Geac terminal. These changes raised serious questions to which we had as yet no answers.

Among the changes we knew we could expect were:

1. All data entry would be performed by acquisition personnel. EDP would be cut out of the data entry aspects of the book order procedure entirely. Was the Geac system streamlined enough to allow the current acquisitions staff to assume this additional duty? Or, as alternatives, would data entry operators in EDP, now free of acquisitions work, be allowed to help in our department; or could we expect that each library agency could be trained to enter their own requests on-line and send much less paper to Acquisitions if any at all?
2. We would no longer have "hard copy" files to rely on. We would lose a "received" file, a file of "orders out" arranged chronologically, copies of purchase order letters, a "cancelled" file; and the book selectors would lose a computer generated item card for their own department's "on order" file. Of course most of this information was available on-line, as well as a good deal more, but were there pitfalls that we should be anticipating? Were the concerns we felt real or a symptom of technophobia?
3. We needed to develop an entirely new set of processing slips for use in Technical Services. How many different kinds did we need? What should they look like? What other library functions relied on EDP's System 3 forms which were going to be eliminated by the Acquisitions changeover?
4. What would acquisitions workers do off-terminal, or when the system was down? We no longer had our traditional filing duties, what would take their place? We didn't have enough terminals to schedule all aides on a terminal all day, even if the library were to allow such scheduling. What could we find for them to do?
5. What were the salary and staffing level implications? Would the workers, or their union, argue that aides were being asked to acquire new competencies and demand additional compen-

sations? As a result of recent staff manipulations, Acquisitions had lost its "assistant head" position. This was acceptable under the old system but what were our options if the new system needed this position restored?
6. Finally, our old system relied on workers who were trained for specific tasks. One aide searched, another checked in primary vendor shipments, another checked in Greenaway and Publisher Plan shipments and so forth. Naturally, there was some cross training and flexibility for vacations and other emergencies, but each worker knew pretty much what to expect each day. The Geac system seemed to require more interchangeable workers. All aides would need to know how to use all of the ACQ functions so that the work could be scheduled efficiently. This seemed to place more emphasis on the supervisor's role in monitoring work flow and assigning tasks on a day to day basis, wherever the need happened to be. How would these changes affect the way our department had traditionally functioned? What would be the impact on staff morale and enthusiasm?

SOME CHANGES APPARENT AFTER TRAINING

The week of training which Geac provided was intense and seemed too short but it was all important to our understanding of how the system was designed to operate. The trainer did not answer any of the questions posed above however. The system had been designed for a "generic" library and it was expected that each site would more or less adapt to the system. Although Geac was, and is, willing to talk to specific sites about specific concerns they would prefer to work with large user groups which can suggest significant alterations to the system which will help several sites. It seems that Geac is hesitant to change their software to assist just one site and understandably so, because any change may have repercussions on the activities of all other sites. So even though the Geac trainer could answer any question about the system itself he was not able to help us plan changes in our own procedures in order to accommodate the Geac System.

Following the week of training we embarked on a long test period which enabled us to fine tune our procedures and finally come to grips with some of our problems.

We learned during this testing interval that:

1. Four terminals would be barely enough to process book orders; there was no possibility of adding the Serials subsystem at the same time. We knew that our IBM system produced an annual average of 35,000 individual records for book orders in recent years. We expected a similar number, with a similar amount of data entry using the Geac System. It looked as though we would need all four terminals to do this.

2. The response time for each "send" was going to be something of a problem because it was variable depending on the overall usage of our processor by other functions which were occurring simultaneously with ACQ. The ACQ system as we knew it then needed at least 17 sends to Search and create a Request for one item. Often the need for a more thorough Search could cause the number of sends to reach 25. (Subsequent software enhancements have reduced the typical number of sends to 10-15 for the procedure.) At the beginning of our test the Search and Request functions would take about 1 minute each. As more and more circulation, cataloging, barcoding and acquisitions activity flooded the processor the entire procedure was typically timed at 5 minutes with occasional occurrences of 7 to 8 minutes for one title. Each day we would see this variety of response times and we began to anticipate problems in planning our work flow.

3. Geac's Invoice function looked straightforward on paper and during training. We soon learned however, that invoicing would be a large consumer of terminal time. Although Geac is working with various vendors towards fully automated, electronic invoicing, at present we are required to recreate a vendor's paper invoice on-line for the system. This can be extremely tedious and difficult work when you consider that it is quite common for us to receive invoices which are 100 lines long, occasionally 200 lines, and, in memory, 300 lines more than once. Each line requires the correct entry of purchase order number, number of copies, and item price and if some data are incorrectly entered the invoice cannot be validated.

The benefit side to this is that we finally have a resolution to our old bugaboo about our invoice totals which do not match the Accounting Office's totals. Now we know that Acquisitions and Accounting are using exactly the same invoice amounts in every case.

4. The Geac System provides no counterpart to our old system of attaching an anticipated discount to a book order *before* the order is encumbered. We now need to enter the full "list" price on each book order. Previously those involved in vendor and discount assignment had become so skilled that nearly any selector could add the "encumbered" amount to the "expended" figure and know that the total was within 5% of what would eventually be actually spent from his or her budget.

Now we would not be able to assess our commitments quite so accurately. While we still might be able to estimate an average discount for some vendors, the total "committed" and "spent" for any individual account is a combination of all vendors and we have no experience in estimating total, across the board, average discounts.

On the other hand, book selectors now have accurate "spent" amounts which are updated every night. This will have to be our benchmark for judging the rate at which the various budgets are being used. I suspect that in the long run it will be a better measure than our old "encumbered plus expended" calculations.

5. Finally, we would need to deal with the difficulty of collecting "average discount" data from the system for most of our large vendors. Even though Geac provides a program for extracting average discount data from the invoices we have entered we will not be able to enter most vendor's line discounts, because we often receive fractional discounts (e.g., 35.5%, 17.2%, etc.).

If a vendor applies a 35.5% discount to the *entire* invoice Geac provides a way of entering that information; but if the vendor uses a different discount on each line of the invoice the system permits only whole, one or two digit numbers. Our only alternative, short of demanding that all our vendors apply discounts in compliance with this restriction, is to forego discount information and enter the actual price of each item after discount when we are creating the on-line invoice record. This provides correct invoice totals but leaves us information poor.

THE NEW SYSTEM – PLACING ORDERS

In order to describe our new system I can briefly describe the steps involved in ordering a title which is new to the library. This can be compared with the similar procedure for our old system described above.

Title selection continues to be made by the various Subject Department heads. A new request form was devised which lays out the bibliographic and budget data in a way which is more suitable to our new system but again the form is optional and selectors continue to send original source data to Acquisitions. In fact we have encouraged the selectors to send ads, bibliographies, reviews and the like to Acquisitions because they often contain information useful for vendor selection. Through the coming year however, we would like to encourage the subject departments to do some original data entry when the source is a standard review service (*Choice, Kirkus, Library Journal, Publishers' Weekly* and some others) and the title is published by one of the large publishing houses.

Acquisitions enters all requests for all types of material in order of receipt in the department. For example, a pack of *Library Journal* cards sent to us from a subject department may need to wait until we enter a branch replacement order which had been received earlier. Although we do attempt to identify "rush" items for expedited ordering no one needs to wait for us to act on an order. If any selector enters a request on-line Acquisitions sees a printout of the request the next day, can make any corrections necessary, authorize the order and have a purchase order in the mail the following day. Any backlog in Acquisitions can be completely bypassed by direct data entry from anywhere in the library. This is an enormous advantage of our new system.

The source material is sorted by type of material in Acquisitions. Vendor assignment is made by the supervisor (unusual, expensive nonroutine items); the order clerk (routine imprints) or an Aide II (audio, video, government documents, among others).

The amount of editing which was found to be necessary has been tremendously reduced by our new system because the data entry is being performed by Acquisitions workers who are familiar with the bibliographic and budgetary elements of a book order. Previously all of these elements needed to be unmistakably identified for EDP workers. Now we edit only in order to highlight information which might be missed by a casual observation. Often a choice between cloth or paper edition will be emphasized, a series entry or an unusual author entry might be underlined. Usually, however, only the publisher, date, ISBN and price are identified by underlining and the appropriate vendor code (BT for Baker and Taylor, for example) is added. In addition the correct book location code is added if necessary (usually this is one or two letters: H for the History Dept., LH for Linden Hills Community Library). The correct account is added, again if necessary (this is usually three letters, -HIS-, but can be more, LIT-FOR, for Literature Dept., Foreign Language account, are examples). This all takes much longer to describe than to do of course, and it is much more efficient than our old system's editing requirements.

We have five boxes, labeled Monday-Friday, in which the source data rests while awaiting data entry. An aide assigned to data entry will select materials from the "oldest" box thus insuring that material is entered in order of receipt. An Aide I performs a Search, creates a Request and authorizes the resulting order.

The Geac SEARCH function is quite efficient. Usually, if a 1987 or 1988 imprint is being ordered, a TITLE search of the ACQ database is all that is required. However, if the title contains unusual elements such as an ampersand, a date, or a numeral, an additional search is indicated. The system provides ISBN, AUTHOR, and SERIES searches as well as TITLE. Moreover, the on-line CATALOG can be searched without leaving the ACQ function. This is useful for searching titles older than 1987 imprints and for capturing bibliographic data for ordering replacement copies.

If the search produces no hits a REQUEST is prepared. Creating a request requires the completion of four screens. The first screen provides fields for entering ISBN, Author, Title, Imprint, Series, Edition, Language (default English), and Media (default nonbook). Subsequent screens call for entry of list price, location (usually one or two characters), number of copies, fund number (14 characters, only 3 to 7 of which need to be entered), vendor, and any specific notes for ourselves, the selector, and/or the vendor. The entire procedure takes about ten "sends" depending on the length of the search. Furthermore, the location, fund and vendor all default to the previous request. Therefore if we batch requests by location, fund, and vendor, little or no additional keying of data is necessary.

If the aide has any questions or problems with the data being entered the request is not authorized and a printout is produced overnight so that the request can be reviewed. But normally the aide who enters the request authorizes it as well and a purchase order is produced overnight and mailed the next day. We have not had any significant problem with this arrangement.

An ideal work flow would allow us to enter all requests received the previous day. Normally we are able to enter all requests within one week, although entering requests is not our top priority as will be explained later.

THE NEW SYSTEM – CHECK-IN

Shipments are unpacked and placed in invoice order (by purchase order number) on book trucks by an Aide I. Items are checked in by calling up the title of the item. Often a title search will produce several orders for the same item and the Aide I will need to find a match for the purchase order number listed on the invoice. An additional command brings up a "Full" display which displays the data necessary to process the book.

If the item being received is NEW the Aide I will note on the processing slip all copies which are still on order. The source of the bibliographic data, the vendor, list price and invoiced price are noted as well. "NEW" books are sent to the Book Selection Area where they are reviewed by the Selector and additional copies are selected for the branch system. Duplicate items are sent directly to the Catalog Department.

As an integral part of the check-in process the Aide is expected to correct the original bibliographic data if appropriate. Shipment errors are set aside for review by the Aide II who can consult with the Order Clerk and then with the supervisor for especially knotty problems. Although no price changes are noted on-line during the check-in process, aides are encouraged to report significant instances or patterns of price increases to the supervisor. The invoice price of the item will be entered later as part of the Invoice function and it can be called up after the Invoice function has been completed.

Our priority list for work assignments starts with a state law requiring payment to be made by any government agency within 35 days of receipt of material. This means that we must unpack shipments, check in material and complete the sometimes lengthy Geac Invoice function in about a week in order to insure that the library's Accounting Office and City Comptroller's Office can complete their duties within this 35 day time frame.

If our check-in is current then we can create requests. If requests are current we enter vendor reports, work on problems, add claims, or enter donated material. Usually, of course, most of these activities are occurring simultaneously but our priorities are quite clear during "crunch" times.

As we ended our first full year on our new system our staff complement had been reduced very slightly from 11 Full-Time-Equivalents to 10.6. We now have one Supervisor, one Serials Order Clerk, one Order Clerk, one Clerk-Typist II, one Library Aide II, four full-time Library Aides I, and three part-time Aides I sharing 1.6 F.T.E.s.

In 1987 we created over 47,000 requests which generated 44,429 book orders and we spent 99.5% of the book budget.

WHAT WE KNOW SO FAR

Just prior to activating our new system we had raised some questions we couldn't answer at the time. After a full year on-line we now know that:

1. The Acquisitions Department staff was able to handle the data entry work load, with a little help. EDP agreed to provide a data entry operator for 4 hours each day; all library agencies were given training on the ACQ system which allowed them the option of placing orders on-line as staff time and terminal schedules allowed.

For the short term (that is, four to six months) we realized that we would have an enormous work load problem because most of the material ordered during the last months of 1986 would need to be checked in on the Geac system in early 1987. This required us to create full records for each of these titles so that we could show these items as paid from the 1987 book budget. We calculated that our work load for the first few months on the Geac system would be almost double what we should expect to be "normal." As it happened we did experience a 3-4 week backlog in processing new requests in early 1987 and we did require some overtime hours to catch up, but our prediction that this would be a short-term problem was accurate and the current work load seems to be appropriate for our current staff.

2. The loss of the traditional paper files for Acquisitions activity was a short-term crisis. Primarily, the fears seemed to be the loss of "on order" information which was formatted by agency, that is: titles on order for the Literature, or History Department, etc., and secondarily, the access to budget data, both current and historical. The Geac ACQ system provides a report program which prints out all activity on selected account numbers for designated date parameters. The Acquisitions Department working with EDP, agreed to run this program weekly for *all* account numbers and distribute it to the selectors. Our original plan was to accumulate the printout up to the month level. That is, the first week's printout would be contained in the second week's which was accumulated again the third, until the fourth week. The fifth week's printout would be just that one week's activity and the cycle would start again. This plan did help the users of the system bridge the gap between systems but it soon became too unwieldy for Acquisitions or EDP to generate as planned. The accumulation schedule needed to be dropped in March because some print runs were approaching a thousand pages. Under the weight of ever larger weekly printouts, and with some training and increasing familiarity with the system, the book selectors agreed to allow us to quit this procedure entirely. Although there is no hard copy report of titles on order for any individual agency it seems that we have all adjusted to the situation and learned to appreciate the amount of information available to us now which wasn't before.

The budget reports were a somewhat different story. Geac provides a printout of budget information by account number but this printout is not formatted for distribution to a wide audience. The program is quite easy to run, unlike the report which was described above, and EDP provides it to Acquisitions at the end of each month. The Acquisitions Department staff reformats the data manually and distributes a monthly budget report which shows budget totals by cost center.

With our experience we could restructure our account numbers in order to use the ACQ System to provide the cost center totals for us but we feel that the half-day of work needed to prepare the monthly budget statement is a smaller price to pay than reassigning everyone's account numbers at this point.

3. The task of devising new forms was ultimately an exercise in communications. Once the users of each form had analyzed their own requirements, the content of each form was established and only the formatting needed to be set. We learned that a form is probably never "finished." Each reprinting of each form has seen minor revisions and perhaps always will.

4. The question of what to do during "down" times is not resolved. During the transition period Acquisitions lost two Aides I who were replaced by four half-time Aides I. During some downtime three of these four have been able to work in other areas of the library because their other half-time position was also in the library and the downtime situation didn't affect that part of their job. Since our serials system is not yet on-line there is usually some serials clerical work which can be assigned—but this will change when serials goes on-line in 1988. There is still some minor filing (copies of paid invoices, for example) and gifts from the public to sort, but downtime is still a problem area with no long-term solutions in sight. Fortunately, downtime is not a significant overall problem. In 1987 unscheduled downtime totalled less than one percent of available hours.

5. It was necessary for the Acquisitions Department to create a new employee position in order to facilitate the work flow. Someone was needed to assist the supervisor in vendor assignment, the monitoring of work flow and work assignments, the resolution of problems; in short, to largely recreate the position of "assistant department head" which had been eliminated earlier. On the serials side, the transfer of the Continuations Clerk allowed us to combine the duties of Continuations Clerk and Periodicals Clerk into one new position. Fortunately we were able to fill both new positions, Order Clerk and Serials Order Clerk, with current Acquisitions

workers who had been at Aide II level positions in the Department. The Aide II level work of both of their old positions was combined into one Aide II position which effectively serves as a half-time assistant to both. This structure looks like it will serve us well in the future. To date there has been no change in the Library Aide I or Aide II salary levels. The new work assignments are seen to be equivalent to previous Aide I and II duties.

6. Any fear about an affect on staff morale seems to have been totally unfounded. Those workers who had reservations about the new system transferred out or retired and those who stayed and those who were hired as replacements were genuinely enthusiastic about implementing the new procedures. The entire process was truly cooperative with input and discussions at all levels. The first year of operation was a stimulating and exciting period because of the attitude of experimentation, cooperation and discovery shown by everyone in the Acquisitions Department.

SUMMING UP — DISADVANTAGES

Although there is no need to be negative in any degree towards the Geac Acquisition system there are some differences between our old and new systems which can be seen as a net loss in capabilities.

One change is in our ability to manipulate the system. As a Geac site we cannot modify the system as we were able to do with our IBM system. Over the last several years several programs were developed in-house which helped supply data for a number of uses. The Geac software is not accessible in this way and we cannot modify or add programs for our own purposes. From Geac's point of view, all users are using the same software so a change for one site will be a change for all. Therefore Geac responds to changes which are requested by several sites, not individual users.

Second, although we enter LOCATION data when we request material there is little data we can retrieve from the system based on LOCATION information. Almost all retrievable data is based on BUDGET (i.e., FUND) and/or VENDOR information. What this means is that the system requires us to set up a unique account number for every specific type of material or location which we want to track. Our selectors have found it necessary to create literally hundreds of accounts in order to monitor data.

Third, as expressed earlier, we often are frustrated by the response time we experience for each "send." There is some hope for resolution of this problem on several fronts however. Geac is working with the system to make it more responsive. New software installed last November dramatically reduced the number of "sends" necessary to complete a request. Recently the library has added an additional Geac 8000 processor which is a twin to the one we had been using. Now the Circulation system has its own processor and no longer competes with ACQ and the other on-line functions. This had a positive and sometimes dramatic effect on our response time. Down the road we foresee moving all our functions to a Geac 9000 processor which we hope will bring additional benefits to all library users.

Fourth, we are finding the claiming procedure is quite cumbersome on the Geac system. Our old IBM system provided a simple claiming procedure which relied on a manual (or visual) check of old order forms. The Geac system requires a multi-stepped and, so far, poorly understood procedure to first identify candidates for claim or cancellation and then another operation to add a claim to an individual record and finally a third operation to actually print the claim forms. Because claims had a low priority during our initial year on the system we are quite far behind with our claims at the moment and are finding it difficult to catch up. Once we are caught up I anticipate a good deal of effort will need to be made to keep us current.

SUMMING UP—ADVANTAGES

On balance I feel that the pluses of our new system outweigh its minuses. Some of the advantages we have identified already and some we foresee as potential future improvements.

First, we are experiencing better turnaround times from vendors than we ever had before. If we start counting from the time Acquisitions first receives a request from a selector we can usually show a two-week improvement from that point to check-in date, sometimes more. Part of the improvement is improved efficiency within the library due to the Geac system but also due to the fact that vendors seem to respond well to Geac purchase order forms which list one title per slip. Down the road, vendors are working with Geac towards more integration and communication so that, eventually, truly on-line electronic ordering and invoicing may be practical realities.

Second, the efficiencies gained in-house are significant. For example, the search used to be a multi-stepped, largely manual procedure. Now it is a quick, one-time, on-line operation which is more effective than the old one.

Third, there is system-wide access to the system. Any site can determine which titles have been ordered, received, cancelled, etc., for any other site in the library system. Added to this is the capability for any selector to enter an on-line request for a title and know that a purchase order will be in the mail in two days.

Finally, each selector has accurate, up to date budget information for any account. There is almost endless flexibility in the account structure, any number of accounts can be created for either long-term or short-term use and money can be transferred between accounts very easily. Geac's background in developing software for financial institutions is quite evident in the elegant and effective simplicity of their BUDGET function.

Even after only one year of operations we feel that the Geac Acquisition System is superior to our previous system which had had over 12 years of in-house improvements and modifications. The turmoil of the planning stages, the staff training and the implementation was a reasonable price to pay for the improvements we've gained.

DYNIX

Automated Acquisitions in an Integrated Online System

Pauline J. Iacono

SUMMARY. The Ramsey County Public Library (Roseville, MN) used the OCLC online acquisitions system for six years. While it worked well and was much more efficient than a manual system, it did not provide a way to deliver order information to public services staff and patrons. In 1986 they installed a DYNIX integrated system and in 1987 the DYNIX acquisitions module. All order and "in process" information now appears in the PACs. The features of the DYNIX system are described and the ordering process used by Ramsey County is detailed. The use of the integrated acquisitions system allowed the reorganization of the department, job enrichment opportunities for Library Assistants, and the reassignment of some hours to public services.

THE RAMSEY COUNTY PUBLIC LIBRARY

The Ramsey County Public Library is a suburban library system in the Minneapolis/St. Paul metropolitan area. There are five libraries in the system and the Administrative Offices and Technical Services are in separate, leased quarters.

Pauline J. Iacono is Technical and Computer Services Librarian at the Ramsey County Public Library, 1910 W. County Road B, Roseville, MN 55113.

© 1989 by The Haworth Press, Inc. All rights reserved.

Our selection, acquisitions and cataloging are centralized and we order, catalog and process 10,000 titles and over 60,000 items each year. All types of library materials—books, paperbacks, recordings, periodicals and audio/video materials—are cataloged and all, except videos, may be requested by our patrons.

In 1978 the Library committed itself to a retroconversion project using OCLC, intending to produce a COM catalog to replace the cumbersome and expensive-to-maintain card catalogs. The COM catalog itself was planned to be an interim step to an online catalog some years down the line. The conversion took five long years, but the benefits in later years have been great.

ACQUISITIONS

In 1980, as in many libraries, all materials were ordered using a purely manual acquisitions system. It was labor intensive and difficult to use, whether you wanted to know how much had been spent in an account, or if you simply wanted to know if a title was on order. One of the most constricting parts of the system was that all the ordering information was in only one place—a 3 × 5 card file in the Acquisitions Department. A great deal of staff time was spent filing or pulling slips from those files, or searching to find out what was really on order. A manual fund accounting system was also maintained although it rarely agreed with the account balances we received from the County, where checks were written.

In 1981 we were chosen to be a Beta test site for the new OCLC online acquisitions system. A staff member was sent to Dublin for training and OCLC provided a third OCLC terminal for use with the acquisitions system. Shortly after the installation of the OCLC acquisitions system, Technical Services moved from the headquarters library into leased quarters. One of our OCLC terminals was installed at the headquarters reference desk so they, too, could have access to OCLC information.

The advantages of an online acquisitions system quickly became apparent. We had fund accounting that actually reflected discounts and non-filled orders; we had a fast, online way of knowing what was on order; and, best of all, we had the OCLC database to use as a basis for ordering. But even as we were discovering its advantages, we also saw what it was lacking—a way to get that ordering information into our catalog for everyone to use. The COM catalog was only produced twice a year (with monthly supplements), and while new items were the most in demand by our patrons, they were not listed until they were received and cataloged, often several months later. In addition, we also still had to maintain the manual request or holds system. Request cards were filled out for each title wanted and kept on file in the requests department at the headquarters library which each week conducted "raids" at the branch libraries in order to fill the requests for the system.

Nevertheless, having the information online was better than any access we had ever had before, and since the headquarters library had an OCLC terminal they were able to logon to the acquisitions module and see not only what we already owned, but also what we had on order. In an attempt to also make this information available to the branch libraries, we installed a telephone line directly into the acquisitions department and checked "on orders" for them on demand. We used the OCLC acquisitions module quite successfully for nearly six years. Even though it cost an average of $12,000.00 per year to use, we believed the benefits of the automated system made it worthwhile. When OCLC made the announcement that it was planning to take the system off line our major concern was that it remain for us to use until we had our own system operating.

THE ONLINE SYSTEM

As we planned our ideal online system we had one overriding requirement—that it be integrated. We wanted a system with circulation, cataloging, Public Access Catalog (PAC), acquisitions and serials modules that interacted with each other using data created only once. As it happened we chose the DYNIX system, even though acquisitions and serials were in development and not yet available. We brought our first library up with the circulation module in January of 1986, the other four libraries within four months, and PACs were installed at each location shortly thereafter. We continued to use OCLC acquisitions since the DYNIX module was not yet completed. We had volunteered to be a Beta test site for the DYNIX acquisitions module as soon as it was ready because OCLC had announced a firm date when acquisitions would be taken off line. (Recently, OCLC changed its mind and said acquisitions would remain online indefinitely.)

Since the online catalog in our own system was now available to all staff and patrons, we made the decision to update and download records from OCLC into our system as soon as a title was ordered. At last we had a way (sort of) to let everyone know what was on order. It was particularly important to us because patrons were now able to place their own requests by using the PAC and the circulation module had an extremely efficient request system. With the "on orders" in the PAC we had almost all of the requests automated. There was still no way to handle requests for things we didn't own, but we were confident there would be eventually. Attaching our holding symbol and downloading from OCLC before we had the material in hand (and then being careful to delete it if we couldn't get something) was an extra step for Technical Services, but it was one we were willing to take in order to make the record available in the PAC.

ONLINE INTEGRATED ACQUISITIONS

Fourteen months after the installation of the DYNIX system, in March of 1987, we installed the first version of the DYNIX acquisitions module. In our planning for the conversion to the new module we decided to run the two systems concurrently for six months — using OCLC only to receive or claim items already ordered on it, and using DYNIX for all new orders. The DYNIX acquisitions module has a desiderata file, hierarchical fund accounting, vendor files which also track vendor performance, "order blanks" to speed the ordering process, an electronic interface with Baker and Taylor, online invoice files, and a wide variety of reports.

Desiderata

The Desiderata file was the first thing we discovered about the DYNIX acquisitions module, and our request system was finally complete. The Desiderata file is a place online where requests for materials not in our collection can be requested. It is not available to patrons because we prefer to have a reference librarian research those titles first to see if it would be better to recommend purchase or to request an interlibrary loan. Once the librarian determines that a purchase request should be entered they are asked to fill out a short online form listing as much information as they can find. The Desiderata records do not appear in the PAC, but patron requests can easily be placed on them once the first librarian creates the record. Since it uses the same patron file that the circulation module uses, all that is required is the entry of a barcode.

Each week Technical Services personnel go through the new records in Desiderata, verifying the title and completing whatever information is missing from the record. (We always make certain, for example, that an ISBN number is included since we must have it for our electronic ordering.) The list of new titles is given to the selection librarian, who determines if an item will be ordered, how many copies will be purchased, and which branches will receive them. Order records are created from the Desiderata records which then appear in the PAC and can have requests placed on them by patrons. When the item is received on the system, any patron holds that were attached to the Desiderata record are automatically placed at the head of the holds queue.

Whenever a new, sure-to-be popular title is announced, it is entered into the Desiderata file. Then, when patrons begin to ask for it, requests can be quickly and easily placed. The reference librarians also use the Desiderata file for requesting replacement copies for their locations.

Fund Accounting

Setting up the hierarchical funding in the middle of a fiscal year was a bit tricky, especially since we had funds encumbered on the OCLC system, but after three months we cancelled all remaining orders on OCLC and added those monies to the DYNIX system. We didn't come out quite even at the end of the year, but it was close enough.

On DYNIX we can add money to accounts, transfer funds between accounts, set up notational accounts (for gifts, etc.) and even set up accounts outside of the materials budget. The fund accounting also contains a log of all transactions affecting accounts which can be printed out by date and item, or by account or by operator. If the auditors were ever interested we could keep them busy for days!

Vendor Files

A record is set up for each vendor the library uses. It contains the name and address of the vendor, the name and address of any contact or sales person, discounts, minimum order requirements, our customer number and any contract numbers required for ordering. These records do not have to be created ahead of time. If, while we are ordering, we find a vendor is not in our file, the record can be created on the fly.

Order Blanks

"Order blanks" contain default information required on the order form that we use to avoid having to fill in all the blanks manually. The "order blank" information is merged electronically by the system when ordering. "Order blanks" usually contain the name of the person doing the ordering, the vendor name, the account the item is being charged to and the number of copies being ordered. There may be several for one vendor depending on the kinds of materials being ordered. For example, we have one "order blank" to use when we order adult books from Baker and Taylor and an entirely different one to use when ordering reference books.

Ordering

When we started to use the DYNIX acquisitions system, our practice of updating and downloading OCLC records began to take place even earlier in the ordering process. In any acquisitions system some kind of bibliographic record must be created. A record already in the catalog can be used, or one can be input by hand. Since we were going to need that OCLC record for cataloging later we decided to download it into our system as the first step and use it as the basis for the order record too.

The ordering process, as it has evolved in the last year, is very simple. A library assistant takes the ordering tool to OCLC, finds a record and downloads it into our system. She notes the OCLC number on the review. Our interface loads those records into the DYNIX system in real time, so by the time she has finished she can begin to order. At the DYNIX terminal she chooses the "order blank" appropriate to the items being ordered and begins. A search of our DYNIX catalog by OCLC number locates the appropriate bibliographic record and it is "selected." The system uses the data on that record and the data on the "order blank" to fill in the order record. The only step remaining is to add the cost of the item and change the number of copies if it is more or less than the order blank specified. When the order record is filed in the catalog, the system creates holdings records noting which agency will receive each item ordered, and encumbers the specified fund. The system can encumber the list price, the cost less the stated discount for that vendor, or the list price less the actual discount we seem to be getting from that vendor as shown in the vendor performance data.

Electronic Interface

Purchase orders are then printed and mailed to all vendors except Baker and Taylor. B&T is our major vendor and we have an electronic interface with them. The electronic interface is a marvelous example of software talking to software. The order records, created with DYNIX software, are converted to BISAC records via PKHarmony. Then, using ProComm, we dial the B&T toll free order number and upload our orders using B&T's Acquire software. A few minutes later, a confirmation file for those orders is ready and we download it onto a floppy. After disconnecting from Baker and Taylor, we load the confirmations into our own DYNIX system. We can then look at our order records and immediately see what is being shipped, what is not yet published, what is out of print or what is out of stock. In addition to the advantages of having this information available immediately, we have also found that the delivery time for in stock electronic orders averages eight days. Sometime soon, B&T expects to be able to provide electronic invoicing information as well, which will enable us to download the information we now add manually in the receiving process. We hope that some of our other vendors will begin to offer this service because it saves staff time, and reduces the time it takes to get materials.

Receiving

The receiving process is done in two parts. The actual receiving of materials consists of retrieving the order record and entering the number of copies received. At this point the system changes the status on the holdings records in the catalog to "Just received," and disencumbers and charges the accounts involved. The second part of the process builds the online invoice file. We enter the P.O. number assigned to each title and the actual cost per item from the invoice. Any shipping and handling charges are also entered and the appropriate account is charged. The obvious advantage to an online invoice file is that we have immediate access to detailed information should any questions arise later. Since receiving is done in two parts we are able to use different levels of staff for each process. We can for example, have a page enter the number of copies, and a clerk can do the invoicing later.

Reports

The DYNIX acquisitions system provides many reports on demand. In addition to the fund log mentioned above, it has a New Titles List which gives us an alphabetical listing of all titles received since it was last printed (we provide copies weekly to all our reference desks for patron use), a fund status report, vendor reports (in the printed form it also lists all titles outstanding with any vendor), a list of encumbrances by titles, expenditures by fund, subscription renewals, and a discarded holdings list. The last list can be arranged by agency and used by the branches to see where their holdings are being depleted and need replacing. In addition to the above, our system also has a RECALL function, which lets us create customized reports of any data in the system.

Claiming

The system's claim function can be set to generate automatic or reviewable claims. The library also controls how many claims will be made and at what intervals, and it is possible to review all cancels online before they are actually cancelled. The vendor reports also tell us how many claims have been generated for each vendor, which helps us evaluate the kind of service they offer.

IMPACT ON TECHNICAL SERVICES STAFFING

Because we use OCLC as the source of our bibliographic records, Ramsey County has been able to organize its Technical Services using nonprofessional staff. Currently, there is a full-time Technical Services supervisor, five Library Assistants (two are part-time), five clerks (two are part-time) and three half-time pages.

Until a year ago the department was organized along traditional lines, with one group doing acquisitions and another cataloging and processing. As we began to see how the online system was changing work patterns in Technical Services, it became apparent that other changes could be made as we moved to the new acquisitions module. We decided to merge the two parts of the department and make each library assistant responsible for the ordering and cataloging of one kind of material. The five areas are: adult books, children's books, paperbacks, audiovisual materials, and reference/standing orders/periodicals. Each Library Assistant organizes her workload in whatever way works best for her. One clerk does the receiving and invoicing for everyone and takes care of any returns or invoice inquiries because this seems to work best.

The entire staff of the Technical Services department meets once each week to share information, discuss workflow and other problems because we find that whatever one person does affects everyone else.

Thus far the reorganization has worked well. It provides job enrichment for the Library Assistants by giving them more control over what they do and the acquisitions and cataloging modules have proved so efficient that each of them now spends one day a week in public services. In a year or two we plan to rotate assignments so everyone has an opportunity to experience what it is like to handle another kind of material.

The online system has changed every part of the library. Reference librarians have the latest information available in the catalog. Patrons are learning what a powerful tool the PAC is. The request department has been abolished (the system automatically handled nearly 80,000 requests last year). But no part of the Library has changed as fundamentally as Technical Services. Everything we used to do has had to be evaluated and adjusted. The tedious updating of a COM catalog has been replaced with instant access to a dynamic database; the labor-intensive acquisitions process has been made simple and efficient.

Automated systems are supposed to make one's life easier, and ours certainly has lived up to our expectations. Information about what is "on order" and "in process" is as available as the closest terminal and has become an integral part of our catalog. Materials are ordered, received and processed in weeks instead of months. The workflow through the department has become smooth and even. The Technical Services staff can do their jobs in less time than even before and have the opportunity to be in public services and see why their work is important.

OCLC

Acquisitions—
The Wonders of Automation

Jeanne Harrell

SUMMARY. During the 1980s, many libraries chose to automate their acquisitions department for a variety of reasons. These reasons are noted and applied to a specific academic library's attempts to optimize acquisitions work. The automation planning, implementation, and evaluation processes are examined, specifically as they relate to the implementation of the OCLC Online Acquisitions Subsystem. The resulting organizational changes are discussed, as well as workflow adjustments from preorder searching and ordering to receiving and fund accounting. The author points out certain advantages and disadvantages of the OCLC Acquisitions Subsystem, and explains how the system of choice addressed the objectives of automating acquisitions.

According to Richard Boss, "the primary motives that will prompt libraries to investigate automated acquisitions systems in the 1980's appear to be the hope of realizing cost reduction or cost containment, speeding the receipt of materials, improving fund control, expanding single function systems into integrated systems

---

Jeanne Harrell is Head, Automated Acquisitions, Sterling C. Evans Library, Texas A&M University, College Station, TX 77840.

and being in the forefront of librarianship."[1] This paper explores these objectives for the automation of acquisitions in the context of one library's quest to optimize acquisitions work.

AUTOMATION OF ACQUISITIONS AT TEXAS A&M UNIVERSITY

The administration of Sterling C. Evans Library at Texas A&M University decided to automate the acquisitions process in 1981 using the OCLC Acquisitions Subsystem in order to realize cost containment, to speed the receipt of materials, to improve fund control, to explore the efficiencies of the single record concept, and to be in the forefront of librarianship.

The acquisitions automation process began in 1981 when the Library was selected by OCLC as an evaluator site for the OCLC Acquisitions Subsystem. At the time, OCLC was already in use for catalog card production and interlibrary loan; OCLC had also completed a retrospective conversion project for the Library. After reviewing preliminary documentation from OCLC, it was determined that major changes would be necessary in current procedures and organization in order to perform an adequate test of all aspects of the subsystem.

Since several departments would be affected by any possible change in workflow from preorder searching to voucher typing, a Planning Committee was appointed by the Assistant Director for Collection Development. The committee was composed of the Department Heads of Processing (Cataloging), Copy Cataloging, Monographic Acquisitions, Budget, Resource Development (Materials selection), and Searching. After first attempting to fit the new automated system into the current workflow, the committee determined that a more appropriate goal was "to utilize the system to its potential, disregarding the current organization and workflow processes."[2] Of course, that meant substantial changes in the workflow.

A "Test Group" of twelve staff members from Acquisitions, Resource Development, Budget, and Processing (Cataloging) Divisions evaluated the OCLC Online Acquisitions System from April through June, 1981. During this evaluation process, the participants were temporarily assigned to the Acquisitions Division, where three OCLC terminals and one printer had been installed. The purpose of the group was to determine the potential for improving the existing acquisitions and accounting procedures in the Library. To accomplish this task, the group was:

- To search, order, and receive firm order monographs
- To encumber and expend funds
- To catalog books received

The unusual inclusion of cataloging in this work configuration derived from the need to explore efficiencies of a single record concept. All this was to be accomplished in as few terminal sittings as possible. Figure 1 shows the organization of the Test Group.

After the evaluation period, Library administrators determined that the OCLC Acquisitions Subsystem should be fully implemented. A new department was formed from the nucleus of the Test Group, excluding the Library Assistant from Processing. This group became the Automated Acquisitions Department whose responsibilities include:

- Searching, ordering, and receiving firm order monographs,
- Searching, ordering, and receiving first issues, backfiles, and replacement issues of serials
- Searching, ordering, and receiving special format items such as maps, AV materials, and software
- Encumbering and expending funds
- Producing regular fund reports

The evaluation process revealed that cataloging books immediately on receipt was not feasible because the cataloger had to log off the Acquisitions Subsystem and log onto the Cataloging Subsystem in order to process the books. This change of mode negated any time-saving benefits which could be gained by processing the book upon receipt. Also, the time-consuming task of verifying AACR2 headings when cataloging slowed the process even more.

Several points must be stressed when discussing the evaluation period of the Test Group. First, a major reason for the success of the test and the implementation was the fact that the staff involved were

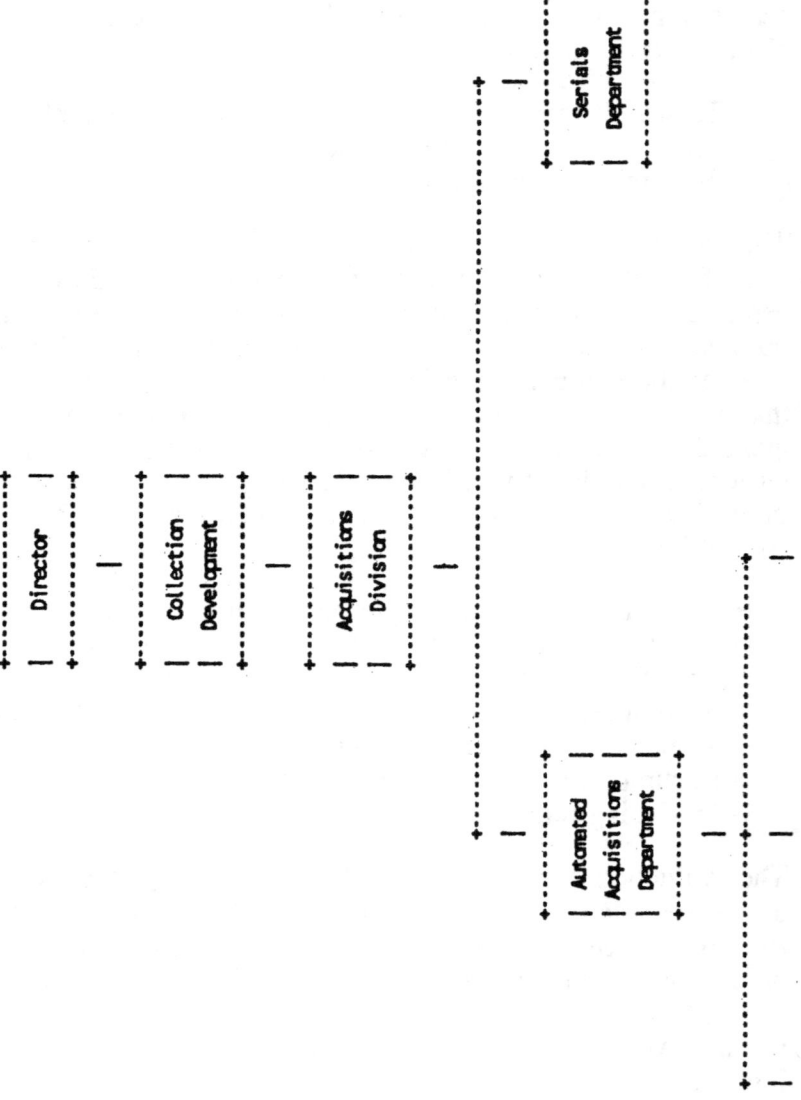

Figure 1. Original Organization Chart of Automated Acquisitions

```
+------------------+  +------------------+  +------------------+
| LA II  RD        |  | Clerk III ACQ    |  | LA II ACQ (S)    |
| (Ordering)       |  | (Reclassed from  |  | (Receiving)      |
|                  |  | Clerk II-Financial)|                   |
+------------------+  +------------------+  +------------------+

+------------------+  +------------------+  +------------------+
| Clerk III ACQ(S) |  | Clerk I    B     |  | Clerk II ACQ(M)  |
| (Ordering)       +- + (Financial Asst.)+- + (Receiving)      |
+------------------+  +------------------+  +------------------+

+------------------+                        +------------------+
| Clerk II ACQ     |                        | Clerk II ACQ(S)  |
| (New Position)   +-                       + (Receiving)      |
| (Ordering)       |                        |                  |
+------------------+                        +------------------+

+------------------+                        +------------------+
| Clerk II ACQ (M) |                        | Clerk II ACQ(S)  |
| (Ordering)       +-                       + (Receiving)      |
+------------------+                        +------------------+

+------------------+                        +------------------+
| Clerk II ACQ (M) |                        | Clerk II ACQ(S)  |
| (Correspondence) +-                       + (Ser. Claimer)   |
+------------------+                        +------------------+
```

KEY

RD - Resource Development
ACQ (S) - Acquisitions, Serials
ACQ (M) - Acquisitions, Monographs
B - Budget Office

included in the planning. Administrators sought staff input from the inception of the idea through its implementation. Second, thorough and ongoing training was provided. Professional staff was available to answer questions as they arose. Third, the staff could see the value of the new system in terms of making the acquisitions process more efficient and effective. If the staff "buy in" to the new system, the implementation will be accomplished much more smoothly.

Predictably, there were problems. One problem cited in the Test Group was the use of too much OCLC and bibliographic jargon with staff who were not familiar with the terms. Time has made many of these new terms familiar and common to Automated Acquisitions staff. Production time slowed down briefly because the group of twelve were sharing only three terminals. Until specific procedures could be worked out, certain bottlenecks occurred. Lastly, the professional staff had to be available constantly for questions until the self-confidence and knowledge base of the Test Group developed.

WORKFLOW USING THE OCLC ACQUISITIONS SUBSYSTEM

After seven years, certain adjustments have been made to the organization as depicted in Figure 1. These changes are displayed in Figure 2. The changes were made in order to address two issues. First, media-specific requirements imposed by the State caused a media approach to be more appropriate. Second, it was determined that two units, each headed by a Library Assistant II, worked more effectively together than three sections, one of which has been headed by a Financial Clerk III. As shown in Figure 2, the Financial Clerk III has become a part of the Serial/Financial Section, thereby providing a secondary supervisory level should the LAII be unavailable. It is hoped that the NAD/Maps position can be upgraded from a Clerk II to a Clerk III in order to provide this same secondary supervisory level for the Monographic/Special Formats Sections.

The workflow for items to be acquired by the Library can be traced most logically by following the path of request cards for needed items. The request card (Figure 3) is filled out either by persons outside the Library (faculty, students) or by one of the three Bibliographers in the Resource Development Division. Classified staff search the request to be sure the Library has not already acquired the item. Then, request cards are given to the Bibliographer in charge of Social Science, Humanities, or Science and Technology. If the bibliographer decides that the Library should acquire the item, he/she assigns an OCLC fund code (i.e., HUM88).

Preorder Searching

After preorder searching is done by the Resource Development Division personnel, the request card is given to a Clerk in Acquisitions (NAD/Maps Clerk on organization chart). This clerk uses established guidelines in determining the best source for materials to be ordered. Although OCLC has an extensive vendor file, the Name Address Directory Clerk must often enter new vendor records. Once the record is entered, it is available to any OCLC user with NAD authorization. The NAD number is then written on the request card and the card is placed in a "To Be Ordered" box by the OCLC terminals. The cards/orders are processed on a first in/first out basis. Rush items are given to a terminal operator to be ordered immediately.

Ordering

The ordering clerks and student workers search the OCLC database for the most appropriate bibliographic record on which to order the item. If not found on the database, an "O" (Ordering) level record is input by the Library Assistant II. This "O" level record can be used by other libraries for ordering purposes, but cannot be used for cataloging except by libraries with authorization to update "O" level records. Libraries are allowed to update their own "O" level records to full cataloging records.

The ordering process is fairly simple once the appropriate record has been located. Figure 4 is the OCLC Acquisitions screen display. The fixed field area is changed to show STATUS: ordered (only six characters are allowed); FORMS: (number of copies for the library), (number of copies to be sent to the vendor). The Name Address Directory number is typed into the SOURCE field, and the

Figure 2. Current Organization Chart of the Acquisitions Division

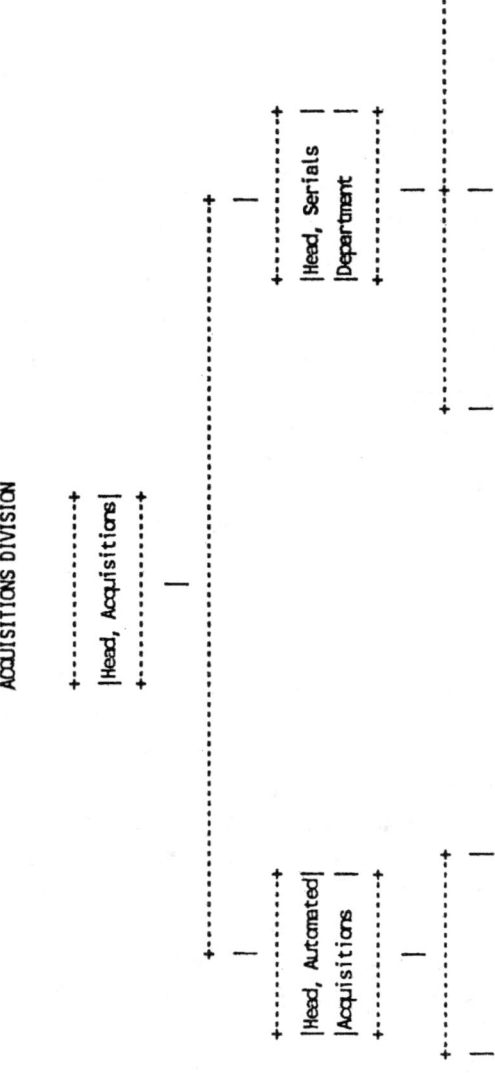

```
+------------------+  +---------------------+
|Mono & Spec Form  |  |Ser. & Financial     |
|LA II             |  |LA II                |
+------------------+  +---------------------+
        |                      |
    +--+-----------+       +--+-----------+
    |  |NAD, Maps  |       |  |Financial  |
    |  |Clerk II   |       |  |Clerk III  |
    |  +-----------+       |  +-----------+
    |                      |
    +--+-----------+       +--+-----------+
    |  |Ordering   |       |  |Receiving  |
    |  |Clerk II   |       |  |Clerk II   |
    |  +-----------+       |  +-----------+
    |                      |
    +--+---------------+   +--+-----------+
    |  |Mono-Ord/PP/Ret|   |  |Receiving  |
    |  |Clerk II       |   |  |Clerk II   |
    |  +---------------+   |  +-----------+
    |                      |
    +--+---------------+   +--+---------------+
    |  |Special Formats|   |  |Tel/Ser Order  |
    |  |Clerk II       |   |  |Clerk II       |
    |  +---------------+   |  +---------------+
    |
    +--+---------------+
       |Mono-Receiving |
       |Clerk II       |
       +---------------+

+-----------------------+  +---------------+  +---------------+
|Serial Bibliographic   |  |Acme Records   |  |Binding Dept.  |
|Records- LA II (1/2)   |  |LA II (1/2)    |  |LA II          |
+-----------------------+  +---------------+  +---------------+
        |                         |
    +--+-------------+        +--+-------------+  +-----------+
    |  |Title Change |        |  |Acme Checker |  |Bindery    |
    |  |Clerk III    |        |  |Clerk III    |  |Clerk III  |
    |  +-------------+        |  +-------------+  +-----------+
    |                         |
    +--+---------------+      +--+-------------+  +-----------+
    |  |Added Volumes  |      |  |Acme Checker |  |Bindery    |
    |  |Clerk II       |      |  |Clerk II     |  |Clerk II   |
    |  +---------------+      |  +-------------+  +-----------+
    |                         |
    +--+-----------+          +--+-------------+  +-----------+
       |Printout   |          |  |Acme Checker |  |Bindery    |
       |Clerk II   |          |  |Clerk II     |  |Clerk I    |
       +-----------+          |  +-------------+  +-----------+
                              |
                              +--+-------------+  +-----------+
                              |  |Mail Checker |  |Bindery    |
                              |  |Clerk I      |  |Clerk I    |
                              |  +-------------+  +-----------+
                              |
                              +--+---------------+  +-----------------+
                                 |Serials Claims |  |Bindery          |
                                 |Clerk II       |  |Clerk I(1/2 time)|
                                 +---------------+  +-----------------+
```

Figure 3. Monographic Request Card

REQUEST FORM

Rush ______

Set in Progress ______

Order Number ______ Dept. ______ Acct. Fund ______

CALL #

Author

Title

Edition

No. of Vols.
Vol. No.

Publisher and Address

Year of Pub.

No. of Copies

Price

Source
o/p Catalog No. ______ Item No. ______

Requested by: ______

Notify:

Phone:

Dept. Representative

1 2 3
Priority

FOR LIBRARY USE ONLY

ISBN ______

LCCN ______

OCLC NO. ______

OCLC ______ ALIS ______

Public Catalog ______

Approval File ______

Not in lib.	Added copy
Copy in lib.	Added vol.
On order	Diff. Edition

SERIALS RECORDS

Active	Inactive
Analyzed	Cat. Sep.

BIP Sup.	Other
FCB	Pub. Cat.

For BIP ______

SEARCHED UNDER:

_____ NUC _____
_____ MANSELL _____
_____ MARC F _____
_____ OCLC _____
_____

SERIES: Traced   Not Traced

_____

REQUEST RECEIVED: _____ ORDERED: _____
APPROVED: _____ ITEM RECEIVED: _____
SEARCHED: _____ CATALOGED: _____

Figure 4. OCLC Acquisitions Screen

```
NO HOLDINGS IN TXA - FOR IN-PROCESS ENTER dip DEPRESS  DISPLAY RECD SEND
OCLC: 15789528        Ord#: NEW           Entrd: 880418  Used: 880418
Type: a  Bib lvl: m   Freq:      Lang: eng  Class:  /  /    Stat: __
Repr:    Enc lvl: 8   Mtrl:      Ctry: nyu  Forms: 1,1  Plan:
  1 010    87-12390
  2 040    DLC |c DLC |d m/c
  3 020    1555700160 : |c $39.95
  4 245 04 The How-to-do-it manual for small libraries / |c edited by
Bill Katz.
  5 260 0  New York : |b Neal-Schuman Publishers, |c 1987.
  6 300    p. cm.
  7 700 10 Katz, William A., |d 1924- |w cn
  8 SOURCE   |a
  9 DESTIN   |a    |c
 10 ORDER    880418
 11 ENCUMBR  |a |b    |d    |e
 12 RECEIPT  |b
 13 EXPEND   |a |b    |d    |e
 14 INVOICE  |b |c    |d
 15 CLAIM    |a
 16 VERIFY   OCLC |b t
 17 REQUEST  |a
 18 REMARKS  |a
```

DESTIN is filled in with the appropriate three character code abbreviated from the full address of the receiving section. The ENCUMBER line is completed to show the fund assigned by the Resource Development bibliographer, the amount to be encumbered, and the number of copies to be ordered. If any special ordering instructions are required, the message is typed into SOURCE subfield f. Some examples could be "Send only volume 2" or "Catalog item no. 125." The last field on the screen is the REMARKS line. This field is used for the initials of the person placing the order and for any notes which must be transferred from the request card, such as "Notify Dr. Jones at 5-1342," "Rush for Reference," "Stevens gift plate," or which Fiscal account number needs to be stamped on the invoice if it is a seldom used account. When the terminal operator taps [PRODUCE] and [SEND], the record reappears with a purchase order automatically supplied.

The orders are transmitted via DX (direct electronic transmission) to the vendors, or the printed action forms are printed once a day in Dublin, Ohio, and mailed to the appropriate vendor, based on the NAD number entered on the record. Originally, the Library filled "2,2" in the FORMS fixed field area to request that two action forms be sent to the Library and two to the vendor. One of the Library forms was filed in the Public Catalog as an "On Order" notice, and one form stayed with the request card until the item was received and processed. That form was then used as a temporary shelf list card until the OCLC shelf list card was filed. First, the Public Catalog "On Order" filing was discontinued; then OCLC decided to change the format of the action form. Rather than the old form, which lent itself to folding into a 3 × 5 size, the new action forms are 8 1/2 × 11. At that point, the Acquisitions (in consultation with Processing and Resource Development) began ordering only the two forms to send to the vendor. The Processing Department now uses scratch cards for shelf list stops. Ordering an action form for the Library is now the exception rather than the rule. The new procedure has reduced OCLC printing costs and eliminated some unnecessary paper.

After the ordering is completed, the request card is placed in an in-process file, arranged by purchase order number, until the material is received. OCLC automatically assigns a unique purchase order number beginning with the year and followed by its next consecutive number. The numbering starts over every January with YY-1 (88-1, 88-2, etc.). The purchase order number is indexed. Indexing makes the order record retrievable not only by author, title, etc., but also by its unique order number prefaced by an asterisk. Unlike the Cataloging Subsystem in which an edited record returns to its unedited version when searched later, the edited acquisitions record remains the way it was edited when searched later by any applicable search term.

Receiving

The receipt process is also quite straightforward. The Monographic Receiving Clerk opens boxes addressed to the Monographic Ordering Section (an address set up in the OCLC ACQ profile and triggered by the three character code in DESTIN). Ideally, there is a copy of the action form in the book or the purchase order number for each item is typed on the invoice. The Clerk then pulls the request card from the in-process file and places it in the item to await terminal processing.

At the terminal, the Clerk retrieves the record by purchase order number and begins the receiving process. The STATUS: is changed to "receiv" or "recprt" (received partially). The EXPEND line is filled in to indicate the fund to be used and the amount actually on the invoice. OCLC provides subfields in the EXPEND line to show the number of copies received, postage, and handling charges. The Acquisitions Subsystem automatically multiplies or adds the appropriate subfields and places the total cost in subfield f. An INVOICE line is filled in to show the invoice number, date, and date expended. A RECEIPT line may also be filled in if a set is only partially received or if other receipt information seems necessary.

When the information is complete, the terminal operator taps [UPDATE] and [SEND] and the appropriate fund is immediately adjusted. The Receiving Clerk also flags the books as to the type of bibliographic copy she discovered (DLC, cooperative cataloging, "O" level), and the book proceeds to Resource Development for pre-catalog searching. Some DLC books are given to the Library Assistant II in charge of Monographs/Special formats for copy cataloging. Following certain Processing Division guidelines, she is allowed to "quick catalog" monographs to be located in the stacks which have straightforward LC call numbers and no series statements.

The Receiving clerk also stamps the invoices with several stamps: date processed, date received, Fiscal account number, media type (mono, serial, etc.), and initials the date processed stamp. If the purchase order number does not appear on the invoice, it is also written above the date processed.

Special formats, such as AV materials and maps, are ordered and received by the same clerks because many of those items have additional paperwork (e.g., purchase requisitions if the materials ordered from any one vendor exceed $250.00). For purchase requisition items, the OCLC order is updated rather than produced, because the order must be processed via a bid from the Central Purchasing Office.

Serials also have special requirements. The same purchase order number is retained on the record until the vendor for the item changes or the maximum of seven screens are filled with data. Then a new purchase order number is initiated. New EXPEND and INVOICE lines are added yearly, and the RECEIPT lines indicate the year or volume paid for.

After monographic items are cataloged and the permanent shelf list cards are filed, processing staff change the STATUS: to "complit." Six months later the order record will be purged from the online system; serial records remain indefinitely.

Fund Accounting

In terms of fund accounting, OCLC allows an unlimited number of funds to be tracked online. Funds can be encumbered and expended on title records, and the accounting program will automatically adjust the fund accordingly. Lump sum expenditures can be processed on individual funds. At any point in time, the fund record can be retrieved to look at the allocation, encumbrances, expenditures, free balance, and cash balance. Encumbrance and Expenditures limits can be set in dollars or in percentages, so that if an order will overencumber a fund, the screen will display a warning that the fund is overencumbered. Overencumbrances can be overridden on the system, but overexpenditures cannot.

Because a moment-by-moment update of the financial information is available, Acquisitions personnel created a method of downloading the name of the fund and the one line which contains the current status of the fund: allocation, encumbrances, expenditures, free balance, and cash balance. This downloading is accomplished on an M300 and manipulated on an IBM-XT using Lotus 1-2-3. The result is a three-page summary fund report and an extended version which reports on the activity in every fund requiring review by the bibliographers in Resource Development. This report is compiled on a biweekly basis and takes only two hours or less to prepare.[3]

The OCLC Acquisitions Subsystem also allows the printing of claim and cancellation action forms by simply changing the status of the record to "clmmat" for claiming materials, "clminv" for claiming missing invoices, and "cancel" for cancellation of orders. The forms are also printed and mailed from Dublin, Ohio. Not all correspondence can be accommodated by the OCLC Acquisition System, but it does reduce the number of letters to be typed. The extensive use of PCs has further automated the Acquisitions Division.[4]

ADVANTAGES AND DISADVANTAGES OF OCLC ACQ

Many of the advantages were evident as the workflow was discussed, but others need to be mentioned as well. Staff time has been saved by automating the accounting process and the ability to view current fund balances as necessary. In addition, OCLC provides offline products, such as the monthly Fund Commitment Record and the Fund Activity Record. Available on microfiche or paper, the activity on each OCLC fund is reported. The list is arranged alphabetically by fund name, and, within each fund, the arrangement is by vendor and then by purchase order number. For archival purposes and various management and problem-solving purposes, these offline products are invaluable.

A second advantage is the ability to view the on-order file from any OCLC terminal. Library staff and patrons can search by title and determine whether a needed item has been ordered. A third advantage for this Library is the fact that all cataloged material and on-order materials are on the same system. When an order is being placed, the terminal operator can look in the upper left corner of the screen and determine at a glance whether the title has already been acquired because TXA will appear there if the item has been cataloged. If the item has already been ordered, but not received, the order record will be retrieved. This integration of the cataloging and ordering systems is a definite advantage of OCLC for Evans Library.

A fourth advantage is the reduction of repetitive keying made possible by the OCLC database. Since the bibliographic data is often already on the screen, only the ordering information must be input. A related advantage is the "constant data" feature. A constant data screen can be set up with ordering or receiving details which apply to several items. By utilizing this feature, the same information can be overlayed onto the order display, thereby saving many keystrokes.

Another related advantage for payments on serial records is the fact that only three lines need to be added to each title screen if the vendor remains the same. This serial expenditure advantage is further enhanced by "constant data" because many of the multiple-item invoices are quite lengthy, so the invoice information and fund name remains the same on each record. Only the volume or year received and the exact cost changes from title to title.

One disadvantage is the expense of using OCLC Acquisitions. The current maintenance fee for an M300 terminal is $504 per year, and the telecommunication fee is $1320 per year for a terminal on a dedicated line connection. There is a charge of $1.21 each time the [Update] [Send] or [Produce][Send] keys are used for a "First Time Use." Printing or transmitting of orders to vendors incurs an additional charge per order. Offline products, such as the monthly microfiche copy of the funds, are an additional cost, as well as the less obvious cost of computer space.

A second disadvantage—response time—is one common to all OCLC users. The response time fluctuates from micro-seconds to several minutes depending on the use of the database, etc. This factor makes it difficult to estimate time needed to accomplish work.

A third disadvantage is related to the use of different modes for acquisitions and cataloging. One must log off the acquisitions subsystem and log onto the cataloging subsystem in order to edit the bibliographic record and produce catalog cards. This aspect of the system originally caused the Acquisitions Division to decide against integrating copy cataloging with receipt of materials.

A fourth disadvantage is the fact that reports cannot be generated as part of the online system. Any reports must be produced by the individual libraries using their resources. Evans Library is fortunate to be able to apply certain software packages and expertise to create its own reports. When OCLC first decided to abandon the Acquisitions Subsystem, OCLC produced a one-time report of purchase orders arranged by status. This valuable report would be especially useful if provided periodically, once or twice a year. Vendor reports, which would be valuable as well, are not provided by the current system.

CONCLUSIONS

In terms of Boss's motivations for automating acquisitions, the automation project at Texas A&M University might be evaluated as follows:

- Cost containment: OCLC Acquisitions is very expensive both in online fees and in the number and level of personnel required to operate it. However, other benefits, such as the existence of one file with all holdings and the quick cataloging program, do justify the cost.
- Speeding the receipt of materials: Especially in its DX version, the use of OCLC ACQS has made receipt of materials expeditious.
- Improving fund control: While the control of funds is excellent, the lack of any ability to manipulate the information to produce reports is frustrating. The necessity for pulling information from a PC to get meaningful management information is not as efficient as some other systems.
- Expanding into integrated system: The availability of on order

information in the same file with cataloged materials has been invaluable to the Library.
- Being in the forefront of librarianship: As a test site for the system, the Evans Library gained high visibility in its use of the system. Further, many presentations and publications have resulted. This body of scholarship has contributed to the Library's reputation as an innovator and leader in librarianship.

Although no systems are perfect, the OCLC Acquisitions Subsystem has provided Evans Library the opportunity to improve its services and streamline its acquisitions procedures. It is indeed unfortunate that the Online Acquisitions Subsystem as we now know it will be modified to eliminate fund accounting when the new OCLC software is put in place. The ACQ350 microcomputer version may be viable for smaller libraries, but large libraries are forced to seek alternatives.

REFERENCES

1. Boss, Richard W., "Issues in Automating Acquisitions," in *Issues in Library Management* (White Plains, NY: Knowledge Industry Publications, 1984), p. 40.
2. Cook, Colleen, "Panel Discussion on Workflows and Staffing of OCLC ACQs Users" OCLC Acquisitions Users Group meeting. ALA Annual Conference, Philadelphia, June, 1982.
3. St. Clair, Gloriana and Nancy Bolland, "A 3-Step Process for Fund Reporting," *OCLC Micro*, 1, no.2 (May 1985), pp. 12-15.
4. Harrell, Jeanne and Gloriana St. Clair, "Revolutionizing Acquisitions Productivity with PCs," *Technicalities*, 7, no.10 (Oct. 1987), pp. 3-7.

MICROCOMPUTER APPLICATIONS

Microcomputer Based Inhouse Acquisitions Program

Helen M. Shuster

SUMMARY. Automated acquisitions programs should be responsive to the needs of individual libraries, incorporating bibliographic, financial and local information with the flexibility to manipulate this data in whatever way is desired by the library. Inhouse microcomputer programs can be developed from generic database software packages such as dBase III+ with excellent results. Worcester Polytechnic Institute's Gordon Library developed a dBase III+ system which answers all management needs relative to budget and collection development as well as providing a streamlined process for purchase and receipt of materials. Various aspects of the design/development process including staffing, level of expertise, time and support are reviewed in addition to a description of the many capabilities of the database itself, such as detailed and hierarchical cost accounting, management reports, claiming control and collection analysis. The total acquisitions program is described briefly showing how the database interacts with the various steps required in an efficient system.

Helen M. Shuster is Head of Technical Services and Automation, George C. Gordon Library, Worcester Polytechnic Institute, Worcester, MA 01609.

A good automated acquisitions program should be flexible enough to manipulate the central database to extract (in detail or in summary form) all the information necessary for management decisions on budget and collection development as well as providing a streamlined process for the actual purchase and receipt of materials. The system developed at the Gordon Library of Worcester Polytechnic Institute (WPI) was in response to the need for both information and efficiency. Even though the library was a member of a multi-library automated network looking towards a totally integrated system, and already used an online circulation system with a public access catalog as the next component, there were many reasons to automate the acquisitions process independently without waiting for an acquisitions module to be developed by the vendor of the online system.

This paper will discuss the issues involved in setting up and implementing an inhouse system using off the shelf relational database and spreadsheet software (specifically dBase III+ and Lotus 1-2-3 at WPI) on a hard disk microcomputer; describe the database design, design process, what can be accomplished with the existing structure; and finally review the major procedures involved in the total acquisitions program and how these interact with the database.

The main reasons for developing an inhouse acquisitions system at WPI were the need to do the following:

—Document expenditures for budgetary control in a precise, efficient and expeditious fashion.
—Justify expenditures to higher administration officers.
—Predict future expenses.
—Evaluate and relate recent acquisitions to the total collection.
—Access and manipulate any piece of the acquisitions data to provide quick answers to budget or bibliographic questions.
—Produce easily created multifaceted reports.
—Maintain tighter control over steps in the acquisitions process.

In developing the system two years ago we knew that we would not be able to link with a major bibliographic source for the automatic transfer of acquisitions data, nor would we be able to access cost information in a similar manner. However, these considerations were less of a priority because there were good sources for this information in the library. OCLC has been used for years to verify acquisitions orders along with various print catalogs for price information and even though this data had to be input manually, it was the flexible manipulation of the data for management purposes that was the top priority. Since that time we have purchased a software package called OCLANG which does transfer the OCLC data into the database via download onto floppy disk. Some libraries might want the on order information located in the public access catalog and this was also not possible. In actual fact, the WPI reference staff preferred not to have on order information accessible to users as it usually caused more confusion than it was worth.

All of the initial needs were met by the local inhouse system which was created using dBase III+ and Lotus 1-2-3 on a 20 megabyte hard disk AT&T 6300 microcomputer.

TIME

One of the most crucial considerations is the time factor. It is important to allow plenty of time to learn new software, especially if programming is needed and this needs to be learned by library staff because there is no one else around to do it. Professional staff must be willing to spend additional after work hours if necessary to concentrate on the programming, prepare documentation or whatever else needs to be done to meet a deadline. Hours must be specifically assigned as well as allowed to support staff to work on the project. The regular work of the department has to continue as well as planning for the new system and it is important not to overload support staff. Most of the burden, therefore, must be borne by the professionals, or more lead-in time must be allowed for.

How much time is required to create and implement the program depends, to a certain extent, on the level of expertise within the library or whether there are other experts available to assist or write programs. Our level of expertise was minimal three years ago when we began. We had used an Apple III microcomputer with an inhouse program designed by two undergraduates to interact with Visicalc. The program was very basic and inflexible but it did make us very aware of what we wished it would do, so that a year later we were able to build this wish list into the program. There were three staff members involved at the beginning—the Head of Technical Services and the two support staff who ran the acquisitions area on a daily basis. We had brand new IBM compatible hardware which required MS DOS as its operating system. This in itself was very different from the Apple III which had a built-in operating system so we had to become familiar with DOS commands and the whole concept of an operating system. None of us had used database software so all the concepts, functions and commands of dBase III were completely new territory. One of the support staff had some experience in BASIC programming. We did receive some instruction during the first month after the purchase of dBase III, but all the design and programming was done by the three library staff.

We received the hardware in January, the software in April. The goal was to implement an acquisitions program on July 1 for the new fiscal year. The support staff were very eager to participate and create a really useful program and their input was invaluable, but it took many, many hours to learn dBase and Lotus, understand what they each could do, design the database structure and then learn and implement dBase programming. We were ready on July 1, but in retrospect it would have been easier to allow more time to learn and create the programs. Six months would have been better than three, given the lack of expertise within the library and the unavailability of assistance from elsewhere.

SUPPORT

Many kinds of support are needed when planning a new system. First and foremost, support of the library director is required to encourage and agree to the proposed program. Verbal support alone is insufficient so that the director must either have money in the budget, or be willing to seek additional dollars from the administration or elsewhere. This might be immediate or be included in the following year's budget request. Most often large expenditures require written justification and librarians need to be prepared to think through the entire project and use the envisioned end products to justify purchase of expensive hardware and software. If other uses can be made of the hardware and software at a later date, so much the better.

It is vital to have the support of staff involved in the project. This type of support means involvement, not just lip service. Active involvement in the form of discussions, input of ideas and use of these ideas generally will ensure enthusiasm and cooperation. Support staff or other staff involved in the process being automated are often all too painfully aware of shortcomings of the manual system and are delighted to contribute suggestions of what needs to be done, even if they do not immediately see how it will be achieved. A system chosen or designed by a supervisor who will not use it on a daily basis is never as well received or as well designed as one where the staff are really and truly involved in the choice and who have the opportunity to choose between alternatives. They are much more willing to accept inadequacies if they have been involved from the beginning and see where compromises must be made. It is then their system and one which they are eager to use and, if possible, improve on and enhance.

Hardware and software support would be ideal, but unfortunately there is a wide disparity in the interpretation of both these types of support. Ideally, hardware support should involve assistance in the initial set up and ongoing maintenance. Software support should involve training and assistance throughout the project. If some training in the software can be acquired it should help considerably.

Software manuals are useful to a point depending on their organization, indexing, clarity, etc. It is extremely useful to purchase two or three additional "how to" books which often clarify concepts and functions that are totally incomprehensible in the official manuals and which give better examples and explanations. Several of Alan Simpson's dBase books[1,2] are good as well as Karl Beiser's *Essential guide to dBase III + in Libraries*.[3] Many of these books can be found on the shelves of local bookstores in the computer section.

Local documentation is also very important to the success of the program. It is necessary to create step-by-step instructions for staff members on many of the processes involved. After a while these step-by-step instructions may no longer be used for every day functions, but they are still very important for those processes only performed once a month or more infrequently. In addition, it is extremely useful to record all the program names and contents which match specific databases as well as recording the names of indexes and how and when these should be used. Instructions on how to produce reports, which indexes to set and which conditions to give are really important. When multiple reports are developed, each with a different content and purpose, it is impossible to remember what each report produces unless carefully recorded. Sometimes reports are recreated because even the name is forgotten.

STAFFING

Staffing is also critical to the success of the endeavor. There needs to be one librarian in charge with sufficient enthusiasm and energy to produce results. Equally important is the enthusiasm and motivation to achieve on the part of the support staff. Staff with a thorough knowledge of every step in the manual process are invaluable to the design phase, especially if they are looking for a better way to accomplish new or existing goals rather than recreating the manual system. As mentioned before, it is important to allow enough time to accomplish specific goals so that staff do not get overwhelmed by the problems of coping with the daily workload in addition to learning and designing the new system. Although two support staff were involved in the design phase at WPI, one support staff and the Head of Technical Services accomplished most of the design project and one full time staff member manages the whole program.

CHOICE OF HARDWARE AND SOFTWARE

The hardware and software used were chosen because the Office of Academic Computing at WPI supported them both in terms of hardware discounts and maintenance, and in a software discount. Why choose dBase III+ rather than Lotus 1-2-3 as the foundation for the program? In working with the two software programs we realized we needed the greater ability of a database software rather than the spreadsheet capabilities of Lotus. Lotus does have some database capability but was more difficult to manipulate and edit and the report-producing functions of dBase were exactly what was required. Lotus is used for presentation and manipulation of financial data after it is interfaced from dBase.

DESIGN OF THE DATABASE

In designing the database it is vital to begin by asking what it is you want to do. What types of reports are needed or might be anticipated? What types of information are needed as access points? How might you need to search the database? Do order slips need to be printed? Could an accessions list be printed from the database? If so, what information should it contain? How sophisticated should the monthly budget report be and how should the information be summarized and presented? For example, if you want to produce reports by date of publication it is important to isolate that information by building a field into the database structure for date of publication so that the program can identify and organize reports based on date of publication. Including publication date in the same field as publisher makes the date impossible to index and sort in dBase III+. What other types of reports or groupings of information are needed? Is it important to compare vendor turnaround time? If so, then a field for date of order must be included as well as a date of receipt. It would be no good to have one date field and change the information from encumbered date to paid date when the item is received because then the comparison data would be lost. In a similar fashion if it is important to compare encumbered with actual paid amounts, two fields must be created to contain these two separate pieces of cost information and the encumbered amount must remain in place even after the item is received.

The database structure in use today is not the same as the original. The design changed as more was learned about the software and the needs of the program. This design is described in more detail in an earlier article in *Library Acquisitions: Practice and Theory*.[4] One of the advantages of this type of program is that as needs change or new requirements are discovered, staff can readily adapt the structure or write programs to accommodate these needs instead of relying on outside commercial concerns who may not be at all interested in adapting software to fit the needs of a single library.

The structure may undergo further changes. Staff prefer the current structure where all the information for a single order is in one record rather than in several related databases. Each item ordered has, therefore, its own record in the database which uses three types of fields—Character, Numeric and Date. Character fields are used for text; Numeric fields are for dollar amounts where mathematical functions can be performed; and Date fields are associated with equivalent Character fields so that orders, payments, and claims can be tracked by date (see Figure 1).

Many aspects of the total acquisitions process were taken into account in the design of the WPI program so that it could be multifunctional and answer the many interlinked but different needs involved in the acquisition and evaluation of materials. These aspects are discussed in the two main sections of Management Needs and Operational Needs.

MANAGEMENT NEEDS

Budget Objectives

- Input and edit cost information for each title ordered.
- Maintain up-to-date fiscal information with the ability to provide almost instant answers to many financial questions.
- Produce monthly budget reports grouped by department and fund.
- Extract information for various kinds of financial analysis.
- Produce multifaceted financial reports.

Discussion

It is always important to know the financial history of an item from the date of encumbrance to the date of payment. Each item ordered needs its own specific financial history. A single title order can have several different costs from the time of placing the order to the time of payment for receipt of the item. We wanted to include a field for the anticipated encumbered amount, but be able to change this if a different advertised price was listed on the invoice. A field for the actual cost was needed in addition to the encumbered field. In this way, actual discounts could be more precisely evaluated by

DATABASE STRUCTURE

Field Name	Type	Width	Description
REC NO	N	5	Record number
COPIES	N	2	Number of copies ordered
PO	C	6	Purchase Order number
OCLC	C	10	OCLC number
TYPE	C	3	Type of material – book, A/V etc.
AUTHOR	C	60	Name of single or corporate author
TITLE1	C	60	Title of item ordered, with
TITLE2			additional fields for long title
PUBLISHER	C	30	Name of publisher
YEAR	C	5	Date of publication
EDITION	C	30	Edition number
CALL	C	30	Call number
SUBJECT	C	18	Subject which matches call number
REQ	C	20	Name of person ordering
VENDOR	C	10	Name of vendor
DEPT	C	10	Department of person ordering
FUND	C	3	Fund code
ENCUMB	N	10	Dollar figure for amount encumbered
DORDER	D	8	Date ordered
DCATALOG	D	8	Date cataloged
DPAID	D	8	Date invoice paid
NET	N	10	Dollar figure for amount spent
INVOICE	C	15	Invoice mnemonics
CREDIT	N	10	Dollar figure for credit
CRDP	D	8	Date credit recorded
TOTAL88	N	10	Sum of NET-CREDIT
STATUS	C	10	Status of item reported by vendor
SDATE	D	8	Date of status report
REINDATE	D	8	Date of reinstatement after cancel
CLAIM1	D	8	Date of first claim
CLAIM2	D	8	Date of second claim

FIGURE 1. Database structure.

comparing costs in the encumbered field with costs in the paid field. For items where credits were necessary because of damaged items returned or an incorrect title received, a field for the credit amount was created. Finally, we wanted to summarize the final cost per item in a field which would total net and credit amounts. This would be used for reports.

When the initial record for an item to be ordered is created, the encumbered amount is entered and remains there permanently as does the date of the order. The actual purchase price is entered on receipt of the item as well as the date paid and invoice information. Credits and credit dates are recorded in a similar fashion. An inhouse program verifies the accuracy of input in a matter of seconds so that staff can quickly check the total invoice amount with the dBase total. Once a month, or whenever is necessary, an inhouse program is activated which calculates the actual expenditure for each item and places the sum of NET-CREDIT in the total for the year field.

A monthly accounting report does not need to include detailed information on each item ordered. What we needed was to produce a printed report which summarized expenditures, encumbrances, etc. by fund, and within fund, by department and was created automatically without further keying in of data. The process involves summarizing the costs in dBase and then exporting this summary into a Lotus spreadsheet already set with formulas to calculate the monthly totals, balance remaining, etc. (Table 1).

With date fields specified for each type of cost, reports extracting information on amounts spent or encumbered for certain narrow or broad periods of time can be produced. Answers to questions such as how much did we spend during the past three months on the Math department or how much did we encumber last week can easily be made available in a few seconds or minutes with a few simple commands.

Other types of reports might include departmental lists of titles and their cost and/or encumbrance; comparisons of vendor discounts; lists of costs by call number or by subject; estimate of future costs with percentage increases or decreases either by department, call number, subject, etc. All of these reports and others can readily be produced using a standard report form provided that each type of

TABLE 1. Monthly summary for monographs, January, 1987.

DEPT	ALLOC	ENCUMB	TOTSPENT	BALANCE	TOTJAN	JULYSPENT	TOTSPENT2
ARL	0	4764.18	1651.09	-6415.27	388.25	0	1651.09
ART	900	218.75	0	681.25	0	0	0
BB	7000	1018.45	1223.07	4758.48	304.1	0	1223.07
BM	3000	2389.65	145.9	464.45	22.45	1200	1345.9
CE	7000	3177.2	2815.68	1007.12	1410.25	2000	4815.68
CH	4500	827.95	1399.34	2272.71	695.5	0	1399.34
CM	4500	1881.95	2055.12	562.93	2055.12	1500	3555.12
CS	6500	3286.45	3035.98	177.57	789.25	1000	4035.98
EE	6000	1028.85	2128.34	2842.81	209.95	0	2128.34
FIRE	1000	701.5	317	-18.5	92.05	250	567
GE	22000	6075.15	12686.38	3238.47	1540.83	0	12686.38
HA	12000	1	0	11999	0	0	0
HE		1802.25	1214.14	-3016.39	819.38	0	1214.14
HG		64.7	327.85	-392.55	327.85	0	327.85
HH		623.55	1402.9	-2026.45	473.73	0	1402.9
HM		0	21.6	-21.6	21.6	0	21.6
HP		1644.81	1254.26	-2899.07	803.99	0	1254.26
IN	1200	397.4	871.64	-69.04	350.82	0	871.64
MA	6000	2285.4	285.22	3429.38	285.22	1500	1785.22
ME/MACH	4500	373.2	511.45	3615.35	99.9	0	511.45
ME/MAT	4500	2554.6	2092.1	-146.7	352.75	0	2092.1
ME/ME	7000	3250.25	3940.2	-190.45	1074.32	0	3940.2
MG	4000	529.05	381.61	3089.34	45.45	500	881.61
NU	400	93.5	62.95	243.55		0	62.95
PE	500	101.85	61.85	336.3	16.15	0	61.85
PH	3500	721	2631.32	147.68	804.15	0	2631.32
RE	10000	3450.99	5931.21	617.8	974.14	0	5931.21
RF	4500	1144.65	981.77	2373.58	190.16	0	981.77
SS	4000	2549.23	506.28	944.49	159.67	1000	1506.28
Z		0	231.83	-231.83	3.03	0	231.83
TOTALS	124500	46957.51	50168.08	27374.41	14310.06	8950	59118.08

sort required has an identifiable field. For example, a financial departmental report needs a field where department codes can be identified; a report organized by call number needs a field for the call number for each item so that dBase can index and sort on this field and produce a report either summarizing all items in each general call number area or a specific report listing each call number and its cost. For an example of a vendor discount report see Table 2.

Collection Development Objectives

— Analyze purchased titles by call number and subject.
— Analyze costs by call number and subject.
— Produce reports detailing these analyses.
— Produce monthly accessions list.

A college library without bibliographic specialists in certain subject areas needs other ways of evaluating current acquisitions and relating them to the total collection. Fields for both call number and subject enable price and/or bibliographic data to be manipulated and grouped according to either or both these areas.

A total picture can readily be obtained of the year's acquisitions, both purchases and gifts together or separately, by listing every item in call number and subject order. Call number areas can be reviewed to see whether the library is purchasing sufficient numbers to support the curriculum and if not, whether costs are a factor and whether additional funds need to be assigned or whether departments need to be contacted to see if curriculum needs have changed.

If it is necessary to know in what call number areas departments actually ordered books, a report can be organized to list titles purchased in call number order within department. If, in addition to this, the library needs to know how much is being spent in certain call number areas a detailed report listing each book title and its cost can be totalled for each call number area, or a summary report can list total spent per call number without including the details of cost for each title (see Table 3). This type of analysis is extremely useful in determining actual dollar support of sections of the collection. It is also invaluable for producing this type of information for Accreditation purposes when detailed information is required to document library support of specific Engineering and Science subject areas.

Other useful types of analysis are the ability to average the cost of a single item by either call number, subject, department, etc. Average costs can be computed by dBase and used for budget projections. Current data can be compared to earlier years by producing reports which combine the two databases. For easier presentation and graphing, summary or detailed data can be dumped into a Lotus spreadsheet in a matter of minutes where percentage differences between years can be easily computed. In this way, if expansion in certain subject areas is under discussion, costs and numbers can be estimated and budgeted for fairly accurately (Table 4).

Monthly Accessions Lists can be produced using the date cataloged field to identify all items cataloged in a particular month or period of time. Once subjects are entered into the subject field and call numbers into the call number field from the month's cataloging slips a list is produced from an inhouse program, organized by area of the library, subject and title (Table 5).

OPERATIONAL NEEDS

Objectives

—Maintain a complete file of all orders with access to each piece of data. Reduce/eliminate paper files.
—Produce many different types of reports.
—Keep up to date with claims and status reports.
—Type order forms to send to vendors/publishers.
—Control and organize gifts.

Discussion

The library had maintained several paper files because of the need to organize and extract the acquisitions information in more than one way. A five part acquisitions form was used with each part used for a different purpose and filed in a different file. For example, a title file was maintained so that when items were received the slip could be retrieved by title and sent to cataloging with the book. A fund file was maintained and filed in department order so that

TABLE 2. Comparison of listed and actual costs 1986/87.

PUBLISHER	TITLE	LIST	ACTUAL	DISCOUNT
Ballinger	Competitive challenge : strategies for industrial innovation	26.95	23.45	0.13
Bantam Books	13th Valley : a novel	4.95	4.31	0.13
Birkhauser	Tender ship : governmental management of technological	24.95	21.71	0.13
Brady	Elements of Spreadsheet Style	12.95	11.27	0.13
Butterworths	Proceedings of the Ninth Power Systems Computation Conferenc	165.00	143.55	0.13
Cambridge University Press	Introduction to the mathematics of neurons	49.50	43.07	0.13
Cambridge University Press	Nonlinear diffusive waves	49.50	43.07	0.13

Cambridge University Press	Maximum and minimum principles : a unified approach	79.50	69.17	0.13
Chapman and Hall	Chemistry of the semiconductor industry	99.95	86.96	0.13
Computer Science Press	Program translation fundamentals : methods and issues	36.95	32.15	0.13
Congressional Quarterly	Presidential elections since 1789	15.75	13.71	0.13
Delmar Publishers	Fundamentals of CAD	25.45	22.15	0.13
Elsevier	Production management : methods and studies	53.00	46.11	0.13
Elsevier	Energy models and studies	121.00	105.27	0.13
Elsevier	Analytic techniques for energy planning : proceedings of the	79.00	68.73	0.13
Elsevier	Photoacoustic and thermal wave phenomena in semiconductors	75.00	65.25	0.13

249

TABLE 3. Department purchases by call number.

CALL NO.	TITLE	COST
** DEPT BM		
QC 318 I7 K42 1987	Statistical thermodynamics of nonequiloibrium processes	44.10
QD 96 I5 P66 1985	Aldrich library of FT-IR spectra	450.00
QD 96 R4 W54 1987	Near-infrared technology in the agricultural and food	136.80
QH 585.5 N82 N67 1987	NMR spectroscopy : cells and organisms	211.00
QH 641 C45 1987	Cellular chemiluminescence	375.25
QP 114 E9 K37 1987	Cardiovascular system and physical exercise	121.00
QP 364.7 M6 1986	Monitoring neurotransmitter release during behaviour	65.00
QP 514.2 F58 1987	Human body composition : growth, aging, nutrition, and	62.04
QP 517 M65 S77 1987	Structure, dynamics, and function of biomolecules : the	67.21
QP 519.9 S6 S64 1986	Spectroscopy in the biomedical sciences	119.00
QP 552 M44 M47 1986	Membrane proteins isolation and characterization	18.80

Call Number	Title	Price
QP 86 C73	CRC handbook of physiology in aging	110.05
R 856 R83 1987	Principles of biomedical instrumentation : a beginner's	31.50
R 856.6 A17	AAMI standards and recommended practices	225.00
R 857 M3 T43 1986	Techniques of biocompatibility	247.95
R 857 O6 F8 1986	Functional mapping in biology and medicine : computer	185.00
R 895 S58 1987	Physics in nuclear medicine	43.94
RC 683.5 A9 A27 1987	Essentials of cardiac physical diagnosis	34.50
RC 77.5 C65 1983	Computer-aided electromyography	125.00
RC 78.7 N83 A44 1985	NMR in medicine : the instrumentation and clinical	65.00
RC 78.7 U4 T57 1986	Tissue characterization with ultrasound	225.00
RC 87.9 H54 1986	High frequency ventilation	109.00
RM 837 P48 1987	Photomedicine	342.00
RS 201 C64 M43 1984	Medical applications of controlled release	195.00
TA 1660 I542 1987	Integrated optical circuits and components : design and	70.50
TA 1695 H36 1987	Handbook of molecular lasers	141.00
** Subtotal **		3820.64

TABLE 4. Summary of monographs by classification 1986-1987.

J	**	POLITICAL SCIE	58	1047.15	18.05
K	**	LAW	51	1531.55	30.03
L	**	EDUCATION	30	628.42	20.95
M	**	MUSIC	73	1388.9	19.03
N	**	ART	35	1083.55	30.96
NA	**	ARCHITECTURE	27	820.1	30.37
P-PE	**	LANGUAGE	14	410.41	29.32
P	**	LITERATURE-FOR	28	455.65	16.27
P	**	LITERATURE-GEN	51	1066.79	20.92
PR	**	LITERATURE-ENG	88	2214.11	25.16
PS	**	LITERATURE-AME	94	1489.99	15.85
Q	**	SCIENCE	88	3777.11	42.92
QA	**	MATHEMATICS	194	8505.23	43.84
QA	**	COMPUTER SCIEN	153	6494.18	42.45
QB	**	ASTRONOMY	12	387.53	32.29
QC	**	PHYSICS	99	4944.05	49.94
QD	**	CHEMISTRY	84	5022.64	59.79
QE	**	GEOLOGY	26	258.27	9.93
QH	**	NATURAL HISTOR	53	1915.01	36.13
QK	**	BOTANY	9	477.68	53.08
QL	**	ZOOLOGY	7	293.64	41.95
QP	**	PHYSIOLOGY	52	2668	51.31
QR	**	BACTERIOLOGY	15	863.65	57.58
R	**	MEDICINE	71	3189.12	44.92
S-SK	**	AGRICULTURE	20	914.07	45.70
S-SK	**	FORESTRY	1	42.75	42.75
T	**	TECHNOLOGY	55	2690.1	48.91
TA	**	CIVIL ENG	81	3425.33	42.29
TA	**	GENERAL ENG	167	11678.69	69.93
TC	**	HYDRAULIC ENG	34	1882.23	55.36
TD	**	MUNICIPAL ENG	10	461.72	46.17
TD	**	SANITARY ENG	58	2594.96	44.74
TE	**	HIGHWAY ENG	8	134.05	16.76
TG	**	BRIDGE ENG	1	32	32.00
TH	**	BUILDING CONST	28	1018.3	36.37
TH	**	FIRE SAFETY	17	636.95	37.47
TJ	**	MECHANICAL ENG	85	4367.85	51.39
TK	**	ELECTRICAL ENG	128	5370.81	41.96
TK	**	NUCLEAR ENG	4	165.36	41.34
TK	**	COMPUTER ENG	9	312.19	34.69
TL	**	AERONAUTICS	17	721.76	42.46
TL	**	MOTOR VEHICLES	3	82.4	27.47
TN	**	METALLURGY	19	1147.25	60.38
TN	**	MINING	3	37.82	12.61
TP	**	CHEM TECHNOLOG	66	4601.34	69.72
TR	**	PHOTOGRAPHY	9	358.39	39.82
TS	**	MANUFACTURES	73	3523.83	48.27
TX	**	HOME ECONOMICS	2	21.84	10.92
U-V	**	MILITARY SCIEN	23	533.79	23.21
U-V	**	NAVAL SCIENCE	2	126.74	63.37
Z	**	BIBLIOGRAPHY	37	2059.16	55.65
Z	**	LIBRARY	15	550.25	36.68
	***	Total ***	3212	120875.1	37.63

TABLE 5. Book acquisitions for March, 1988.

SUBJECT	TITLE AND CALL NUMBER
GENERAL	
BIBLIOGRAPHY	Relations of literature and science : an annotated bibliography of scholarship, 1880-1980 c1987 Modern Language Asso. Z 6511 R44 1987
BRIDGE ENG	Fatigue and fracture in steel bridges : case studies c1984 Wiley TG 380 F57 1984
BUILDING CONST	Air conditioning and refrigeration for the professional c1987 Wiley TH 687.5 C48 1988
	Architectural lighting for commercial interiors c1987 Wiley TH 7900 S67 1987
	Manual of built-up roof systems c1982 McGraw Hill TH 2450 G73 1982

253

TABLE 5 (continued)

SUBJECT	TITLE AND CALL NUMBER
	GENERAL
CHEM TECHNOLOGY	Bioseparations : downstream processing for biotechnology Wiley c1987 TP 248.25 S47 B45 1988
	Economic analysis of fermentation processes CRC Press c1988 TP 156 F5 R45 1988
	Heat transfer in air conditioning and refrigeration equipment : presented at the Winter Annual Meeting of ASME ASME c1986 TP 490 H44 1986
	Maximizing flame retardancy via proper processing and product selection : papers presented at Kiawah Island Inn Technomic Pub. Co. c1986 TP 266.5 F574 1986
	Recent developments in chemical process and plant design Wiley c1987 TP 155.7 R43 1987
	Scientific foundations of space manufacturing Mir Publishers c1984 TP 155.7 S35 1984
	Separations in chemical engineering : equilibrium-staged separations Elsevier c1988 TP 156 S45 W36 1988

encumbered and paid amounts could be manually totaled and recorded for the monthly budget report. Each month a staff member went through all slips using an adding machine. A claims file was filed in purchase order or date order and each month a staff member would go through the file to see what should be claimed.

Using the database design, with each piece of information completely accessible because isolated in a field of its own, we knew we could use the single database to serve many different functions, and have access to far more information than existed in the restricted paper environment. Many of the demands on the Acquisitions Department were time consuming to answer or impossible to produce with paper files. When a professor wanted to know whether a certain title was on order but had an incomplete title it was difficult, if not impossible, to locate the order. With dBase it is possible to search by word within a field so this type of question could easily be answered. Other needs, such as answering a question on the status of an order, checking to see which edition was ordered, all this type of question could be readily answered in a few seconds in the database.

In addition to locating information, there is always a need to give faculty, administration, and vendors various reports. These can range from a simple list of gifts to more complex selective type reports. Some of the more complex might be an alphabetical listing of all publishers used; sending lists of on order or received titles to each department; identifying year of publication to see whether up to date material is being purchased—all these could be done in the past but only with a large investment of staff time. The standard report feature in dBase makes it possible to design reports based on single or multiple fields, organize the information in whichever way it is required and have them available within a short space of time.

One of the problems with manual files is that some orders can "fall through the cracks" either at the library or at the vendor and when the person ordering wants to know what the status of that item is after a period of several months, for some reason that particular order has never been claimed or reported on by the vendor or publisher. We needed a system which would identify and print out lists of titles by vendor which had been on order for a certain period of time and had no status report. As dBase allows conditions to be placed and limited choices made in the contents of a report or list, this type of claims report is easily produced once a month (Table 6).

Printed order slips were necessary as we could not transmit orders directly via telecommunications and because one slip was needed anyway for the Cataloging department. dBase can be programmed to print out any of the information contained in the database in whatever format is desired so a program was written to batch print requested orders onto blank form-feed order slips. A simple command activates the program and saves many hours of staff typing time.

As gifts can sometimes be a sizeable percentage of the total acquisitions, we needed a vehicle to control these as well as the purchased items. They are handled somewhat differently in so far that they have no overt costs, status reports, claims to keep track of, but the library needs to know who gave certain items, which ones are added to the collection, what subject areas of the collection are these gifts supporting, etc. These can all be achieved. The staff prefer to use a different database or mini databases for each gift rather than use the same database for purchases and gifts. The structure of the gift database is much less complex and contains fields for bibliographic information and donor. Complete lists of the total gift or partial lists of items added to the collection can be readily produced if a field is maintained which indicates whether the item was added or discarded. Gift lists used to be time consuming to type in the past, especially where alphabetical order was necessary. Items can be added to the database in any order knowing that the program will index and list in any order required. For those items which are retained, call number and/or subject sorts show clearly which sections of the collection are being supported.

PROCESS

As stated in the beginning, one of our goals was to create as efficient a system as possible for the ordering and receipt of materials. It seems appropriate here to outline somewhat briefly the major procedures to show what is involved in using the database and how it ties in with the remainder of the acquisitions processes.

One full time staff member—the Acquisitions Library Associate is able to handle the acquisitions of over 5000 items per year. This includes all steps in the process from the initial receipt, searching and placing of orders and maintenance of all pertinent information on each order in the database to the production of monthly budget reports, other specialized analysis reports, gifts and special projects. Prior to the current system, another staff member was involved in acquisitions for several hours a week, and none of the sophisticated analysis of acquisitions nor the streamlined accounting was possible.

The Acquisitions library associate ordered and received 4306 monographs in 1987. The budget for these was $124,500, and did not include books received through Standing Orders, Technical Reports or A/V materials. The Acquisitions area handles Technical Reports, A/V materials and gifts in addition to the monographs, but records for these are located on a separate database. Continuations and Periodicals have separate budgets, databases and procedures and are handled by other divisions in Technical Services. The size of the 1987 monograph database was 2,536,250 bytes at the close of the fiscal year on June 30 and contained 4306 title orders. Additionally, the gift/AV/technical report database was 223,618 bytes and contained 92 AV orders, 189 technical reports and 464 gift titles. The total for the year was 5050 title records and 2,759,868 bytes. In February of 1988, the 1988 database was 1,900,472 bytes and contained 3259 title orders. In addition the gift/AV/Technical Report database was 345,897 bytes and contained 1266 items making a total to date of 2,246,639 bytes and 4525 title records. The final total for 1988 will obviously be greater than 1987. The practice at WPI is to keep the previous year's database on the hard disk for reference and comparison purposes, but there is obviously more than sufficient space for both databases even with the indexes required. There would be plenty of space on a 20 megabyte hard disk to accommodate a larger acquisitions file and budget as well as store the previous year's database for reference and comparison purposes.

Book orders are received from faculty, librarians and staff, mostly on paper slips. There is one department, however, which has matched the library's database and which sends its book orders to the library on floppy disks. OCLC is the primary source for veri-

TABLE 6. Claim list—April, 1988.

Title	ORDER	Status	SDATE	CLAIM1	CLAIM2
Plant mineral nutrition : an introduction to current concept	09/16/87	NYP,NYP,NYP,NYP	03/01/88	08/07/87	04/13/88
Air and space history : an annotated bibliography	09/16/87	NYP,NYP,NYP,NYP	03/01/88	08/07/87	04/13/88
ICCM & ECCM / Sixth International Conference on Composite	08/11/87	CLAIM	03/01/88	04/13/88	/ /
Anxiety in sports	10/01/87	NYP,NYP,NYP	03/01/88	04/13/88	/ /
Political theory and modernity	10/07/87	NYP,NYP,NYP	03/01/88	/ /	/ /
Modern political thouoght : an introduction	10/07/87	CLAIM,NYP,NYP	03/01/88	/ /	/ /
Money and value : a reconsideration of classical and	10/26/87	BO,BO,BO	03/01/88	/ /	/ /

Sylvia Plath : a biography	11/10/87	NYP	11/20/87	04/13/88 / /
Electro-optic and photorefractive materials : proceedings of	11/10/87	OS,BO,OS,BO,OS, BO	03/01/88	/ / / /
On common ground : caring for shared land from town common	11/10/87	REO,REO	03/01/88	/ / / /
Hydrosoft 86 : hydraulic engineering software : proceedings	11/10/87	REO	04/01/88	/ / / /
Women at work	11/10/87		/ /	04/13/88 / /
Ergonomics in manufacturing	11/10/87	NYP,NYP	02/03/88	/ / / /
Biomechanics of the hand	11/10/87	REO,NYP	03/01/88	/ / / /
Visualized flow : fluid motion in basic and engineering	11/10/87	BO,BO	02/03/88	/ / / /
Topics in boundary element research	11/10/87	REO	01/04/88	/ / / /

fication, bibliographic information and, on occasion, price. The Acquisitions Associate searches all orders on OCLC, using an M300 dedicated terminal, and notes where the library already owns the item. For any item not owned, the bibliographic information is downloaded onto a floppy disk using the "savescreen" function. At the end of the OCLC session, the disk is removed and taken to the AT&T 6300 hard disk unit. We have not attempted to add a hard disk to the M300 because the AT&T microcomputer was readily available for Acquisitions use alone and the M300 is used by Cataloging staff for many hours during the rest of the day. But it would certainly be technically possible to perform the complete process on the M300. The disk with the savescreen information is placed in the A drive of the AT&T, uploaded into the OCLANG software where pertinent fields are speedily extracted and modified into a format acceptable to dBase. A single command then appends the new orders into the dBase database in exactly the order required. Formerly, this information was printed out at the OCLC terminal and entered manually from the copy into dBase.

Once the bibliographic information is loaded, each of the new records is retrieved and edited to add other information such as name of requester, department, date, vendor, etc. Much of this type of repetitive information can be keyed in using function keys to program the text instead of retyping each word or set of numbers time and time again. If prices were lacking, these would have been searched using *Books in Print* or publisher's information and entered manually. The database is also checked for duplication of orders. If it is necessary to monitor expenditures carefully before orders are actually mailed, a single report can be produced itemizing and summarizing costs by department for the current batch of orders. If Department X has only $150 left to spend and the total department amount is in excess of that, then specific items can be temporarily flagged for deletion in order to remain within the budget constraints. These items can be revived and ordered another day when, and if, more money is available.

When all of the data for each order is complete, the program to batch print the order slips is begun. This is a simple two word command whereby only the orders for that day, or whichever days are required, are printed out. Some consideration has been given to transmitting the orders electronically instead of through the mail.

Costs of telecommunication as well as the current need of the Catalog department to have a slip with the item have not indicated that the operation would be necessarily more efficient or cost effective using electronic transmission. The options are still being explored. One slip is filed in title order and one slip is sent to the vendor or publisher.

On receipt of the item ordered, the title order slip is pulled from the paper file, the items matched with the invoice and the individual costs recorded in the database for each item along with the data received. If the nondiscounted price differs from the library's estimated cost, it is changed at this point. Once all the cost information is entered, a simple command to total all net prices for records which have that invoice number is given so that the library associate can check that the price input was correct by matching the total on the screen against the total of the invoice. The item is then sent to the cataloging department along with the title order slip.

At regular monthly intervals a claims report is run by vendor and date. This report lists titles without status reports which have not been received within three months of the date of order. The status report would have been entered as a code by the acquisitions associate as received from the vendor. Periodically, all items not received within a six month period, regardless of status report, are reviewed. In this way, good control can be exercised by the library, with a minimum of effort, over the claiming function.

As has already been mentioned, once a month two programs are run which summarize costs by fund and department. These programs take no longer than a half hour to produce totals even at the end of the fiscal year when there are several thousand records to be included. Once the totals are complete, a simple command transfers the dBase file into a file format readable by Lotus 1-2-3. This new file is imported into a Lotus spreadsheet for easier display and where established formulas calculate the month's expenditure, balance, etc.

CONCLUSION

Much can be accomplished with generic software and the product is often far, far less expensive than a commercial package designed specially for a single purpose. The software is especially cost effective when programs are developed in other areas such as Periodical cost accounting, ILL statistics, library budget accounting, etc. The Acquisitions system designed for WPI could probably be improved with more sophisticated programming, but it works well and we have been able to answer all of the library's and administration's needs for information as well as improving the internal processes. Staff enjoy using the system and derive satisfaction from discovering new methods of using dBase to become more efficient or to analyze the data in a new way. We use the database to serve standard needs of any acquisitions program as well as very specific local requirements. No doubt the future will bring changes in these requirements but the program is flexible enough for major as well as minor modifications and adaptable for transfer into other systems if that should prove necessary. As the library and campus needs change, so will the acquisitions program.

REFERENCES

1. Simpson, Alan. *Understanding dBase III+*. Sybex, Inc., 1986.
2. Simpson, Alan. *Advanced techniques in dBase III*. Sybex, Inc., 1985.
3. Beiser, Karl, *Essential guide to dBase III+ in libraries*. Meckler Publishing Co., 1987,
4. Shuster, Helen. "A versatile dBase III+ acquisitions program at Worcester Polytechnic Institute," *Library Acquisitions: Practice and Theory*, vol. 11, pp. 241-253, 1987.

In Pursuit of Shared Access to the CD-ROM, Dialing *Books in Print Plus*

Julie Nilson
Jon LaCure
Anne McGreer

SUMMARY. This paper describes a feasibility study conducted at Indiana University Libraries to provide dial access to a CD-ROM mounted on a host microcomputer in central technical services. The CD-ROM product chosen for the experiment was *Books in Print Plus*. The paper covers establishing and funding the experiment, selecting the software, identifying and training the participants, running the test, gathering use data, and evaluating the results. It discusses the benefits of using a CD-ROM in a shared environment, and explores some of the constraints. Included are premises for future experimentation and suggestions for other applications. Appended to the paper is a section with enough technical detail to allow the experiment to be replicated at other institutions.

There is a widely held opinion among librarians that remote access to a CD-ROM is not possible. We decided to test the validity of this myth by attempting to develop dial-in access to a centrally located copy of Bowker's *Books in Print Plus*. The issues we encountered included the development of support for the experiment, the problems of territory regarding the CD-ROM, the host microcomputer and telephone line, the establishment of a viable trial, and the technical challenges of the project. This paper summarizes our ex-

---

Julie Nilson is Department Head, Jon LaCure is Acquisitions Assistant for Collection Development for East Asian materials, and Anne McGreer is Manager of the Bibliographic Searching and Exchanges Unit in the Monographic Processing Services Department, Indiana University Libraries, Bloomington, IN 47405.

© 1989 by The Haworth Press, Inc. All rights reserved.

periences at Indiana University Libraries in attempting to puncture this myth. It also contains a section with enough technical detail to allow our experiment to be replicated at other institutions.

The Indiana University Libraries use a variety of bibliographic tools in support of the acquisitions process. Multiple copies of many of these tools are placed in various technical services units in the main and branch libraries. Prominent among those titles which are duplicated is *Books in Print* and its related publications. In Indiana University Libraries' technical services environment, these titles are considered important for selection, collection development, acquisitions, and reference. With the exception of those copies located for public use in reference areas, use by technical services and other library staff is critical but not extensive. Traditionally, a print copy has been maintained within Central Technical Services in the Monographic Processing Services Department. Convenience and the relative health of the materials budget has played a role in the decision of the branch libraries and other departments to maintain subscriptions, to purchase individual years on an irregular basis, or to use some other nearby copy. For example, one branch library, which is located in a building next to the University Bookstore, uses the copy purchased by that agency. The copy in Central Technical Services traditionally has been available for use by library staff on both a walk-in and telephone reference basis. The availability of *Books in Print* in a CD-ROM format opened a number of new areas for consideration.

Investing in *Books in Print Plus* for centralized technical services would provide a more timely, comprehensive product than the printed version. The department had received its first microcomputer and was in a position to explore alternatives to traditional bibliographic print sources. However, the potential of changing from print to a CD-ROM product would mean a change in the way users from other technical services units would be served. The cost of the CD-ROM version also would be substantially higher than the cost of the printed version. We, therefore, decided to develop a research proposal to determine if *Books in Print Plus* could be accessed directly by technical services staff in remote locations. This experiment, if successful, would allow us to continue to provide access to the central copy without needing to devote staff time to training users. It would have the added bonus of allowing use of this copy without requiring a walk across campus to do so. A group consisting of the Head of Monographic Processing Services, the Assistant Head for Acquisitions, the Manager of the Bibliographic Searching and Exchanges Unit, and an Acquisitions Assistant for Collection Development — an individual with great microcomputer expertise — met to discuss the possibility of developing local telephone access to *Books in Print Plus*. On the surface it seemed promising, but it required financial support for an experiment which had equal chances of success or failure.

The Dean of Libraries had established a small fund to encourage and support experimental initiatives in testing and developing new library services. Under the auspices of this Pilot Project Program, an application was made for funding to acquire software, to provide technical support, to write a brief user's manual, and to gather use data and general feedback. The Monographic Processing Services Department planned to contribute generous amounts of staff time, the use of its microcomputer for the duration of the experiment, and a telephone line regularly used by one of the department's units. This plan would limit department access to both the microcomputer and to *Books in Print Plus*. The proposal was brief and somewhat speculative as to the anticipated results. It, however, fit nicely within the parameters of the Pilot Project Program and was funded readily. As with most such efforts, the funding was the easiest part. Subsequent challenges included selecting the remote operation software for the test, identifying a willing group of participants, establishing a reasonable trial period, and obtaining the cooperation of department members in relinquishing use of the Leading Edge microcomputer during specified hours and in setting it up for the dial-in participants.

CHOOSING THE SOFTWARE

A special class of software, sometimes called remote access software, is required to run *Books in Print Plus* from a remote location. Some of these software products, *Carbon Copy* for example, require that the same program be used on both the host and the remote. Since typically the host program costs more than $100 and the remote program somewhat less, this can amount to considerable expense if numerous users are involved. It also means that both computers must be IBM compatible. *PC-Anywhere* was chosen for this project because it seemed to be the only full featured package that allowed any computer or terminal to function as a remote. The only requirement was that microcomputers have software capable of basic terminal emulation such as VT-100. It also compared favorably with other packages in benchmark tests performed by *PC Magazine*.[1]

THE PARTICIPANTS AND TRIAL PERIOD

Once we had chosen the software and developed a plan for a test, we were ready to solicit volunteers who were willing to participate in the experiment and to provide feedback. An announcement was placed in the Libraries' *IUL News* describing the project and calling for volunteers. Several individuals from the main and branch libraries responded and agreed to attend an organizational meeting. The meeting included interested parties who had access to IBM or PC compatible microcomputers with modem and printer as well as individuals who were not planning to use the system but were curious about how it might work. Volunteers represented collections in the sciences, social sciences, and humanities.

Before the meeting, the software had been tested and a brief user's manual was drafted. At the meeting, seven remote sites were identified and the participants were provided with the necessary software and documentation. Two hours a day were selected (8:00-9:00 a.m. and 1:00-2:00 p.m.) as dedicated time on the Leading Edge for remote access. The participants agreed to a tentative test period of six weeks.

To implement Monographic Processing Services' part of this project's operation, departmental staff had to be trained and scheduled to set up the Leading Edge with the *PC-Anywhere* diskette. The CD-ROM player and printer had to be turned on, and the telephone instrument connected to the Leading Edge had to be disconnected. A calendar was established with a schedule of who was responsible for this set-up procedure each time. At the end of each hour, the telephone had to be reconnected and the *PC-Anywhere* diskette stored away. In addition, the entire department was informed about the unavailability of the Leading Edge and its telephone line during the hours dedicated to the remote users. Department staff were cooperative and supportive in contributing to the success of the experiment.

During the test period, the participants had few problems operating the system. The major issue seemed to be access time. Some participants, particularly branch library managers, found themselves or their staff too busy with other daily activities during the times of the test to be able to use it. Others found the system busy when they tried to access it.

EVALUATION

At the end of the six week test period, another meeting of the participants was held to gather evaluative information and discuss reactions. By this time, enough enthusiasm had been expressed about the way the system worked, and about the newly acquired access to this CD-ROM tool with its many search keys, that we reached an agreement to extend the test period and to include one additional participant. There were several requests for extended hours, which were constrained by the department's various other claims on the Leading Edge.

The participants were provided with a screen log in which the date, time, user, number of searches, and comments could be recorded. The use data gathered during the six week test period showed that four of the volunteers accessed the system 26 times and conducted 123 searches. The other volunteers used the system at least one time, presumably to see how it worked. Since the heavy users claimed most of the days and hours set aside for the test, it was clear, in retrospect, that we should have limited the number of participants, expanded the hours for the test, or assigned exclusive times to each user.

The participants took advantage of the additional search keys available in the CD-ROM version. Although preorder verification was an important use, other uses included identifying prices to bill unreturned items, correcting citations in the bibliography of a book, searching unfilled ILL requests for possible purchase, and searching patron requests. Comments from the participants included, "... timesaver when I am able to use it since we use BIP at the bookstore . . ." "... enjoy using this system. Enables me to do many things in a very small amount of time." There also were many positive comments about the expanded capabilities provided by the CD-ROM version of *Books in Print*.

We identified several major technical issues which needed to be evaluated. They included problems with terminal emulation, the question of security, and the possibility of freezing operations on the host.

PC-Anywhere, and its remote software *Aterm*, causes slightly slower operations at the remote site. However, if terminals or microcomputers using terminal emulation software are used at the remote site, getting information on and off the screen can take an inordinate amount of time at 1200 baud. Besides speed there are other problems associated with terminals. The most important are the differences in the keyboards and in the number of lines in the display. *PC-Anywhere* handles both of these problems adequately, but it is difficult for the casual user to remember all the key stroke combinations involved in reproducing the IBM keyboard, so that one line at the top or bottom is not invisible. Each remote site, depending on the hardware and software used, has the potential of presenting a different set of problems, which must be solved on a site-by-site basis.

Security is another aspect that needs to be considered. It is possible for the remote user to break out of the host's software, especially if batch files are used. When this occurs the remote has complete control over the host. Although we did not anticipate this happening, we decided not to leave sensitive or valuable data and programs on the host and to back up the hard disk frequently. We did not test any software-based security system. We felt that this additional level of complexity was undesirable.

Finally, it is possible for the remote user to freeze the host. This occurred most often using terminal emulation, but it can happen using *Aterm*. For example, attempting to print to the host printer when it is turned off or out of paper can freeze the host. The problem can be resolved by keeping a disk in drive A with DOS and an autoexec batch file to run *PC-Anywhere*. This allows the remote user to reboot the host and continue to use *Books in Print Plus*.

FINAL ANALYSIS AND FUTURE PLANS

Due to the overall positive reaction of the project participants, the next step was to seek support for establishing this service on a reasonable and regular basis. Two hours a day of access was not enough to serve the needs of the experimental group let alone to expand the service to include all branch libraries and other technical services locations. Also, the department would need to acquire an additional microcomputer to provide access on an extended basis. Any equipment acquired ideally should perform at a rate faster than the Leading Edge used for the pilot project.

The final report of the project was presented to the Library Administration and was discussed at the Library Administrative Council. With the many funding priorities facing all areas of the library, it was important to determine that there was broad interest in and support for establishing this service. The project report was discussed thoroughly and it was determined that there was enough interest to prompt establishing the service for those areas which wished to participate. Several suggestions were made for looking at particular microcomputers which were believed to have potential for faster processing. There also was concern that the support equipment selected should not be so expensive that the cost of the extended service didn't exceed the cumulative costs of our present mode of access.

Identifying a moderately priced, readily serviceable, faster microcomputer which is compatible with the CD-ROM proved more of a problem than anticipated. However, a short list was developed and a selection recommended to the administration. We are now anticipating the installation of this service on a permanent basis by the summer of 1988. It is our expectation that once it is operational, a number of additional uses will be developed.

OTHER POTENTIAL USES FOR THE SYSTEM

One feature of Bowker's *Books in Print Plus* that might have special significance in a dial-up environment is the ability to use a word processor to edit citations from the data base and write them to files on the host. Bowker limits this feature somewhat by only allowing three word processors, *Brief, Wordstar,* and *Word Perfect,* none of which are in use in our department. However, renaming *PC Write's* "ed.com" to "ws.com" seemed to convince Bowker's software that we were using *Wordstar* and we were able to use *PC-Write* without any problems.

We experimented briefly with this feature. The potential seems to exist for a remote location to call up the data base, find the book or books wanted and write the citation to a local file on the remote. Since the information would be in machine readable form, it could be incorporated into a data base, or used to generate an order for the book. We anticipate that some locations will use this feature in the *Books in Print Plus* software to have their order requests delivered to the printer in Monographic Processing Services. The edit feature could be used to call up a word processor for the purposes of adding a fund, rush, notify or shelving instructions. We speculate that this might be considered important for certain "rush" orders that otherwise would be handled via campus mail. We also speculate that remote users might print their own file copies of orders from the bibliographic information in *Books in Print Plus*.

Another interesting area of investigation is the possibility of linking into the campus communication system. With more computers connected directly into this high speed system, it may be possible to bypass the telephone lines. Microcomputers have been connected to our campus system as single user host nodes, so it is technically possible; although far beyond the scope of our experiment, this could lead to direct access to CD-ROM data bases by the general library user. The single user problem might be solved in much the same way that it is on larger bulletin board systems by using several computers linked by a local area network and rollover telephone numbers. The remote access and database retrieval software would need to be installed on each node, but they should be able to share access to one or more CD-ROM players.

CONCLUSION

Our experiment demonstrated that remote access to a CD-ROM is possible. It opened new areas for future analysis, including the comparative cost of maintaining multiple subscriptions to print copies versus the cost of establishing a CD-ROM based service. It provided the essential first step in challenging the belief that use of a CD-ROM is limited to the location of the microcomputer where it is mounted. We encourage others to venture into this uncharted territory.

REFERENCES

1. Stone, M. David, "Computing at a distance," *PC Magazine*, March 31, 1987, p. 249-262.

APPENDIX

The Software

PC-Anywhere has no built in bulletin board like functions. If the host wants a log, announcements, or user comments, the necessary programs have to be written. We chose to operate the system with a series of short programs all driven by a DOS batch file. This seemed particularly appropriate since Bowker's *Books in Print Plus* operates from a batch file which could be incorporated into ours. Since it was difficult to anticipate how we might need to manipulate the log, we wanted it in ASCII format. ICON was chosen over other programming languages because of the ease with which it could manipulate ASCII strings and the very short time required to get a function up and running.*

---

*ICON is available on many local bulletin board systems, BIX, or directly from University of Arizona, either through their bulletin board or via anonymous FTP to ARIZONA.EDU for those with access to ARPANET.

Setting Up

Most of the necessary installation of *PC-Anywhere* can be accomplished from the initial screen. The baud rate, comm port, and modem type need to be set. Terminal type should be "ask caller" in a system with callers using various computers and communication software packages. A separate installation program allows you to modify such things as colors, keyboard sequences, and terminal selection. However, in most cases the default setting should suffice for this kind of operation.

The programs provided here will probably need to be modified for local needs. Anyone with elementary programming skills should be able to modify the write statements to control the screen output and log content. If more complex bulletin board features are desired, a programmer with experience in the PC environment will probably be necessary.

BIP-RO.BAT

```
echo off
rem BIP-RO.BAT is called by PC-Anywhere
rem It runs Bowker's BIP+ software from a remote location
rem making s a log of the callers names and time on the system
cls
cd\icon
iconx getname
rem getname opens log and writes time and date
type messages
pause
cd\bowker
cdrom
banner bipm.pic
bk
relcdrom
cls
cd\icon
iconx getcmt
cd\anywhere
alogoff
```

GETNAME.ICN

```
# getname.icn – 5 October 1987
# This program gets user's name, branch or department, time, and date
```

```
# Writing to a file called "log"
#    called by BIP-RO.BAT


procedure main ()
    outtext := open ("log", "a")
       write (&dateline)
    write (" ")
    write ("First Name: ")
        firstname := read ()
    write ("Last Name: ")
        lastname := read()
    write ("Branch or Department: ")
        branch := read()
            write (outtext, "TIME ON: ", &dateline)
            write (outtext,"FIRST NAME: ",firstname)
            write (outtext, "LAST NAME: ",lastname)
            write (outtext,"BRANCH: ",branch)
    write (" ")
end
```

GETCMT.ICN

```
# Getcmt.icn — 5 October 1987
# This program records any user comments and time logged off
# Writing to a file called "log"
#    called by BIP-RO.BAT


procedure main()
    outtext := open ("log", "a")
    write (" ")
    write (&dateline)
        write (outtext, "TIME OFF: ",&dateline)
    write (" ")
    write("We would like to hear your questions or comments.")
    write ("Please leave an e-mail address or phone number")
    write ("if you would like a personal reply.")
    write (Enter a <carriage return> at the end of each line.")
    write ("Use 'bye' on a line by itself to end.")
    write ("|---1---2---3---4---5---6---|")
        while comment := read() do
            if match ("bye",comment) then break
            else write (outtext," ",comment)
                write (outtext,"--------------")
    write (" ")
    write ("Thank you for your call.")
    write ("You are now being logged off.")
end
```

Microcomputer-Based Acquisitions Systems: Where Have We Come From; Where Are We Going?

Norman Desmarais

SUMMARY. This article discusses the development of microcomputer-based acquisitions systems. It describes the features common to many of them and projects possible future improvements and developments. It summarizes research done for the author's *Automated Acquisitions Systems*.

The first automated acquisitions systems were developed exclusively for minicomputers and mainframes because only this size computer had sufficient memory to store and process the large data files an acquisitions department requires. The large capital outlay needed to purchase such systems far exceeded the resources of all but the largest and most well-endowed libraries.

EARLY DEVELOPMENTS

As microcomputers decreased in costs and increased in power and memory capacities, vendors and systems developers began working on automating various library functions. This turned out to be a very difficult task, especially for vendors because acquisitions work has so many exceptions, intricacies, and subroutines. In addition, every librarian has his/her own way of doing things and wants

---

Norman Desmarais is Acquisitions Librarian, Phillips Memorial Library, Providence College, Providence, RI 02918.

This article summarizes research done for the author's *Automated Acquisitions Systems*. — Westport, CT; London: Meckler Corporation, 1988. — (Essential Guide to the Library IBM PC; 11).

the system customized to his/her procedures and to his/her purchase order format. Meeting all these specifications presents a major challenge to a vendor who wants to develop a system flexible enough to satisfy the requirements of most librarians.

Automating acquisitions rarely got top priority. Cataloging, circulation, and online catalogs received primary consideration because of their greater visibility and generally more time-consuming, labor-intensive, repetitive tasks which lent themselves to automation. Even today, many minicomputer systems do not have acquisitions modules.

Initial efforts concentrated on expediting the repetitious steps in purchase order production. While some librarians applied electronic memory typewriters or word processing packages to produce their orders, others used database management programs and developed their own acquisitions databases. It did not take long to realize that access to a bibliographic database or other source of bibliographic information in machine readable form from which to download would significantly decrease processing time.

Meanwhile, microcomputer costs remained out of reach for most small and medium size libraries. To bring some degree of automation to these libraries and help them expedite orders to them, some vendors like Baker & Taylor and BroDart developed hand-held devices to accept International Standard Book Numbers (ISBN) and transmit them over toll-free telephone lines. Vendors would supply the bibliographic records on confirmation slips, at an added cost if requested. These forms also served as multi-part order forms for filing in the library and departmental catalogs.

Even though some libraries may be interested only in expediting the production of purchase orders to save staff time, this is not the sole function of an automated acquisitions system. True acquisitions systems distinguish themselves in the improved management of the various order files and fund accounting as well as in the ability to perform the varied acquisitions tasks.

Interfaces

Virtually all systems on the market interface with some bibliographic utility such as OCLC, RLIN, etc., or some other source of data from which to extract and manipulate records and/or to upload them to the utilities. Some require a separate module to do so. In addition to interfacing with these utilities, many modules also have or will make available interfaces with optical disc laserbases such as *BiblioFile*, *Any-Book*, or *Books in Print Plus*.

Those systems which interface with the bibliographic utilities permit retrieval of records to disk for subsequent uploading into the acquisitions modules. Those which draw on a vendor's database provide the ability to download bibliographic records into the local databases. They also have a feature to place orders online with the respective producers of the modules such as Baker & Taylor and Midwest Library Service. Others plan to add online ordering capabilities. However, even though BISAC (Book Industry Standards Advisory Committee) has developed standards for electronic order transmission, we will need to wait for their more universal acceptance and implementation. Without such general acceptance, each acquisitions system requires a different interface program for each source or vendor.

Ordering

All microcomputer-based acquisitions systems allow the operator to modify records and to display and update an order immediately after entry or modification. Those with multi-level password protection may restrict this activity to certain personnel.

While all modules supply one or more fields for entering local notes or comments, each one treats this differently. Some have more flexibility than others by providing more, longer, or variable length fields. They all furnish workforms or templates for data entry. Almost all (*Card Datalog* and Baker & Taylor's *Search and Order* excepted) accommodate default values for certain fields of newly entered orders. Some provide constants, defaults, or macros to facilitate data entry in other fields.

All systems allocate space to indicate any special handling requirements (rush, notify—, etc.); but each one handles it differently. This also applies to ordering multiple copies for multiple locations on the same PO (purchase order). Generally, the user needs to create separate purchase orders for each item going to a different location or charged to a different account or needs to indicate this information in a field designated for notes, comments, or special handling.

Most systems include a directory to include the name and address (and sometimes the account numbers, names of account representatives or contact people, and telephone numbers) of the most frequently used vendors. The programs draw on this data to insert it into the appropriate places on the purchase orders and/or cover letters to eliminate unnecessary keystrokes. Some modules (*Bib-Base, Card Datalog, Any-Book, Unicorn, Nonesuch,* and *MATSS*) let the operator select a default vendor/supplier or provide the ability to accept the information at order entry time and keep it constant until it is changed on subsequent orders.

Fund Accounting

A prime feature of a true acquisition system is its ability to perform fund accounting functions. This includes posting encumbrances against the proper fund accounts, providing information regarding budgeted amounts for each one along with the encumbrances posted against them, expenditures and available balances. Each module performs this important task in a different way; so librarians may want to monitor these figures until they are certain the reports satisfy their requirements. Such systems also automatically update all financial records after the transactions or if price or quantity change.

Many packages (*Bib-Base, Any-Book, Purchase, Unicorn, Nonesuch,* and *MATSS*) also have special programs or utilities to perform year-end procedures to close out a fiscal year and to transfer any open orders to the new fiscal year. Most modules which provide this feature archive the previous year's information in addition to transferring funds and encumbrances to the new fiscal year. Some programs permit charging a previous year's orders to an accounting cycle different from the current one. Those which provide this feature also archive the previous year's data in addition to transferring funds and encumbrances to the new fiscal year. This archival capability provides an audit trail or a machine readable history file on tape or disk to trace transactions for a specified fund account, vendor, order, or invoice.

Systems have different ways of alerting the operator when funds go over budget. Some (Sydney's *Micro Library System*, *Booktrak*, *Nonesuch*, and *MATSS*) warn him/her at the time of data input. Most require displaying the fund account files to determine the status of each one. Others require calculating the balances to determine this information. In addition, only a few (*Bib-Base*, *Micro Library System*, and *MATSS*) have the facility to convert prices to and from foreign currencies. Only *Any-Book* can calculate estimated discounts at the time of order creation based on vendor discount policies.

While most of the programs handle discounts at the time of receipt, they process this information differently. Some compute it on the basis of the difference of encumbered and received prices and post the percentage in the record. Others calculate a flat discount over the entire invoice while others calculate the discounts on a record-by-record basis, spreading a flat discount over all records in proportion to their relative expense on the invoice. A few compute an average discount and post it against each record on the invoice with various procedures to allocate odd cents. A less desirable alternative requires one to calculate flat discounts manually on a per-item basis and record this figure as the received price.

While some modules do not accommodate adjustments for credits or fund transfers, those that do handle it differently. Generally, they let the operator edit the data to calculate the changes in the records. In addition, each module has a different path to access financial information. Most require running a report to get a display or printout of all the fund accounts or individual ones. They also offer a variety of access points with some providing more flexibility than others.

Receiving/Paying

All systems update the On-Order/In-Process files to record receipt and/or payment. They unencumber funds and post expenditures to the proper accounts. They also provide fund balance information along with balances for expenditures and encumbrances. Here again, one should monitor this information as it may not always meet local requirements.

Claims

All systems offer the ability to produce cancellations and reorders, each in its own way. Most packages prepare claims and cancellations on a set schedule or on demand and according to specification. They also furnish a space in the record for local notes regarding claims, non-supply, etc.

Access Points

All systems provide access to the order files by the traditional methods: author, title, author/title, ISN, and purchase order number. Some have even more access points such as LCCN, accession number, call number, keyword, or truncated search key (*Bib-Base*, *Micro Library System*, *Any-Book*, *Purchase*, *Nonesuch*).

Most modules grant access to the fund accounts by fund number. They also usually have some kind of error detection for duplicate orders. As error detection may "overlook" some duplicates in a single-point check, one may want to think carefully about relying on this feature. For example, a check on ISBN alone will not reveal a duplication of title for different bindings or editions of a work. Nor will a title check alone detect variations in titles such as a work produced in British and American editions.

Management

One of the strengths of an automated acquisitions system along with the abilities to produce purchase orders and to track fund accounting is the ability to exercise better control over departmental operations. All modules provide comprehensive information about every item on order and in process. This includes a record of the date of receipt by the library and the final cost. Units with multi-level password control may limit access to this information to authorized personnel only.

While none of the modules tracks the date of shipment by the vendor, most librarians will probably not use this feature even if the producers offer it. The modules usually provide a space to record the date of payment and the invoice number. Some even record the check number or payment voucher number.

Many systems let the librarian set up a separate status code to identify items under consideration and to segregate them from ordering in a different fiscal period or when funding becomes available.

Reports

Automated acquisitions systems generally supply online reports summarizing fund accounts (allocations, encumbrances, expenditures, balances). Sometimes they also have online reports listing records on hold for locally-defined reasons. This usually requires setting up a separate "hold" account or a dummy fund to group these items. Acquisitions modules vary considerably in the types and detail of the offline reports they provide. Most of them can produce reports for orders outstanding for more than a specified time period and sort them by vendor for possible claiming or reordering.

The fund reports provide the ability to calculate financial information for individual funds or groups of funds. Such data along with purchase-volume information could serve collection development librarians in determining average costs of materials by fund/account/department/branch. Systems vary in the ease of operating the reporting mechanisms. Some require more manual calculations than others to produce a report. By the same token, these fund reports also provide cumulative statistics for monthly and yearly reports which represent time-consuming activities in a manual system. None of the programs we know of give total numbers of records and items added, edited, or deleted during a particular time period. At best, they list total numbers of records in the database by category and/or status. This may prove sufficient for most librarians' needs.

While several systems offer some form of vendor performance analysis to track turnaround time, fulfillment rate, discount, average cost, etc., there is great variation in the type of information produced and the manner of providing it. Some supply the raw data and let the user calculate such items as the average cost and discount separately on the basis of information in the reports (*BibBase, Unicorn, MATSS*). Others may track fulfillment rate (number of items received, back-ordered, cancelled, etc.) as a percentage of total items ordered, leaving the user to calculate the average costs and discounts. In addition, many systems include features to create selection lists, bibliographies, or accessions lists if desired.

We know of only one acquisitions system (*Bib-Base*) that accommodates the entire ALA character set—a feature which permits the printing of diacritics and other special characters. The display of diacritics on the screen and their printing is a function of the software which probably very few programs can handle, as the use of special characters requires redefining the keyboard. If this is an important consideration, prospective purchasers should inquire about it from the respective vendors.

Electronic Ordering

Some vendors have developed microcomputer-based electronic ordering systems which facilitate the placing of orders but do not do any of the acquisitions activities such as fund accounting, receiving/paying, vendor analysis, and management reports. These software packages (*BaTaSYSTEMS ACQUIRE, BOOKEASE™, FlashBack, PC-Order,* and *PC-Rose®*) are vendor-specific in that they place orders only with the vendor of the software. Librarians dealing with several vendors would need several different packages to order from different ones.

Generally these programs require the input of the ISBN and quantity and sometimes other verifying information such as author or title to determine if the ISBN and the bibliographic information match. They allow placing the orders with the vendor electronically over telephone lines and getting status confirmation. After receiving order confirmation and the downloaded bibliographic record, the operator can print order forms locally if desired for filing in departmental or public access catalogs.

These programs were developed as stand-alone systems to operate on IBM PC/XT/AT and compatible microcomputers. With the exception of *BOOKEASE*, the vendors have adapted them to function with *Books in Print Plus* by extracting the necessary information from the bibliographic record for batch ordering. (Although *BOOKEASE* is not modified to work with *Books in Print Plus*, the producer can easily do so.)

Several book vendors would also like to develop interfaces with some of the more popular acquisitions systems. We can expect to see some of them appear on the market in the not-too-distant future as the BISAC standards become more widely accepted and used.

A useful addition to these programs would be the ability to poll the vendor's stock to determine if a title is readily available and to indicate that it should not be back-ordered if not readily available.

FUTURE POSSIBILITIES

As the costs of memory for microcomputers and of optical disc systems continue to decrease and as more libraries install CD-ROM drives, we can anticipate the development of programs that capitalize on the strengths of each medium. In addition to *Books in Print Plus* and *Any-Book* (which incorporates an acquisition system), we could see other existing CD-ROM products like *Cumulative Book Index*, *BiblioFile*, and the various MARC databases getting new applications in acquisition work. We can also expect new CD-ROM tools in the very near future.

The marriage of large quantities of magnetic memory and the large storage capacities of optical discs will see the application of artificial intelligence techniques to large bibliographic laserbases. Some such systems already exist for bookstores (Del Mar Group's *Smart Systems* and *Bookseller's Assistant*) and public access catalogs (The Library Corporation's *The Intelligent Catalog*). Their application to bibliographic databases in an acquisitions environment could facilitate collection development by suggesting titles for purchase, to develop profiles of buying patterns, or to produce selection lists somewhat like an approval plan.

The optical disc's large capacity for indexing overhead could provide the ability to search titles (or any other field, for that matter) by keyword to track incomplete or erroneous citations. While few acquisitions librarians may need Boolean search capabilities on a regular basis, we have become so accustomed to hearing about these features and seeing them in operation in database management programs that we will require them of our acquisitions software. The storage of directory listings of publishers, vendors, bookstores and the ability to transfer relevant information into the purchase order could eliminate much tedium in verifying sources, names, and addresses. Integration of other tools such as dictionaries could serve to verify spelling in an application program or to suggest alternate spellings of a word which the requester cannot remember properly.

In addition to seeing greater flexibility in interfacing with various software packages such as spreadsheets and word processors, we should see greater integration of sources on optical discs. Instead of having a separate disc for in-print material and another for out-of-print or paperbound, we should see products incorporating all of this data on a single disc or possibly two.

We are seeing greater use of "hot keys" or macros. The development of memory-resident programs which let the user define keys or short-cuts can supplement programs and further enhance some existing systems. One of the requirements for such programs should be the ability to place them into memory or to remove them at will in order to avoid disrupting the operation of other programs with which they may conflict.

As BISAC standards become more widely accepted and used, we should see further development in electronic ordering capabilities permitting more local systems to telecommunicate orders directly to their vendors. We can also anticipate links with inventory control systems to determine whether or not the vendor has a particular item in stock. Such programs should include the capacity to specify whether or not to backorder a title or to reroute it to another vendor.

When BISAC completes its work on standards for electronic billing, we should begin seeing capabilities developed to interface with various acquisitions systems for automatic invoicing over the telephone lines. Some vendor produced systems have already implemented variations on this idea for customers ordering from them. Baker & Taylor permits viewing billing information online or printing an invoice. Midwest Library Service sends a floppy disk along with its shipment of materials for uploading into its *MATSS* system and/or for printing invoices.

Recent years have seen rapid progress in automating acquisition processes. Vendors continue to develop new systems and enhance existing ones with new or improved features. Increasing memory capacities and computing power coupled with decreasing prices lead us to anticipate more flexible and more user-friendly modules. Local storage of large databases in optical format will also open new horizons for acquisitions librarians.

For Product Safety Concerns and Information please contact our EU
representative GPSR@taylorandfrancis.com
Taylor & Francis Verlag GmbH, Kaufingerstraße 24, 80331 München, Germany

www.ingramcontent.com/pod-product-compliance
Lightning Source LLC
Chambersburg PA
CBHW071806300426
44116CB00009B/1223